S0-BYN-636

THE CIVIL WAR IN GEORGIA

The Civil War in Georgia

} **A NEW GEORGIA ENCYCLOPEDIA COMPANION**

EDITED BY John C. Inscoe

A Project of the New Georgia Encyclopedia

Published in association with the Georgia Humanities Council
and the University System of Georgia/GALILEO

THE UNIVERSITY OF GEORGIA PRESS   *Athens & London*

Published in 2011 by the University of Georgia Press

Athens, Georgia 30602

www.ugapress.org

© 2004–11 by the Georgia Humanities Council and
the University of Georgia Press

All rights reserved

Designed by Erin Kirk New

Set in New Baskerville Std by
Graphic Composition, Inc., Bogart, Georgia

Printed and bound by Thomson-Shore

The paper in this book meets the guidelines for
permanence and durability of the Committee on
Production Guidelines for Book Longevity of the
Council on Library Resources.

Printed in the United States of America

15   14   13   12   11   P   5   4   3   2   1

Library of Congress Cataloging-in-Publication Data

The Civil War in Georgia : a new Georgia encyclopedia companion
/ edited by John C. Inscoe.
   p. cm.
Includes bibliographical references and index.
ISBN-13: 978-0-8203-4138-5 (hardcover : alk. paper)
ISBN-10: 0-8203-4138-x (hardcover : alk. paper)
ISBN-13: 978-0-8203–3981-8 (pbk. : alk. paper)
ISBN-10: 0-8203-3981-4 (pbk. : alk. paper)
1. Georgia—History—Civil War, 1861–1865.
I. Inscoe, John C., 1951–
E559.C5 2011
975.8'03—dc22   2011009442

British Library Cataloging-in-Publication Data available

} Contents

THE NEW GEORGIA ENCYCLOPEDIA, an online multimedia publication, is a project of the Georgia Humanities Council in partnership with the University of Georgia Press, the University System of Georgia/GALILEO, and the Office of the Governor.

The NGE provides an accessible, authoritative source of information about people, places, events, historical themes, institutions, and many other topics relating to

- the arts
- business and industry
- cities and counties
- education
- folklife
- government and politics
- history and archaeology
- land and resources
- literature
- media
- religion
- science and medicine
- sports and recreation
- transportation

THE **NEW GEORGIA**
ENCYCLOPEDIA
www.georgiaencyclopedia.org

} Acknowledgments

There is no scholarly endeavor as inherently collaborative in nature as an encyclopedia. That is certainly the case with this volume, as it is for the larger online project from which it is drawn, the New Georgia Encyclopedia (www.georgiaencyclopedia.org). Kelly Caudle, the NGE's project manager and managing editor, and Sarah McKee, the project editor, should by all rights have been listed as coeditors of this volume, given their input in every phase of its development and implementation. The three of us worked closely in determining what content to include, how to organize it, and how to adapt it from our online site to this print version. Sarah deserves special credit for her careful oversight of every phase of the process; her creativity and good judgment are evident throughout, most notably in the brief excerpts scattered throughout the text, which we hope lure readers back to the many other relevant articles in the NGE.

There are many others, of course, who have contributed to the creation of this book. First and foremost, we thank the more than sixty contributors—including established scholars, students, and history enthusiasts—for their carefully researched and thoughtful entries covering myriad aspects of the Civil War in Georgia. We also thank Stephen Berry, an associate professor of history at the University of Georgia, for shepherding the students in a 2009 graduate class through the writing of several articles, which provide depth and variety to this presentation of Georgia's Civil War story.

We are deeply grateful to the NGE's fact checkers, most of whom are university reference librarians, who have helped to ensure that the information presented in these entries is as accurate and reliable as possible. In particular we would like to recognize Kristin Nielsen and Patrick Reidenbaugh of the University of Georgia Libraries, both for their efforts to complete the fact checking of new entries so that they could be included in this book and most especially for their longtime dedication and invaluable contributions to the encyclopedia as a whole.

We are grateful to Nicole Mitchell, the director of the University of Georgia Press, for her enthusiastic support of this volume, as well as for the NGE itself over the past decade. She offered welcome advice and direction, as well as copious patience, during the process of revising and organizing our online content into a book manuscript. It was a pleasure to work with Jon Davies, as he shepherded us efficiently and with good cheer through this volume's production. We appreciate the input at various other stages of production by his colleagues Erin New, Kathi Morgan, John Joerschke, John McLeod, and Pat Allen, as well as the good work of cartographer David Wasserboehr.

And finally, we offer our sincere appreciation for the contributions of our project partners, the University System of Georgia/GALILEO and the Georgia Humanities Council. In particular, we thank GALILEO director Merryll Penson and her staff, whose technical guidance and support are essential to the success of the NGE. We are also grateful to the Georgia Humanities Council, the copublishers of this book and enthusiastic champions of the NGE. Council president Jamil Zainaldin and vice president Laura McCarty have been integral to every aspect of developing and implementing the New Georgia Encyclopedia, as well as this volume.

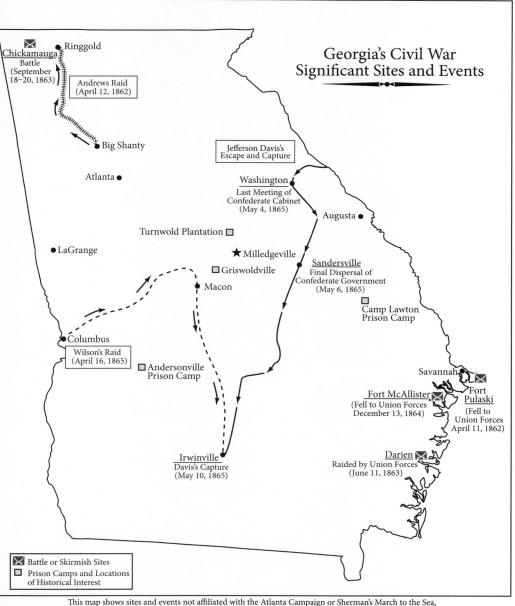

Georgia's Civil War
Significant Sites and Events

Ringgold

Chickamauga
Battle
(September
18–20, 1863)

Andrews Raid
(April 12, 1862)

Big Shanty

Atlanta

Jefferson Davis's
Escape and Capture

Washington
Last Meeting of
Confederate Cabinet
(May 4, 1865)

Augusta

Turnwold Plantation

LaGrange

★ Milledgeville

Griswoldville

Sandersville
Final Dispersal of
Confederate Government
(May 6, 1865)

Macon

Camp Lawton
Prison Camp

Columbus

Wilson's Raid
(April 16, 1865)

Andersonville
Prison Camp

Savannah

Fort McAllister
(Fell to Union Forces
December 13, 1864)

Fort
Pulaski
(Fell to
Union Forces
April 11, 1862)

Irwinville
Davis's Capture
(May 10, 1865)

Darien
Raided by Union Forces
(June 11, 1863)

Battle or Skirmish Sites
Prison Camps and Locations
of Historical Interest

This map shows sites and events not affiliated with the Atlanta Campaign or Sherman's March to the Sea,
maps of which are available on pages 78–79 and 95.

} Introduction

Georgians, like all Americans, experienced the Civil War in a variety of ways. With the exception of the Battle of Chickamauga in 1863, the state avoided major military conflict until 1864, when for nine months Union general William T. Sherman's troops moved across Georgia to devastating effect, pushing slowly and painfully toward Atlanta, and then more rapidly toward Savannah and the coast. The Atlanta campaign and March to the Sea changed the course of the war, as John Fowler notes in the overview essay that opens this book. Both events had a direct impact on national politics (particularly on U.S. president Abraham Lincoln's reelection) and, perhaps more debatably, on Southerners' continued commitment to the Confederate cause. Sherman's incursion also left a legacy that was far more traumatic and indelible for the state than would have been the case had the war come to an end earlier, as many assumed it would.

Yet, long before Sherman made his appearance, the people of Georgia felt the hard hand of war, and in ways that had little to do with invading armies or battlefield clashes. Naval encounters and guerrilla conflicts characterized the early years of the war in Georgia, while the prisons and hospitals, factories and plantations on the state's home front provided critical support to the Confederacy. The historian F. N. Boney succinctly describes the state's significance to the Confederacy in his book *Rebel Georgia*: "As Virginia dominated the upper South, Georgia was the cornerstone of the deep South. These states were the two essential Confederate bastions; if either crumbled, the war was lost." Finally, just as the institution of slavery was central in bringing on the war, so too did its demise at the end of the war play an integral role in shaping Georgia's postwar society. The liberation of nearly half the state's wartime populace, more so than any other aspect of Southern defeat, created an economy that was radically different from the antebellum order that Southerners had gone to war to uphold.

These are the stories told here. Through selected articles from the *New Georgia Encyclopedia* (www.georgiaencyclopedia.org), this book reveals Georgia's experience of the war, on both the battlefield and the home front, and demonstrates how activity in the state proved vital to the Confederacy as a whole. The content and arrangement of these articles also reflect the new ways in which the Civil War, a defining event in Southern, indeed, U.S., history, has come to be studied, documented, and analyzed.

The Civil War is understood and chronicled very differently in 2011, the beginning of its sesquicentennial, than it was in 1961, the beginning of its centennial. For much of the twentieth century, historians focused largely on the military aspects of the war. As military scholars are quick to remind us, war is first and foremost defined by battles, campaigns, and military strategies. These topics, along with biographies of generals and other military leaders, both Union and Confederate, dominated Civil War scholarship for decades. Such works joined those by Bruce Catton and Shelby Foote, whose masterful, multivolume narratives were largely military in focus, as well as those by Emory University historian Bell Wiley, who wrote two celebrated studies of the common soldier's experiences: *The Life of Johnny Reb* (1943) and *The Life of Billy Yank* (1952).

The content of this book reflects not only such traditional military examinations of the war but also the significant expansion of Civil War studies since the centennial. Recent scholarship explores the nonmilitary facets of the war years in greater depth and variety, putting considerable emphasis on such topics as home-front conditions, emancipation, dissent, Unionism, gender roles, and guerrilla warfare. Another recent trend is an increased focus on how Americans, and particularly Southerners, remember and commemorate the war. The Civil War's legacy is constantly evolving; what began during Reconstruction has continued into the twenty-first century, and historians today are far more conscious of how memory—whether as public commemoration, individual reminiscence, historic preservation, or literary and cinematic interpretation—shapes the war's multiple meanings. At the outset of the sesquicentennial these new historical perspectives allow us to appreciate the conflict as a complex and multifaceted experience for Georgians and for all Southerners—soldiers and civilians, men and women, blacks and whites.

This book begins with an overview of the Civil War in Georgia, followed by articles arranged into three chronological sections. Subsections within the three main sections further group articles by subject matter or theme. The first section, entitled "Prelude to War," chronicles the events leading up to the war and the prominent roles played by the state's native sons in the sectional crisis of the 1850s, as well as its culmination in 1860–61 with Georgia's decision to leave the Union and join the new Confederate nation.

The second section, "The War Years," covers the battles, campaigns, and military strategies that defined the conflict in Georgia. While the Atlanta campaign and Sherman's March to the Sea are central to that coverage, those events are set within the broader context of other significant military activity in the state, both before and after the turbulent year of 1864. Also covered in this section are the multiple forms of military support and services, and the many facets of home-front activity and civilian experience that took place in Georgia, capped by the most momentous event of all—emancipation.

When the war ended in 1865, Georgians began the long process of rebuilding their lives and communities. The volume's third section, "The War's Legacy," explores the immediate aftermath of the war in Georgia, beginning with Reconstruction, and continues into the twenty-first-century efforts of historians, reenactors, archaeologists, curators, park rangers, writers, and filmmakers, whose work provides us with new perspectives on the conflict.

While most articles appear here in their entirety, several (most of which appear as boxes) have been slightly condensed from their online versions, and some have been formed by consolidating sections of broader articles; in such cases multiple authors are credited. Because our original intent was that each article should stand alone in terms of relevant content, certain basic information appears in more than one place. Although many individuals in Georgia played key roles in the Civil War and its later commemoration, biographical entries are not included in this volume due to space constraints. We encourage readers to visit the *New Georgia Encyclopedia* online for full entries on the men and women who figure prominently in Georgia's Civil War story and for further treatments of topics related to the war.

} Overview:
The Civil War in Georgia

The South, like the rest of the country, was forever altered by the dramatic events of the Civil War. Few states, however, were more integral to the outcome of the conflict than Georgia, which provided an estimated 120,000 soldiers for the Confederacy, as well as 3,500 black troops and a few hundred whites for the Union cause.

Georgia's agricultural output was critical to the Confederate war effort, and because Georgia was a transportation and industrial center for the Confederacy, both sides struggled for control of the state. Some of the most important battles of the war were fought on Georgia soil, including Chickamauga, Resaca, and Kennesaw Mountain, while the battles of Peachtree Creek, Bald Hill (Atlanta), Ezra Church, and Jonesboro were significant turning points during the Atlanta campaign of 1864. Perhaps most important, one can argue that the Civil War's outcome was decided in Georgia with the Atlanta campaign and U.S. president Abraham Lincoln's subsequent reelection.

Georgians' Road to War

When Lincoln's election to the presidency triggered the secession crisis in the winter of 1860–61, most Georgians initially hoped for yet another sectional compromise. The Georgia legislature, however, following a directive from Governor Joseph E. Brown, appropriated $1 million for military expenses and called for the election of delegates to a state convention to discuss secession. The majority of Georgia's political leaders at this point, including Francis S. Bartow, Henry Benning, Governor Brown, Howell Cobb, Thomas R. R. Cobb, Wilson Lumpkin, Eugenius A. Nisbet, and Robert Toombs, advocated secession. Their efforts focused on exciting white Southerners' fears of slave insurrection and abolition, which could potentially lead to black equality and intermarriage.

Despite the best efforts of such antisecessionists as Alexander Stephens and Benjamin Hill, the die was cast. The secession convention vote on January 19, 1861, took Georgia out of the Union as expected, though by a closer vote than many had anticipated. Infantry regiments were authorized, and the convention appointed Bartow, the Cobb brothers, Nisbet, Toombs, Stephens, and four others as delegates to a convention of other seceded states to meet in Montgomery, Alabama, on February 4. At Montgomery, the delegates organized the Confederate States of America, and Georgians played an important role in creating the provisional Confederate government. Howell Cobb served as president of the convention, and Thomas R. R. Cobb was the main architect of the Confederate Constitution. Toombs and Stephens were prominent in the proceedings, but to their disappointment the presidency of the new nation fell to Jefferson Davis of Mississippi. Still, Stephens won the vice presidency, and Toombs accepted the office of secretary of state.

The War Begins

After secession, most Georgians hoped to avoid war and peacefully leave the Union, but the firing on Fort Sumter, the harbor in Charleston, South Carolina, made conflict inevitable. Governor Brown's call for volunteers on April 18 brought an enthusiastic response, and by October 1861 around 25,000 Georgians had enlisted in Confederate service. At first, Georgians experienced the war on far-off battlefields in Virginia and Tennessee. Soon, however, the war came to Georgia by sea. A Union naval force under Admiral Samuel F. Du Pont, commander of the South Atlantic Blockading Squadron, established a base of operations on Hilton Head Island, South Carolina, in the fall of 1861, to launch attacks along the south Atlantic coast. Alarmed, President Davis sent General Robert E. Lee to Savannah to organize the defense of Georgia and upper Florida. Lee lacked the resources to do much, however, and before long Union forces began capturing key points along Georgia's coast. By March 1862 Union troops had seized all of Georgia's coastal islands, and on April 10, 1862, Union batteries on Tybee Island wrecked Fort Pulaski, leading to the fort's surrender and the closure of Savannah as a functioning port.

By the war's second year, the Union also targeted Georgia's railroads. In April 1862 Union spy James J. Andrews led twenty saboteurs in a daring raid. In Big Shanty (present-day Kennesaw, in Cobb County) they seized the *General* locomotive and steamed northward. Western and Atlantic Railroad officials pursued them and, after a nearly ninety-mile chase, caught the Andrews gang near Ringgold before they could significantly damage the rail line. Confederate soldiers captured most of the saboteurs, and Andrews and seven of his raiders were hanged as spies in Atlanta. A year later, a Union cavalry force under Colonel Abel D. Streight attempted to cut the Western and Atlantic rail line near Rome, but Confederate general Nathan Bedford Forrest captured the Union force before it could do any real damage.

Georgians Battling Richmond

Meanwhile, the hardships and realities of war began to wear on Georgians. In April 1862 the Confederate government in Richmond initiated conscription to replenish depleted ranks. This was the first national draft in American history. Governor Brown argued that the draft was unconstitutional and despotic. He fought it and tried to maintain control of the state militia and other state troops. As the age limits of the draft were expanded, Brown protested anew. He relentlessly labored to field some viable separate state force and further circumvented conscription by recruiting militia members, who became known as "Joe Brown's Pets."

Despite attacks from pro-Davis nationalists, Brown remained popular and won a fourth straight term as governor in 1863. But Brown was not the only Georgia statesman battling the Davis administration. Vice President Stephens spent much of his time at his home in Georgia denouncing Davis's despotism. Toombs had quickly become bored as secretary of state and left to command a military brigade in Virginia, but he soon resigned and spent the rest of the war also denouncing the Davis administration. Even moderate Herschel V. Johnson joined the critics of the Richmond government. These men did much to hinder Confederate efforts and inflame anti-Davis sentiment.

Home-Front Mobilization

While Brown struggled with the centralization policies of the Confederate government, he also worked to increase the state's wartime production, especially with the manufacture of military supplies and equipment. Georgia quickly became a vital production center for the Confederate war effort. Atlanta, the state's rail center, emerged as a home front, and the city contained one of the South's few rolling mills, a quartermaster's depot, and several major military hospitals. Additionally, Augusta, Columbus, Macon, and Savannah were vital industrial centers. Augusta was home to the Confederate Powder Works, the largest gunpowder factory in the Confederacy; one of the largest textile mills in the South; and an arsenal. Columbus had the Confederate Naval Iron Works, Columbus Naval Yard, cotton and woolen mills, and the South's largest shoe factory. An arsenal in Savannah produced munitions until 1862, when operations were moved to Macon after the fall of Fort Pulaski. Macon also boasted a laboratory for bullet design and testing and was a depository for Confederate gold. The industrial village of Griswoldville, near Macon, manufactured weaponry before being destroyed by Union troops.

Financing the war was another struggle for the Brown administration. Like the rest of the Confederacy, Georgia tried to pay for the war with bonds and treasury notes instead of taxes. This led to massive inflation as paper money poured into the economy and the price of necessities soared beyond the reach of the masses. By early 1864 in Atlanta, for example, firewood sold for $80 a cord, corn for $10 a bushel, and flour for $120 a barrel; by contrast a Confederate private received $11 a month.

Governor Brown worked tirelessly to aid common whites and made sure that needy soldiers and their families received money and salt to preserve foodstuffs. Yet the hardships of war touched the lives of every citizen, male and female, white and black. Georgia soldiers saw action in every major campaign of the Civil War, and although Georgia units were engaged in the battles of the western theater, most served in the eastern theater in the Army of Northern Virginia. These men faced chronic shortages of food, clothing, and medicine as the ravages of combat and sickness relentlessly depleted their ranks. At home, white women faced the dilemma of managing farms and providing food for themselves and the war effort without adequate labor. Indeed, Georgia women had to step into multiple roles, providing support to soldier aid societies, working in hospitals or factories, and caring for their families.

Social and Military Upheavals

The war also challenged slavery and the plight of African Americans. Slavery broke down during the war, with slaves using the absence of white males to secure better working and living conditions. While most slaves remained on farms and plantations, many served the war effort of both sides as cooks, teamsters, servants, and laborers. Moreover, as Union forces penetrated the state, many slaves ran away to seek their freedom with the advancing Northern troops. Overwhelmed by the influx of freedpeople, Union forces set up "contraband" camps to provide food and shelter. In 1862 Union authorities began to authorize black enlistment, and many black recruits emerged on the coast and in northwest Georgia.

While both Confederate and Union forces sought to find ways to use black labor, freedpeople continually looked for ways to assert their own desire for freedom, dignity, and economic stability. Crucial to maintaining and enhancing their physical freedom was ownership of land. In Savannah, Union general William T. Sherman issued his controversial Special Field Order No. 15, giving freedpeople control of abandoned lands in the Sea Islands and signaling a new era of black independence throughout the South. While radical elements of the Republican Party applauded this measure, the idea of taking property from whites, even Confederates, and giving it to African Americans proved far too drastic for the majority of white Americans, North and South. Therefore, the order was rescinded following the war.

Adding to the chaos of the home front was the growing presence of Confederate deserters who, after 1863, hid in remote areas of the state, from the mountains in the north to the swamps and piney woods in the southeast. Equally harsh, Confederate and Unionist guerrillas of north Georgia made a hellish existence for many civilians. Georgia's Appalachian counties had long been a stronghold for Unionists, and as the war continued to turn against the Confederacy, these areas became ever more hostile toward the Confederate government. War weariness led to other forms of dissent from Georgia civilians, who by late in the war joined with more ideologically committed Unionists to resist government-imposed conscription, impressment, and taxes-in-kind.

Union Military Incursion

The first full-scale military operation in Georgia took place in the late summer of 1863. In September a Union army under Major General William S. Rosecrans captured Chattanooga, Tennessee, and swept into Georgia. Later that month, Confederate forces under General Braxton Bragg defeated Rosecrans at the Battle of Chickamauga and followed the retreating Union troops back to Chattanooga. The situation eventually led Lincoln to remove Rosecrans and appoint Ulysses S. Grant as commander of all Union forces in the western theater. Using reinforcements, Grant shattered Bragg's forces at Missionary Ridge, sending them fleeing to Dalton in north Georgia.

In May 1864, the beginning of the Atlanta campaign, the Union launched simultaneous advances in Virginia and Georgia designed to crush the last remaining Southern resistance. General Sherman began the invasion of Georgia with more than 110,000 men. His objective was to capture Atlanta and destroy the Confederate Army of Tennessee under the command of Bragg's replacement, General Joseph E. Johnston.

Using his superior numbers to outflank the Confederate defenses of Dalton, Sherman began a long series of flanking maneuvers designed to bypass Johnston's fortified positions. Only once, at the Battle of Kennesaw Mountain, did the Union troops attempt a large-scale frontal assault. Its failure led to a return to the war of maneuver. By July Sherman had pushed Johnston to Peachtree Creek at the outskirts of Atlanta. An anxious President Davis replaced Johnston with General John B. Hood. An aggressive commander, Hood attacked Sherman repeatedly during the battles of Peachtree Creek, Bald Hill (Atlanta), and Ezra Church. Although the attacks failed to destroy the Union troops, they did stymie Sherman's advance.

Meanwhile, in August, the Confederates managed to defeat two Union cavalry raids headed for Macon and Andersonville. By the end of the month, however, Sherman broke the last Confederate rail line supplying Atlanta at Jonesboro, forcing the Confederates to abandon the city. The fall of Atlanta helped to ensure the reelection of Lincoln, thus making the Atlanta campaign arguably the most important of the war in terms of political consequences.

After evacuating Atlanta, Hood's army marched north into Tennessee, hoping to disrupt Sherman's supply lines and draw him away from Georgia. Sherman briefly followed but then swung back to Atlanta after sending Major General George H. Thomas northward with sufficient forces to crush Hood's army near Nashville, Tennessee, by the end of the year. Meanwhile, in mid-November, Sherman launched his March to the Sea. Having destroyed Atlanta's capacity as a rail and industrial center, Sherman and 60,000 men marched southeastward against token opposition, cutting a sixty-mile-wide swath through Georgia to Savannah. Along the way, rail lines, bridges, factories, mills, and other wartime resources were annihilated. Despite orders, private property was also looted and destroyed. The Union soldiers foraged liberally off the land, although instances of murder and rape were rare.

On December 21, 1864, Union forces finally reached Savannah. Triumphantly, Sherman telegraphed Lincoln: "I beg to present you as a

Christmas gift the city of Savannah with 150 heavy guns and plenty of ammunition and also about 25,000 bales of cotton." In February 1865 Sherman moved northward out of the state to crush resistance in the Carolinas.

The War's End

The last significant military action in Georgia came from Alabama, with Union major general James Harrison Wilson's cavalry force capturing Columbus on April 16, wrecking its industrial center, and moving on to Macon. Wilson's Raid occurred one week after the surrender of the Confederacy at Appomattox. By early May, Governor Brown formally surrendered the state's remaining military forces. Union forces quickly arrested Brown, Stephens, and Cobb, but Toombs escaped to Europe. Also captured was Captain Henry Wirz, the commandant at Andersonville Prison, which had the highest mortality rate of any Civil War prison; Wirz was the only person to be executed for war crimes committed during the Civil War.

Jefferson Davis held the last meeting of the shadow government at Washington in Wilkes County. On May 10 Wilson's forces captured him at Irwinville. The long war had finally ended, and the emancipation of the slaves was completed in 1865. Although Georgians realized that the nation would remain united and that slavery had ended, other questions remained to be answered as they sought to build a new Georgia from the rubble of the old.

JOHN D. FOWLER

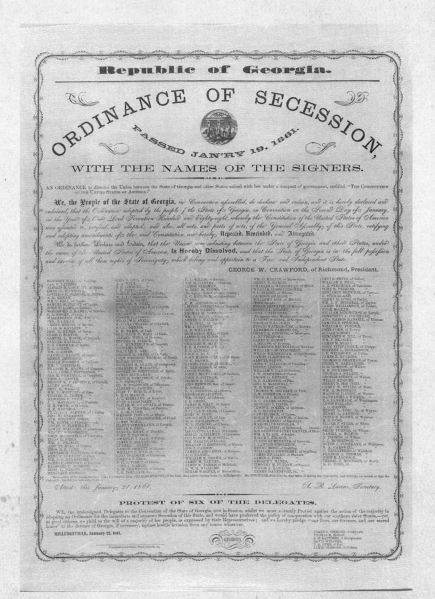

Georgia's Ordinance of Secession, signed in Milledgeville on January 21, 1861. Courtesy of Hargrett Rare Book and Manuscript Library / University of Georgia Libraries.

THE CIVIL WAR WAS VERY MUCH A POLITICAL WAR, one brought on by the simultaneous failure of national political leadership and the triumph of Southern politicians pushing regional agendas. Following an overview of antebellum slavery and a socioeconomic snapshot of the state in 1860, this opening section focuses on the political issues, processes, and decisions that led Georgia out of the Union in January 1861 and negotiated its place within the Confederate nation created only a few weeks later.

By the 1850s national debates over the institution of slavery, which had formed the bedrock of Georgia's agricultural economy for a century, intensified as the United States continued to acquire new western territories. During this sectional crisis, many white Georgians, along with other Southerners, argued vehemently to maintain protections for slavery in the face of rising abolitionist sentiment in the North. The crisis finally culminated in secession. On January 19, 1861, Georgia became the fifth state to secede from the Union in the aftermath of Abraham Lincoln's election to the presidency, and the state joined with six others in Montgomery, Alabama, to form the new Confederate nation on February 1. The opening shots of the war in April at Fort Sumter, outside Charleston, South Carolina, and President Lincoln's subsequent call for troops to put down the rebellion brought four more states into the Confederacy by May.

In the end, the decision to leave the Union was made eleven different times by eleven different states over a period of five months. Despite the major national developments that fueled the secession movement across the South, there were significant variables in how the secession process played out in individual states. Differences in leadership, shifting sentiments, geographic variables among a state's populace, and other factors all contributed to how and when Georgia and other states chose to take themselves out of the Union. Thus, while Georgia shared much along the road to disunion and war with its fellow Deep South states, certain circumstances, personalities, and socioeconomic realities also determined the route it took and the role it played within the larger Confederacy.

} Slavery

When the Georgia Trustees first envisioned their colonial experiment in the early 1730s, they sought to avoid the slave-based plantation economy that had developed in other colonies in the American South. The allure of profits from slavery, however, proved to be too powerful for white Georgia settlers to resist. By the era of the American Revolution (1775–83), African slaves constituted nearly half of Georgia's population. Although the Revolution fostered the growth of an antislavery movement in the Northern states, white Georgia landowners fiercely maintained their commitment to slavery even as the war disrupted the plantation economy. At the constitutional convention in Philadelphia, Pennsylvania, in 1787, Georgia delegates joined with South Carolina's to insert clauses protecting slavery into the new federal charter. In subsequent decades slavery would play an ever-increasing role in Georgia's shifting plantation economy.

Cotton and the Growth of Slavery

For almost the entire eighteenth century Georgia's plantation economy was concentrated on the production of rice, a crop that could be commercially cultivated only in the Lowcountry. During the Revolution planters began to cultivate cotton for domestic use. After the war the explosive growth of the textile industry promised to turn cotton into a potentially lucrative staple crop—if only efficient methods of cleaning the tenacious seeds from the cotton fibers could be developed. By the 1790s entrepreneurs were perfecting new mechanized cotton gins, the most famous of which was invented by Eli Whitney on a Savannah River plantation owned by Catharine Greene in 1793. This technological advance presented Georgia planters with a staple crop that could be grown over much of the state. As early as the 1780s white politicians in Georgia were working to acquire and to distribute fertile western lands controlled by the Creek Indians, a process that continued in the nineteenth century with the expulsion of the Cherokees. By the 1830s cotton plantations had spread across most of the state.

As was the case for rice production, cotton planters relied upon the labor power of enslaved African and African American people. Accordingly, the slave population of Georgia increased dramatically during the early decades of the nineteenth century. In 1790, just before the explosion in cotton production, some 29,264 slaves resided in the state. In 1793 the Georgia Assembly passed a law prohibiting the importation of slaves. The law did not go into effect until 1798, when the state constitution also went into effect, but the measure was widely ignored by planters, who urgently sought to increase their enslaved workforce. By 1800 the slave population in Georgia had more than doubled, to 59,699; by 1810 the number of slaves had grown to 105,218.

The 48,000 African slaves imported into Georgia during this era accounted for much of the initial surge in the slave population. When Congress banned the African slave trade in 1808, however, Georgia's slave population did not decline. Instead, the number of slaves imported from the Chesapeake's stagnant plantation economy as well as the number of children born to Georgia slave mothers continued to outpace the number of slaves who died or were transported from Georgia. In 1820 the slave population stood at 149,656; in 1840 the slave population had increased to 280,944; and in 1860, on the eve of the Civil War, some 462,198 slaves constituted 44 percent of the state's total population. By the end of the antebellum era Georgia had more slaves and slaveholders than any state in the Lower South and was second only to Virginia in the South as a whole. The lower Piedmont, or Black Belt, counties—so named after the region's distinctively dark and fertile soil—were the site of the largest, most productive cotton plantations. Over the antebellum era some two-thirds of the state's total population lived in these counties, which encompassed roughly the middle third of the state. By 1860 the slave population in the Black Belt was ten times greater than that in the coastal counties, where rice remained the most important crop.

Slaveholders

Although slavery played a dominant economic and political role in Georgia, most white Georgians did not own slaves. In 1860 less than one-third of Georgia's adult white male population of 132,317 were slaveholders. The percentage of free families holding slaves was somewhat higher (37 percent) but still well short of a majority. Moreover, only 6,363 of Georgia's 41,084 slaveholders owned twenty or more slaves. The planter elite, who made up just 15 percent of the state's slaveholder population, were far outnumbered by the 20,077 slaveholders who owned fewer than six slaves. In other words, only half of Georgia's slaveholders owned more than a handful of slaves, and Georgia's planters constituted less than 5 percent of the state's adult white male population.

These statistics, however, do not reveal the economic, cultural, and political force wielded by the slaveholding minority of the population. Slaveholders controlled not only the best land and the vast majority of personal property in the state but also the state political system. In 1850 and 1860 more than two-thirds of all state legislators were slaveholders. More striking, almost a third of the state legislators were planters. Hence, even without the cooperation of nonslaveholding white male voters, Georgia slaveholders could dictate the state's political path.

As it turned out, slaveholders expected and largely realized harmonious relations with the rest of the white population. During election season wealthy planters courted nonslaveholding voters by inviting them to celebrations that mixed speech-making with abundant supplies of food and drink. On such occasions slaveholders shook hands with yeomen and tenant farmers as if they were equals. Nonslaveholding whites, for their part, frequently relied upon nearby slaveholders to gin their cotton and to assist them in bringing their crop to market. These political and economic interactions were further reinforced by the common racial bond among white Georgia men. Sharing the prejudice that slaveholders harbored against African Americans, nonslaveholding whites believed that the abolition of slavery would destroy their own economic prospects and bring catastrophe to the state as a whole.

Propping up the institution of slavery was a judicial system that denied African Americans the legal rights enjoyed by white Americans. Since the colonial era, children born of slave mothers were deemed chattel slaves, doomed to "follow the condition of the mother" irrespective of the father's status. Georgia law supported slavery in that the state restricted the right of slaveholders to free individual slaves, a measure that was strengthened over the antebellum era. Other statutes made the circulation of abolitionist material a capital offense and outlawed slave literacy and unsupervised assembly. Although the law technically prohibited whites from abusing or killing slaves, it was extremely rare for whites to be prosecuted and convicted for these crimes. The legal prohibition against slave testimony about whites denied slaves the ability to provide evidence of their victimization. On the other hand, Georgia courts recognized slave confessions and, depending on the circumstances of the case, slave testimony against other slaves.

The relative scarcity of legal cases concerning slave defendants suggests that most slaveholders meted out discipline without involving the courts. Slaveholders resorted to an array of physical and psychological punishments in response to slave misconduct, including the use of whips, wooden rods, boots, fists, and dogs. The threat of selling a slave away from loved ones and family members was perhaps the most powerful weapon available to slaveholders. In general, punishment was designed to maximize the slaveholders' ability to gain profit from slave labor. Evidence also suggests that slaveholders were willing to employ violence and threats in order to coerce slaves into sexual relationships.

Over the antebellum era whites continued to employ violence against the slave population, but increasingly they justified their mastery in moral terms. As early as 1790, Georgia congressman James Jackson claimed that slavery benefited both whites and African Americans. The expanding presence of evangelical Christian churches in the early nineteenth century provided Georgia slaveholders with religious justifications for human bondage. White efforts to Christianize the slave quarters enabled masters to frame their power in moral terms. They viewed the Christian slave mission as evidence of their own good intentions. The religious instruction offered by whites, moreover, reinforced slaveholders' authority by reminding slaves of scriptural admonishments that slaves should "give single-minded obedience" to their "earthly masters with fear and trembling, as if to Christ."

This melding of religion and slavery did not protect slaves from exploitation and cruelty at the hands of their owners, but it magnified the role played by slavery in the identity of the planter elite. In 1785, just before the genesis of the cotton plantation system, a Georgia merchant had claimed that slavery was "to the Trade of the Country, as the Soul [is] to the Body." Seventy-five years later Georgia politician Alexander Stephens noted that slavery had become a moral as well as an economic foundation for white plantation culture. The "corner-stone" of the South, Stephens claimed in 1861, just after the Lower South had seceded, consisted of the "great physical, philosophical, and moral truth," which is "that the negro is not equal to the white man; that slavery—subordination to the superior race—is his natural and normal condition."

Alexander Stephens, of Taliaferro County, served as the vice president of the Confederacy during the Civil War. An ardent defender of slavery, Stephens also opposed separation from the Union right up to the time Georgia seceded in January 1861.—From online entry "Alexander Stephens"

WWW.GEORGIAENCYCLOPEDIA.ORG

Slaves

Depending on their place of residence and the personality of their masters, slaves in Georgia experienced tremendous variety in the conditions of their daily lives. Although the typical (median) Georgia slaveholder owned six slaves in 1860, the typical slave resided on a plantation with twenty to twenty-nine other slaves. Almost half of Georgia's slave population lived on estates with more than thirty slaves. Most Georgia slaves therefore had access to a slave community that partially offset the harshness of bondage. Slave testimony revealed the huge importance of family relationships in the slave quarters. Many slaves were able to live in family units, spending together their limited time away from the masters' fields. Frequently Georgia slave families cultivated their own gardens and raised livestock, and slave men sometimes supplemented their families' diets by hunting and fishing. Christianity also served as a pillar of slave life in Georgia in the antebellum era. Unlike their masters, slaves drew from Christianity the message of black equality and empowerment. In the early nineteenth century African American preachers played a significant role in spreading the Gospel in the quarters.

Throughout the antebellum era some 30,000 Georgia slaves resided in the Lowcountry, where they enjoyed a relatively high degree of autonomy from white supervision. Most white planters avoided the unhealthy plantation environment along the coast, leaving large slave populations under the supervision of a small group of white overseers. Slaves were assigned daily tasks and were permitted to leave the fields when their tasks had been completed. Lowcountry slaves enjoyed a far greater degree of control over their time than was the case across the rest of the state, where slaves worked in gangs under direct white supervision. The white cultural presence in the Lowcountry was sufficiently small for slaves to retain significant traces of African linguistic and spiritual traditions. The resulting Geechee culture of the Georgia coast was the counterpart of the better-known Gullah culture of the South Carolina Lowcountry.

The urban environment of Savannah also created considerable opportunities for slaves to live away from their owners' watchful eyes. Slave entrepreneurs assembled in markets and sold their wares to black and white customers, an economy that enabled some slaves to amass their own wealth. A number of slave artisans in Savannah were "hired out" by their masters, meaning that they worked and sometimes lived away from their masters. Savannah's taverns and brothels also served as meeting places in which African Americans socialized without owners' supervision.

This cultural autonomy, however, was never complete or secure. The rice plantations were literally killing fields. On one Savannah River rice plantation, mortality annually averaged 10 percent of the slave population between 1833 and 1861. During cholera epidemics on some Lowcountry plantations, more than half the slave population died in a matter of months. Infant mortality in the Lowcountry slave quarters also greatly exceeded the rates experienced by white Americans during this era. In addition to the threat of disease, slaveholders frequently shattered family and community ties by selling away slaves. More than 2 million Southern slaves were sold in the domestic slave trade of the antebellum era.

Away from the Lowcountry, health patterns were much less grim, but slaves tended to experience greater degrees of white supervision. Three-quarters of Georgia's slave population resided on cotton plantations in the Black Belt. These slaves typically experienced some degree of slave community but also were surrounded by far greater numbers of whites. Some one-fifth of the state's slave population was owned by slaveholders with fewer than ten slaves. These slaves doubtless faced greater obstacles in forming relationships outside their owners' purview. Whatever their location, slaves in Georgia resisted their masters with strategies that included overt violence against whites, flight, the destruction of white property, and deliberately inefficient work practices. Slaves in Georgia experienced hideous cruelties, but white slaveholders never succeeded in extinguishing the slaves' human capacity to covet freedom.

The Beginning of the End

By the late 1820s white slaveholders in Georgia—like their counterparts across the South—increasingly feared that antislavery forces were working to liberate the slave population. In the months following Abraham Lincoln's election as president of the United States in 1860, Georgia's planter politicians debated and ultimately paved the way for the state's secession from the Union on January 19, 1861. Statesmen like Senator Robert Toombs argued that secession was a necessary response to a long-standing abolitionist campaign to "disturb our security, our tranquility—to excite discontent between the different classes of our people, and to excite our slaves to insurrection." Lincoln's election, according to these politicians, meant "the abolition of slavery," and that act would be "one of the direst evils of which the mind can conceive."

Ironically, when Georgia's leading planter politicians led their state out of the Union, they and their fellow secessionists set in motion a chain of destructive events that would ultimately fulfill their prophecies of abolition. The arrival of Union gunboats along the Georgia coast in late 1861 marked the beginning of the end of white ownership of black slaves.

JEFFREY ROBERT YOUNG

Wanderer

The *Wanderer* was the last ship to bring slaves from Africa to Georgia and one of the last ships to smuggle bondsmen to American soil. On November 28, 1858, the *Wanderer* arrived at Jekyll Island, where its crew smuggled ashore 409 slaves acquired in West Africa.

The incident is especially noteworthy because the federal Slave Importation Act, passed in 1807, had officially banned the foreign importation of slaves into the United States. News of the *Wanderer* and its cargo quickly spread across the country and contributed to the sectional tensions between the North and the South that would soon lead to secession and the Civil War.

Late in 1857 Colonel John D. Johnson, a New Orleans sugar baron who was also a member of the prestigious New York [City] Yacht Club, commissioned a 238-ton luxury sailing vessel to be built on Long Island for his personal use.

Despite the ship's attributes, Johnson, for whatever reason, did not keep the *Wanderer* for long. In 1858 he sold the vessel for $25,000 to William C. Corrie of Charleston, South Carolina.

Shortly after his purchase, Corrie was approached by business associate Charles A. L. Lamar of Savannah, who proposed that together they retrofit the *Wanderer* and convert it into a slave ship. Lamar, scion of a prominent Savannah family, was a "fire-eating" radical who had long opposed the U.S. government's restriction on the importation of slaves. Corrie agreed to his associate's proposition.

Corrie returned the *Wanderer* to New York and oversaw its transformation from luxury yacht to slave transport, which included storage space for 15,000 gallons of drinking water and a second, hidden deck inserted beneath the main deck. After further alterations made in Charleston, the *Wanderer* set sail for Africa. Still flying the triangular pennant of the New York Yacht Club, the former luxury ship arrived at the mouth of the Congo River, in present-day Angola, on September 16, 1858.

Eluding British naval patrols along the coast, the *Wanderer* and its crew easily sailed up the Congo to areas where slaves were readily available. Corrie and Lamar contracted with a representative for an illegal New York slave-trading firm, Captain Snelgrave, to provide 500 Africans. The Americans paid for the slaves at a rate of fifty dollars per head, with rum, gunpowder, cutlasses, and muskets. The entire transaction was completed in less than a month, and by mid-October the *Wanderer* had begun its return voyage to the United States.

The ship arrived at Jekyll Island (a more clandestine point of entry than Savannah) on November 28, 1858. The entry point had been arranged by Henry DuBignon Jr., who owned Jekyll Island and had conspired with Corrie and Lamar from the beginning. Of the 487 Africans on board, 78 perished en route. Within a matter of days Lamar and Corrie dispatched the survivors to slave markets in Savannah and Augusta, as well as to markets in South Carolina and Florida.

After locals spread the word that they had spotted newly imported Africans on native soil, and evidence revealed that the crew of the *Wanderer* had presented counterfeit documentation to the authorities, Lamar, Corrie, and his conspirators were tried in federal court in Savannah on three separate counts of piracy in May 1860. Prosecutors were unsuccessful in proving their case, however, and the local jury returned a verdict of not guilty. No doubt Lamar's status as one of Savannah's leading citizens played a pivotal role in the acquittal.

The *Wanderer* incident incensed many Northerners and contributed to the increasingly strained and deteriorating relationship between the North and the South. U.S. president James Buchanan responded to the *Wanderer* incident by proposing that the federal government adopt a more aggressive stance against the slave trade.

KATHERINE E. ROHRER

} Georgia in 1860

Georgia, uniquely situated among Southern states on the eve of the Civil War, played a vital part in the formation of the Confederacy. A geographic lynchpin that linked Atlantic seaboard and Deep South states, the "Empire State" was the second-largest state in area east of the Mississippi River (Virginia was larger until West Virginia broke away in 1861), and the second-largest Deep South state (only Texas was larger). In population, slave and free, Georgia was the largest in the Deep South. Both geographically and demographically, Georgia encompassed as much diversity as any Confederate state, and these factors had an important impact on how the state experienced the war years and what it contributed to the Southern war effort.

Population

Georgia's population passed 1 million residents for the first time in 1860. Census figures that year indicate that more than 591,000 of those residents (56 percent) were white, and nearly 466,000 (44 percent) were black. These figures reflect a 16.7 percent increase in the state's 1850 population, a somewhat slower growth rate than Georgia had seen in the 1820s, 1830s, and 1840s, due largely to outmigration by Georgians headed west.

In terms of geographical distribution, nearly 60 percent of the populace lived in the Black Belt, a broad swath running diagonally through the state's center from South Carolina toward the southwest along the Alabama and Florida line. The vast pine barrens or wiregrass region of southeastern Georgia was the state's most sparsely populated area, with only 5.6 percent of the state's total population; the narrow strip of six coastal counties had about the same percentage of the population as the southeastern counties, though concentrated in a far smaller area. The upcountry and mountain counties together claimed nearly a third of the populace.

Slaves outnumbered whites in both the Black Belt and the coast (making up 55 percent in the former and 59 percent in the latter). About a fourth of the wiregrass and upcountry counties' populace consisted of slaves, and only 13 percent of mountain residents were enslaved, with several of the northernmost counties claiming slave populations of less than 5 percent.

Like the rest of the South, Georgia remained overwhelmingly rural in the mid-nineteenth century, averaging a population density of fewer than 16 people per square mile. In 1860 nearly 8 percent of Georgians lived in towns or cities of more than 2,000 people, up from 4.6 percent in 1850. Savannah remained Georgia's largest city, as it had always been, with the highest concentration of slaves (around 35 percent). With 22,292 residents, Savannah was nearly twice the size of Augusta, the second-largest city in the state, with 12,493 people. Columbus, with 9,621 residents, was only slightly larger than rapidly growing Atlanta, with 9,554. (Atlanta had nearly quadrupled in size since 1850 and would almost double in size by 1862; by 1880 it had become the state's largest city.) Macon was the state's fifth-largest city, with a population of 8,247. Slaves made up roughly a third of all of these cities' populations, except Atlanta, where only 1 in 5 residents were enslaved. Free blacks made up a mere 0.3 percent of the state's black population in 1860, and they were concentrated largely in urban areas, especially Savannah and Augusta.

Nearly 99 percent of white Georgians in 1850 were American by birth; slightly more than three-fourths of those were born in Georgia. By 1860 newcomers to the state included an increasing number of Northerners, attracted by business opportunities in growing cities like Atlanta. The largest foreign-born concentration was in Chatham County, where nearly a third of its free residents, primarily Irish laborers and a small but influential group of German Jews, were born abroad.

Class and Wealth

Georgia remained a sharply divided society in terms of wealth and resources, with a pronounced hierarchical social structure dictated by the institution of slavery. Although more than 60 percent of white families in the state owned no slaves, the 37 percent who did, and especially the small tier of large planters, skewed the average to suggest that Georgia was among the wealthiest states in the Union. The per capita wealth of white Georgians in 1860, for example, was nearly double that of New Yorkers or Pennsylvanians. On average, slaveholders in the state owned property worth nearly five times that of a typical landholder in the North. Slave property in Georgia was worth more than $400 million in 1860 and accounted for at least half the state's total wealth.

A mere 6 percent of white Georgians held nearly half the state's property, in land and slaves. They made up the planter class, generally defined as those who owned 20 or more slaves and whose plantations ranged from 200 to 500 improved (or farmable) acres. While the largest holdings in Georgia were smaller than those of planters in Mississippi or Louisiana (only twenty-three Georgia planters owned more than 200 slaves, and only one owned more than 500), a number of Georgia families still ranked among America's richest citizens. Much of this concentration of wealth was on the Sea Islands, and yet the newly opened lands of western and southwestern Georgia, which had been frontier areas only a generation or so before, were home to an ever-increasing number of the state's largest and most profitable plantations by 1860. Nearly 40 percent of the Black Belt's slaves were located along the Flint River and the Alabama border.

Slaveholders who did not fall into the planter class but owned more than five slaves comprised 21 percent of free households; along with planters, they held approximately 90 percent of the state's wealth, according to one estimate. Many of these slaveholders were professionals, including lawyers, politicians, and doctors, or businessmen who lived in towns or cities while still maintaining plantation operations nearby.

Nearly three-fourths of the state's white population consisted of yeomen and the landless poor, who claimed less than 10 percent of Georgia's wealth. The yeoman class included farmers who owned fewer than five slaves and, for the most part, fewer than 100 acres of improved land. Many such residents were concentrated in the less-productive mountain counties and the wiregrass region. These areas were also home to many dirt or subsistence farmers, who raised just enough to support their families but nothing of any commercial value. The number of landless whites increased over the antebellum period and made up nearly half of the white populace by 1860. Many of these were farm tenants, who made up as much as 40 percent of the agricultural workforce in some of the state's more marginalized counties. Others were sons waiting to inherit land from their fathers, laborers who drifted from one county to another looking for work, or overseers hired to manage large plantations.

Agriculture

Nearly 75 percent of Georgia's white male populace between the ages of twenty and seventy, and more than 90 percent of its slaves, were directly engaged in agricultural pursuits in 1860, and as noted above, the vast majority of the state's productivity and wealth grew from its plantation economy. Cotton remained king. Georgia had led the world in cotton production during the first boom in the 1820s, with 150,000 bales in 1826; later slumps led to some agricultural diversification. Nevertheless, Georgians raised 500,000 bales in 1850, second only to Alabama, and nearly 702,000 bales in 1860, behind Alabama, Mississippi, and Louisiana. All of these states were beneficiaries of another boom in cotton prices in the late 1850s. The vast majority of cotton production in Georgia fell within the Black Belt (4 of every 5 bales were produced there), although the upcountry and coastal islands were also steady producers.

Corn, claiming 40 percent of the state's cultivated land, rivaled cotton as an agricultural commodity and was the mainstay of smaller farmers outside the Black Belt. Much of that corn was grown to feed hogs, with more than 2 million raised throughout the state in 1860. As a result, pork was the most-consumed meat by Georgians, black and white, as was true for most antebellum Southerners. Hogs and other livestock were raised in the mountains and in the wiregrass and sold to plantation markets as the most viable cash commodity produced by small farmers.

On the coast, rice continued to be among the most lucrative of crops, and Georgia trailed only South Carolina as the nation's largest rice producer. After a lag of several decades, rice made a dramatic comeback in the late antebellum period, moving from 39 million pounds produced in 1850 to more than 52.5 million pounds ten years later. A number of secondary crops, including tobacco, wheat and oats, and sweet potatoes, were grown in abundance throughout the state; more sweet potatoes were grown in Georgia than anywhere else in the world in 1860.

Cotton played an important role in Georgia's entry into the war, its wartime experience, and its postwar efforts to rebuild. Once the war began, the Confederacy attempted to use cotton as a weapon by starving the North of the crop and by courting European support with it.—From online entry "Cotton"

WWW.GEORGIAENCYCLOPEDIA.ORG

Industry

The most pervasive forms of industry in late antebellum Georgia remained those most closely tied to agriculture, including the gristmills and sawmills that produced the flour, cornmeal, and timber consumed both locally and in ever-widening markets within the state. The combined value of flour and meal totaled more than $4.5 million, according to the 1860 census, more than any other manufactured product in the state.

Southerners' campaign to bring cotton mills to the cotton fields, rather than sending their cotton off to New England, began in the 1810s, and early efforts at building textile mills in Georgia took place in the 1820s and 1830s. But it was only in the 1850s that the industry came of age, fueled both by the cotton boom of that decade and by more efficient applications of steam and water power in fall-line cities like Augusta, Columbus, and Macon, as well as in smaller communities like Athens, Roswell, and Sparta. In 1860 Georgia led the South in the number of textile workers, with 2,800 (more than half of them female) employed in thirty-three mills.

The lumber industry also experienced a boom in the 1850s, with pine and cypress products accounting for an annual worth of $2.4 million. In 1860 sawmills employed 16 percent of the state's industrial workforce, most of which was concentrated in southeastern Georgia's pine barrens and coastal counties. Savannah was the beneficiary of much of this production and had emerged by 1860 as one of the nation's most active market and production centers, with sawmills, lumberyards, and a thriving export trade to England. Brunswick and Darien were secondary ports fueled primarily by timber floated downriver for processing there. Naval stores operations and turpentine distilleries were also driven by the state's pine forests. In the mountains, marble quarries and small-scale mining enterprises of iron, copper, and coal were under way, though they became significant parts of the state's industrial output only after the war.

Slaves made up much of the state's industrial workforce. Many were hired by companies on annual contracts to work in mines, sawmills, railroad construction, and other enterprises, both urban and rural. Only the textile industry resisted opportunities to employ many slaves, and it was the focus of an ongoing debate as to the benefits or detriments of putting slaves into factories. The 1860 census indicates that 5 percent of Georgia's slaves spent the majority of their time employed in industry rather than agriculture.

Among the most important developments that would shape the war in Georgia was the dramatic expansion of railroad tracks in the state during the 1840s and 1850s. By 1860 the state had the most extensive system of rail lines in the Deep South and was second only to Virginia in the South as a whole. Eighteen railroad companies had constructed 1,400 miles of track at a cost of more than $26 million in private and public funding. These lines were vital to the state's economic and industrial expansion and had much to do with driving Atlanta's rapid growth as well as its strategic importance during the war.

JOHN C. INSCOE

 # Sectional Crisis

Georgia played a pivotal role in the sectional crisis of the 1850s, in which Southern politicians struggled to prevent Northern abolitionists from weakening constitutional protections for slavery. The crisis ultimately led to the outbreak of the Civil War. During this period, however, and for much of the antebellum era, Georgians maintained a relatively moderate political course, often frustrating the schemes of Southern radicals. The passage in 1850 of the Georgia Platform, which endorsed the Compromise of 1850, helped to avert secession for a decade.

The Mexican War and Its Aftermath

The national debate over slavery intensified in the wake of the Mexican War (1846–48). By 1840 the national Whig and Democratic parties had crystallized in Georgia, creating a strong two-party system that would last in the state for the next decade and a half. The Whigs were led by George W. Crawford, who served as governor from 1843 to 1847, and by rising stars Alexander Stephens and Robert Toombs. The Democrats were headed by the equally capable Howell Cobb, Herschel Johnson, and George W. Towns. The two parties remained evenly matched for much of the 1840s, but the Mexican War placed Georgia Whigs in a defensive position from which they never recovered.

Echoing their Northern counterparts, Stephens and other Whigs criticized the war for provoking dangerous questions regarding the status of slavery in the western territories, which the United States stood des-

Robert Toombs, a native of Wilkes County and one of the most ardent secessionists in the U.S. Senate, helped to lead Georgia out of the Union on the eve of the Civil War. This was surprising; although Toombs was a slaveholding planter, he had dedicated the majority of his political career to preserving the Union.—From online entry "Robert Toombs"

WWW.GEORGIAENCYCLOPEDIA.ORG

tined to acquire by defeating Mexico. And while it was a Pennsylvania Democrat who in 1846 offered to Congress the so-called Wilmot Proviso, a measure seeking to ban slavery from these newly acquired territories, many more Northern Whigs than Northern Democrats seemed to favor it. Partially as a result of appearing tied to an antislavery party, Georgia Whigs lost the governorship in 1847 to States' Rights Democrat George W. Towns. They would never win it back.

As the Whigs predicted, the 1848 Treaty of Guadalupe Hidalgo, ending the Mexican War and bestowing the Mexican Cession (the territorial package that the United States acquired from Mexico), brought slavery to the forefront of a national debate. Politicians seeking sectional compromise instead of the controversial Wilmot Proviso suggested either popular sovereignty within the territories or an extension to the West Coast of the line established by the 1820 Missouri Compromise, which generally prohibited slavery above latitude 36°30' north.

South Carolinian John C. Calhoun and his radical Southern followers refused compromise, however, and insisted that the U.S. Constitution guaranteed the legality of slavery in all national territories. Calhoun then called for a politically united South to pressure the federal government into accepting his position on the territories, threatening secession if Congress attempted to prohibit slavery's westward expansion. Seeking his own course, however, U.S. president Zachary Taylor, a Louisiana Whig elected in 1848, unexpectedly began preparing the Mexican Cession's California territory for immediate statehood in 1849. California appeared destined to enter the Union as a free state, a development that would upset the sectional balance in the U.S. Senate at the expense of the South. Congress, with Georgia's Howell Cobb serving as House Speaker, resisted Taylor's machinations for fear that a free California would provoke Southern disunion.

Furious over Taylor's nationalist agenda, Calhoun's radicals scheduled a Southern Rights convention to meet in June 1850 at Nashville, Tennessee, where they hoped to rally the region's political leadership and perhaps begin preparations for secession. Georgia's politicians broke party lines over the question of joining the Southern Rights movement. Some, like Herschel Johnson and Governor Towns, eagerly jumped on the Southern Rights bandwagon, while many others, including the powerful triumvirate of Cobb, Stephens, and Toombs, rejected the radicals' call. In stark contrast to their divided political leaders, the vast majority of white Georgians continued to support the Union, and only 2,500 people even bothered to vote in the April election for state delegates to the Nashville convention.

Back in Washington, D.C., Kentucky senator Henry Clay sought to end the sectional controversy over the Mexican Cession by formulating a series of compromise proposals. Under the resulting Compromise of 1850, passed in September with the support of congressmen Cobb, Stephens, and Toombs, California was admitted as a free state while a decision regarding the status of slavery in the Utah and New Mexico territories was indefinitely postponed. Additionally, the slave trade was abolished in Washington, D.C., to satisfy Northerners, while a tighter Fugitive Slave Law was designed to appease Southerners. Nevertheless, many Southern radicals (known as "fire-eaters") quickly dismissed the Compromise of 1850 for unevenly benefiting the North, and they continued to advocate secession.

Mistakenly believing that white Georgians supported the radical cause, Governor Towns scheduled elections for a December 1850 state convention in the hopes of launching the state toward secession. But the plan backfired dramatically as Georgia voters elected a resoundingly pro-Union delegation by a convincing 20,000-vote majority. At the December convention, all but 19 of the 264 delegates signed the Georgia Platform, which pledged support for the Union and the Compromise of 1850 under the conditions that the federal government would not try to prevent the expansion of slavery into new territories and would enforce the strengthened Fugitive Slave Act. The result of a strong popular mandate and a document that satisfied the North and the South, the Georgia Platform effectively stifled the radical movement and ended talk of secession. For good measure, in 1851 Georgians elected Unionist Democrat Howell Cobb for governor over States' Rights candidate Charles McDonald by a decisive 18,500 votes.

With the national crisis cooling off after the passage of the Georgia Platform, state politicians seemed to settle back into their old partisan camps. Yet for the rest of the decade Georgia Democrats would continue growing in dominance while the Whigs slipped further into decline. In 1852 Alexander Stephens and Robert Toombs rejected the Whig Party's presidential nomination of Virginian Winfield Scott, whose political alliances with antislavery Northerners pointed to a repeat of Taylor's nationalism. Both leaders eventually drifted into the Democratic ranks.

Nevertheless, even after the national Whig Party dissolved in the wake of Scott's devastating defeat by Democrat Franklin Pierce, Georgia Whigs continued to muster a sizeable anti-Democratic front under a number of different party labels. In 1853 Whig Charles Jones Jenkins ran for governor on a Unionist ticket and nearly upset Democrat Herschel Johnson. The gap widened in 1855 when Garnett Andrews, running under the anti-immigrant American Party label, failed to unseat Johnson despite the fact that less than 2 percent of Georgia's population was foreign born. The Democrats would keep the governor's chair for the rest of the 1850s, and the Whig Party's moderating influence over Georgia politics steadily eroded.

The End of Moderation

Despite its moderate tendencies in the 1840s and 1850s, Georgia remained deeply wedded to the institution of slavery. By 1860 one-third of Georgia's white families were slaveholders, roughly half the state's total wealth was invested in slavery, and 462,000 slaves made up nearly 44 percent of Georgia's total population. The rise of the antislavery Republican Party in the mid-1850s therefore pushed white Georgians to abandon their tradition of political moderation.

Starting in 1854 controversies surrounding slavery in the western territories again unleashed a storm of national controversy that this time would culminate in civil war. In a highly miscalculated move, Democratic senator Stephen Douglas of Illinois proposed to organize the territories immediately west of his home state under the doctrine of popular sovereignty, a proposal that violated the cherished 36°30′ line established by the Missouri Compromise. The resulting Kansas-Nebraska Act of 1854 infuriated many white Northerners who feared that Douglas had opened the door for slavery's westward expansion, which would close off a potential future frontier for white free labor.

Northern resentment quickly gave rise to the Republican Party, a purely sectional organization intent on banning slavery from the western territories. Proving the party's electoral strength, Republican presidential candidate John C. Frémont came shockingly close to winning the election in 1856 despite the fact that Delaware, Maryland, Virginia, and Kentucky were the only slaveholding states to place his name on their ballots.

As national politics became increasingly wrought with sectional antagonism, Georgia's tradition of political moderation disintegrated. State politicians viewed the Republicans as antislavery fanatics seeking to destroy slavery even in the South, and many considered secession a necessary remedy in the event that the Republicans captured the presidency. State politics began to reflect the changing mood. After maneuvering the Democratic nomination away from moderate Howell Cobb, states' rights advocate Joseph E. Brown handily defeated pro-Union candidate Benjamin Hill in the 1857 gubernatorial election. A self-made businessman and small slaveholder from the north Georgia mountains, Brown crafted a popular Jacksonian political style by denouncing state banks during the 1857 recession, providing increased funding for Georgia's woeful public schools, and lowering taxes. Riding a wave of popular support, Brown easily won reelection in 1859 by crushing opposition candidate Warren Akin, the last of the neo-Whig challengers. The ardent States' Rights Democrat would thus occupy the governor's chair during the greatest political crisis in Georgia history.

The Presidential Election of 1860

Compounding sectional antagonisms exponentially, abolitionist John Brown was captured leading an attack on a federal arsenal at Harpers Ferry, Virginia, in October 1859. It soon became clear that Brown had planned to use the arsenal to arm a massive slave insurrection. Despite the dismal failure of Brown's raid and his subsequent execution in December, the incident cast an ominous shadow over preparations for the presidential election of 1860.

The national Democrats proved incapable of agreeing on a platform position regarding slavery in the territories and sundered along sectional lines. The remaining regular Democrats nominated Stephen Douglas for president (with Georgia's Herschel Johnson for vice president), while the Southern faction selected Kentucky's John C. Breckinridge, thus dividing the Democratic Party along sectional lines. Soon thereafter a group of Unionist ex-Whigs selected a third presidential candidate in Tennessean John Bell. The Republicans nominated another ex-Whig, Illinois' Abraham Lincoln, on a platform that reaffirmed the Wilmot Proviso. As with Frémont in 1856, Lincoln's name did not appear on Georgia ballots.

With Johnson as his running mate, Douglas campaigned personally in Georgia but was rewarded with only 11,500 votes. On the other hand Unionist John Bell captured roughly 43,000 ballots, showing that the old Whig banner still retained some viability in the state. Breckinridge, whose candidacy was largely equated with supporting Southern secession, managed to win Georgia with 52,000 votes.

Yet despite Breckinridge's victory, the combined vote totals of Unionist candidates Douglas and Bell surpassed the Kentuckian's tally, suggesting that the majority of Georgian voters were not yet ready to forsake the national Union. Lincoln won the presidency by garnering a majority of the Electoral College despite receiving virtually no support from any Southern state. Upon learning of Lincoln's victory, Governor Brown recommended the allocation of $1 million for the state's defense, which was appropriated by the state legislature, and scheduled January 2 elections for a special state convention to discuss secession. The struggle over Georgia's future in the Union had begun.

KYLE OSBORN

Georgia Platform

With the nation facing the potential threat of disunion over the passage of the Compromise of 1850, Georgia, in a special state convention, adopted a proclamation called the Georgia Platform. The act was instrumental in averting a national crisis and demonstrated that compromise and conciliation remained viable alternatives to secession and war.

Southern radicals called on the South to reject the Compromise of 1850 as an assault on the constitutional right of slavery and urged their states to secede from the Union. Georgia was best prepared to respond to events, having established a provision for a special convention to deliberate alternatives; the convention, held in Milledgeville, would be a testament to the skill and moderation of a handful of Georgia statesmen.

Howell Cobb, Alexander Stephens, and Robert Toombs represented Georgia in Congress and wielded a great deal of political influence within the state. Their roles in these events not only aided the passage of the Compromise of 1850 in Washington but also ensured the defeat of the radical secessionists in Georgia. The culmination of their efforts was the Georgia Platform.

The November elections for the special convention to be held in December 1850 demonstrated an overwhelming support for the pro-Union position in Georgia. In a five-day session the convention drafted an official response to the tensions threatening the Union. All but nineteen delegates voted for the Georgia Platform. The genius of the document lay in its balance of Southern rights and a devotion to the Union.

The platform established Georgia's conditional acceptance of the Compromise of 1850. Much of the document followed a draft written by Charles Jones Jenkins and represented a collaboration between Georgia Whigs and moderate Democrats dedicated to preserving the Union. In effect, the proclamation accepted the measures of the compromise so long as the North complied with the Fugitive Slave Act and would no longer attempt to ban the expansion of slavery into new territories and states. Northern contempt for these conditions, the platform warned, would make secession inevitable.

This qualified endorsement of the Compromise of 1850 essentially undermined the movement for immediate secession throughout the South. Newspapers across the nation credited Georgia with saving the Union. Nevertheless, the conditions upon which the Georgia Platform rested would fail the tests of time, bringing in the next decade a replay of events with different results—secession and war.

GEORGE W. JUSTICE

 # Secession

Georgia's secession from the Union followed nearly two decades of increasingly intense sectional conflict over the status of slavery in western territories and over the future of slavery in the United States. Secession had been seriously mentioned as a political option at least as far back as the Missouri crisis of 1819–21, and threats to disrupt the Union were commonplace in every sectional crisis from the nullification era (1828–33) onward. While white Georgians, along with other white Southerners, disagreed over whether secession was a constitutional right (embodied in the national compact that grew out of the 1787 Constitutional Convention) or a natural right of revolution (arising from the inherent power of the people to form and abolish governments), in a practical sense this distinction mattered less than the fact that secession was widely recognized as a legitimate potential remedy for perceived Southern grievances. Thus, when Abraham Lincoln, the candidate of the antislavery, Northern Republican Party, won the 1860 presidential election, states in the lower South moved quickly to call state conventions to consider secession. Georgia's state legislature set

January 2, 1861, as the election date for a state convention, which was to meet on January 16.

Opposing camps formed rapidly in the campaign for the election of county delegates to the state convention. Immediate secessionists, mostly former Democrats headed by Howell Cobb, Thomas R. R. Cobb, Joseph E. Brown, Henry Rootes Jackson, Robert Toombs, and others, believed that Lincoln's election violated the spirit of the U.S. Constitution and provided clear evidence that a tyrannical Northern majority intended to trample on Southern rights and ultimately abolish slavery. Honor and safety depended, immediate secessionists argued, on severing ties with the Union as quickly and completely as possible, to protect the South from its enemies and promote Southern unity. Immediate secessionists had the advantage of a decisive plan of action and a strong set of allies in neighboring Deep South states—South Carolina, Mississippi, Florida, and Alabama would secede before Georgia's state convention even met.

Herschel Johnson, a political leader in Georgia, was a candidate in the fateful 1860 presidential election that set secession into motion. He served as the running mate for Democratic presidential candidate Stephen Douglas, who lost the election to Abraham Lincoln.—From online entry "Herschel Johnson"

WWW.GEORGIAENCYCLOPEDIA.ORG

Cooperationists, a varied collection of former Whigs and conservative Democrats, were led by Alexander Stephens, Herschel Johnson, and Benjamin Hill. Cooperationists agreed that the South faced great dangers and that Republicans would have to be forced to provide strong guarantees that would protect slavery and Southern rights if Georgia was to remain in the Union. In other words, cooperationists differed from immediate secessionists more in tactics than in underlying principles. Cooperationist plans for delay and deliberation typically involved the holding of a convention of the Southern states as a vehicle for framing ultimatums to extract concessions from the Republican Party. The secession of nearby states, however, made the logic of cooperationist proposals suspect and weakened their resolve; they were far less active during the campaign than their immediate secessionist counterparts.

White Georgians spoke very clearly on the issues at stake in 1860–61. A series of debates was held in the state capital of Milledgeville in mid-November 1860, soon after news of Lincoln's election reached Georgia. There and in later county conventions throughout the state, speakers denounced Northern aggression; reiterated familiar claims regarding Southern rights to expand slavery into the territories; vigorously defended Southern honor; conjured up the horrors of abolitionism, race war, and racial amalgamation; and insisted upon security for the South's peculiar institution. Liberty and freedom, for the white male voters of Georgia, meant preserving their right to hold slaves and to rule their family households without interference from outside forces, most especially from the federal government, which in their view had fallen into the hands of abolitionist fanatics. Republican and Northern hostility to slavery was cited as the sole compelling reason for contemplating secession, and white Georgians agreed that what they interpreted as repeated and unprovoked assaults upon slavery must cease or the Union must be dissolved.

On January 2, 1861, a miserably rainy day, Georgia voters went to the polls and selected delegates to a convention that would decide the state's response to Lincoln's election. Low voter turnout due to the poor weather may have affected the election's outcome. The exact results of the January 2 election, in terms of total votes cast for each side statewide, will probably never be known: there were voting irregularities, and some of the candidates held ambiguous positions.

Although the unofficial count released—not until April—by Governor Joseph E. Brown showed a lopsided victory for the immediate secessionists, the best evidence indicates that they won, at best, a tiny majority of the ballots cast, 44,152 to 41,632. Outside of the mountain counties (strongly cooperationist) and the coastal counties (overwhelmingly for immediate secession), voting patterns were mixed. Black Belt counties that had supported the Whig Party in the 1830s and 1840s and had voted against John C. Breckinridge, the Southern Democratic candidate in the 1860 presidential election, tended toward cooperationism, while Democratic counties in the Black Belt that had supported Breckinridge generally favored immediate secession. Although only about 40 percent of white families in Georgia held slaves (a considerably higher percentage than in the South as a whole), no clear-cut divisions along slaveholder/nonslaveholder lines appeared at the polls.

The Georgia state convention opened on January 16, 1861. It was an august assemblage, including Alexander Stephens, Robert Toombs, Eugenius A. Nisbet, Herschel Johnson, and Benjamin Hill; former governor George W. Crawford presided. Despite the closeness of the election, it soon became clear that the secessionists had a controlling majority.

The crucial vote occurred on January 18, when Nisbet offered resolutions for immediate secession and Johnson countered with a proposal for a convention of the Southern states. Johnson's plan embodied the cooperationist formula of seeking redress for grievances in the Union, while reserving secession as the ultimate remedy. Georgia's conditions for remaining in the Union, as outlined by Johnson, included constitutional amendments opening all territories to slavery and providing for the unrestricted admission of new slave states, along with the repeal of personal liberty laws (laws that impaired the ability of slave owners to recover fugitive slaves) in the Northern states. After debate, the convention passed Nisbet's resolutions by a 166 to 130 vote.

The next day, January 19, 1861, the delegates voted 208 to 89 to adopt an ordinance of secession. On January 21 the ordinance of secession was publicly signed in a lengthy ceremony, making Georgia the fifth state to leave the Union, following South Carolina, Mississippi, Florida, and Alabama. By the first of February, Louisiana and Texas would go out as well.

The convention adjourned temporarily to allow a committee time to write the new constitution and to await the outcome of the Confederate Convention at Montgomery, Alabama, in February 1861. Georgians played a prominent part in those proceedings. Howell Cobb presided over the convention, which formed a provisional Confederate government and chose Jefferson Davis of Mississippi as president and Alexander Stephens of Georgia as vice president.

Reconvened in March, the Georgia Secession Convention, now a constitutional convention, ratified the new Confederate Constitution and voted to submit the new Georgia constitution to the people by ballot in July. The delegates adjourned for the last time on March 23, 1861. Nearly three weeks later, on April 12, Confederate batteries fired on federal troops at Fort Sumter, and thus began hostilities in the Civil War.

ANTHONY GENE CAREY
GEORGE W. JUSTICE

 # State Constitution of 1861

The first order of business for Georgia legislators after the state seceded from the Union on January 19, 1861, was to create a new state constitution. Although the process began merely with amending the 1798 constitution to accommodate the state's independence from the Union, the delegates to the convention quickly formed a committee to draft an entirely new constitutional document. The delegates made no distinctions between their authority to decide the question of secession and their power to amend or replace the existing state constitution. After the business of secession had concluded, the delegates immediately turned their attention on January 21 to writing a new constitution.

The committee charged with drafting the new constitution was chaired by Thomas R. R. Cobb and included Benjamin Hill and Linton Stephens (the half brother of Alexander Stephens, the Confederacy's new vice president). After several days of deliberation, the body adjourned both to allow a committee to draft the new constitution and to await the outcome of the Confederate Convention, consisting of delegates from the seven seceded states, which met in Montgomery, Alabama, in early February to establish a government and draft a constitution for the newly formed Confederacy.

After Georgia seceded from the Union on January 19, 1861, **Thomas R. R. Cobb** was elected to the Provincial Congress of the Confederate States of America in Montgomery, Alabama. He served on the committee that drafted the Confederate Constitution, and the original manuscript is believed to be in his handwriting.—From online entry "Thomas R. R. Cobb"

WWW.GEORGIAENCYCLOPEDIA.ORG

The constitutional convention reconvened in Savannah in early March and ratified the Confederate Constitution drawn up in Montgomery. It also adopted the new Georgia constitution and voted to submit it to the people for ratification. Voters approved the document in July, but with a very low turnout and by a very close margin.

Patterned largely after the Confederate Constitution, the Georgia Constitution of 1861 was the first state constitution to be submitted to the people for ratification. It also took away the amending power of the legislature, stipulating instead that all amendments had to be made by a constitutional convention elected specifically for that purpose. Though earlier constitutions had enumerated only four or five personal liberties, the Constitution of 1861 incorporated a lengthy bill of rights, drawn up by Cobb. Adopted as Article 1, much of this portion of the constitution remains a part of the state constitution today. Among other things, the concepts of due process and judicial review were included for the first time.

The new constitution made several stipulations regarding slavery. It prohibited the foreign importation of slaves into the state. (The Confederate Constitution did likewise, despite the efforts of some who hoped to revive the foreign slave trade, which the U.S. Congress had banned in 1808). It also stated that the "General Assembly shall have no power to pass laws for the emancipation of slaves." It did grant the legislature the right to ban free blacks from coming into the state.

The convention dissolved after approving the new constitution on March 23. After its ratification in July, the constitution remained in effect throughout the Civil War. The Reconstruction era would see three new state constitutions written and approved: one in 1865, one in 1868, and the last in 1877.

LAVERNE W. HILL
MELVIN B. HILL JR.
GEORGE W. JUSTICE

Milledgeville

In 1802 Creek lands in the central part of the state were ceded to Georgia. No sooner had this territory been divided into counties than a drive to move the seat of government was initiated. On December 12, 1804, lawmakers passed an act to move the capital from Louisville to a new town, to be named Milledgeville in honor of the current governor, John Milledge.

Some 3,240 acres were appropriated for the new capital in Milledgeville; lots were sold and the proceeds were used to construct the new statehouse. Construction of the capitol took two years, and by the fall of 1807 the building was ready to be occupied. In October fifteen wagons carrying the treasury and public records of the state left Louisville for Milledgeville.

For sixty years Milledgeville served as Georgia's capital city, despite campaigns in the 1840s and 1850s to move it to either Atlanta or Macon.

Milledgeville remained Georgia's official state capital throughout the Civil War. It was there, on January 19, 1861, that Georgia convention delegates passed the Ordinance of Secession, and the state joined the Confederate States of America, to the accompaniment of wild celebration, bonfires, and illuminations on Milledgeville's Statehouse Square. Nearly four years later, on a bitterly cold November day, Union general

William T. Sherman and 30,000 Union troops marched into Milledgeville. When they left a couple of days later, the statehouse had been ransacked (but not burned); the state arsenal and powder magazine had been destroyed; the penitentiary, the central depot, and the Oconee bridge were burned; and the surrounding countryside was devastated. Many official state records were loaded on trains, which pulled out just before Sherman's troops reached the city.

With Union forces in control of Milledgeville, the state government fled to various other locations. The General Assembly held a special session from February 15 through March 11, 1865, at Macon's old city hall. In November the governor, Joseph E. Brown, fled Macon to escape Sherman's troops on their March to the Sea. He took refuge at his plantation in Cordele but was back in Milledgeville by December.

Joseph E. Brown spent nearly eight years in the Governor's Mansion in Milledgeville. He served two two-year terms as governor before the war and was reelected to two more terms during the war years.—From online entry "Joseph E. Brown"

WWW.GEORGIAENCYCLOPEDIA.ORG

In May 1865, following the surrender of the Confederate army to the Union, Governor Brown called the legislature to convene later that month at the statehouse in Milledgeville, but he was arrested by Union troops, and the legislature did not meet. Subsequently, Union troops took charge of state government in Georgia. A new constitution was adopted, elections were held, and in December 1865, the legislature met at the Milledgeville capitol.

In 1868, during Reconstruction, the capital was moved to Atlanta—a city emerging as the symbol of the New South as surely as Milledgeville symbolized the Old South.

EDWIN L. JACKSON
ROBERT J. WILSON III

Old Governor's Mansion

The Old Governor's Mansion is located in Milledgeville, the state's capital from 1807 to 1868. In 1835 the Georgia legislature resolved to construct the first official residence for the governor. Construction on the home began in 1836 and was completed in 1838 or 1839. It is considered one of the finest examples of the Greek Revival style in the nation. The building, a three-story stucco-over-brick structure, features a central rotunda and a massive Ionic portico.

The mansion served as the home of ten governors and their families, until the removal of the capital to Atlanta in 1868. Governor George R. Gilmer was the first to occupy the house, in 1839, near the end of his second term. Governor Brown resided in the mansion longer than any other governor. His four consecutive terms spanned the end of the antebellum period, the Civil War, and its immediate aftermath. During the Civil War the mansion became the stage for celebrations, speeches by Confederate generals, and Governor Brown's efforts to secure Georgia's autonomy while a part of the Confederate States of America. In November 1864 Union general William T. Sherman and 30,000 troops marched into Milledgeville. During his brief stay, Sherman was based at the mansion before continuing his March to the Sea.

With the removal of the capital in 1868, the mansion was virtually abandoned to state-appointed caretakers. For nearly a century (1891–1987) it served as the home of the president of what is now Georgia College and State University. The building is the oldest structure on the university's campus.

In 1973 the Old Governor's Mansion was designated a National Historic Landmark by the Trust for Historic Preservation; it underwent major renovations in the early 2000s and now serves as a historic house museum open for public tours.

JAMES C. TURNER

SECTION 2 }} The War Years

Battle of Resaca, fought in Gordon County on May 14–15, 1864. Color lithograph originally published by Kurz & Allen, circa 1889. Courtesy of Library of Congress, Prints and Photographs Division.

THE CIVIL WAR IN GEORGIA is often closely associated with the extended incursion by Union general William T. Sherman's troops in 1864—including both the Atlanta campaign and the subsequent March to the Sea. Yet the war fought on Georgia's soil entailed much more than the turbulence of 1864. It included earlier military engagements and the equally vital institutional structures in the state that supported the Confederacy, as well as civilian activity on the home front. The articles in this section cover all these aspects of the war years, in subsections that focus on military actions, military support, and home-front activity within the state.

Military action in Georgia began with naval operations that proved critical to the state, with a Union blockade posing as great a challenge on the Chattahoochee River as it did on the Atlantic coast. The theft of a train, known as Andrews Raid, an incident that lasted all of seven hours one day in April 1862, captured much attention at the time, and ever since, due to the sheer drama and derring-do involved, while guerrilla warfare wreaked havoc on certain parts of the state far longer than any other form of military engagement.

The most massive clash between Union and Confederate forces in Georgia, the Battle of Chickamauga, took place in 1863, followed the next year by Sherman's arrival and the first major battle of the Atlanta campaign, at Resaca. The campaign's most intense and destructive battle occurred at Kennesaw Mountain, and a relatively minor skirmish, but one that has become an important archaeological site, took place at Pickett's Mill. After capturing Atlanta, Sherman's troops embarked on their March to the Sea, which ended with the equally momentous, if far less destructive, occupation of Savannah by the end of the year. One of the final military actions of the war, Wilson's Raid, took place at Columbus in March 1865. And while not strictly a military maneuver, Confederate president Jefferson Davis's flight from Richmond, Virginia, and his capture in south Georgia were at least symbolically as important in bringing the Confederacy to an end as was Confederate general Robert E. Lee's surrender at Appomattox, Virginia.

Military support in the state, such as prison camps, hospitals, and manufacturing enterprises, played a substantial role in Georgia's war effort. Meanwhile, very different segments of military manpower helped shape the course of the war in the state, including Georgia blacks, both slave and free, who served in the Union army and Confederate deserters, who took a toll on both military efforts and morale for much of the war's duration.

Civilians also played significant roles in Georgia's war effort, in both positive and negative ways, and it is here that much of the recent scholarship on the war demonstrates the complexity of activity and sentiments on the home front. Newspaper editors, for example, wielded tremendous influence in shaping public opinion throughout the war. Dissenting white Georgians, for a variety of reasons and in a variety of ways, opposed the war effort and protested the many sacrifices that they were asked to make on behalf of the Confederacy. Much of that opposition—but not all—came from Unionists, those who on ideological grounds remained at some level devoted to the Union as both an entity and a cause.

Women also played important and varied roles during the war years. Through Scarlett O'Hara, the iconic heroine of Margaret Mitchell's novel *Gone With the Wind* (1936), the multiple challenges that the war posed for wealthy Southern women are well known, but only in the last couple of decades have historians begun to shift their focus from the experiences of plantation mistresses to those of poor white and black women, who often suffered far more during the war years. Finally, the most consequential impact of the war was felt by Georgia's more than 400,000 slaves, as they made the transition from slavery to freedom. As with most aspects of the home-front experience, emancipation took place in diverse ways and under varying circumstances, and recent scholarship has brought to light the myriad ways in which slaves themselves often shaped the terms and situations of their new status as freedmen and freedwomen.

Although emancipation began during the war years, its repercussions were felt in equally dramatic ways after the war, for both black and white citizens of Georgia. This, in concert with the state's other Civil War experiences, both military and civilian, marked an irrevocable shift in the economic and social landscape of Georgia and continues to influence it today.

MILITARY ACTIONS

Taylor and Huntington stereograph of Fort McAllister, 1864. Courtesy of Georgia Archives, Vanishing Georgia Collection, bry008–90.

} Fort Pulaski

A massive five-sided edifice, Fort Pulaski was constructed in the 1830s and 1840s on Cockspur Island at the mouth of the Savannah River. Built to protect the city of Savannah from naval attack, the fort came under siege by Union forces in early 1862 and was ultimately captured on April 11.

Origins and Construction

Following the War of 1812, the U.S. government began planning a system of coastal fortifications to defend the nation's coast against foreign invasion. Because Savannah was the major port in Georgia, navy officials recognized the need for a fort on Cockspur Island to protect the city from attacks coming up the Savannah River. In 1829 construction began on the new fort, named for Count Casimir Pulaski, a Polish immigrant who fought during the American Revolution (1775–83).

Responsibility for most of the early work on Fort Pulaski fell on the shoulders of Lieutenant Robert E. Lee, recently graduated from the U.S. Military Academy at West Point, New York. Lee oversaw the preliminary construction, choosing the site and designing a system of drains and dikes to support the weight of the masonry fort. In 1831 Lieutenant Joseph K. Mansfield took charge of Pulaski's construction and oversaw the project for the next fourteen years. When finished in 1847, the fort could mount 146 cannons, some on the parapet atop the 7.5-foot-wide walls and others in casemates inside the walls.

Count **Casimir Pulaski**, frequently hailed as the founder of the American cavalry, served in the Continental army during the Revolutionary War. He died during the siege of Savannah in October 1779. During the 1850s the city of Savannah erected a fifty-five-foot obelisk in Monterey Square to honor Pulaski.—From online entry "Casimir Pulaski"

WWW.GEORGIAENCYCLOPEDIA.ORG

Civil War

In January 1861, shortly before Georgia seceded from the Union, state troops occupied Pulaski to keep Union forces from garrisoning it. During the fourteen years since the fort's completion, its condition had deteriorated considerably. Its moat had filled with mud, and not a single cannon was mounted in place. Five companies of troops from Macon and Savannah formed the garrison. Helped by slaves impressed from nearby rice plantations, these men cleared the moat and began to mount guns along the fort's walls. By the time Colonel Charles H. Olmstead took command of Pulaski in December 1861, its defenses had improved dramatically.

Fort Pulaski faced its first threat in November 1861, following the capture of nearby Port Royal, South Carolina, by Union forces. General Robert E. Lee, commanding Confederate forces in the region, ordered Tybee Island and other islands near the fort abandoned because they could not be adequately defended. Lee believed, however, that Fort Pulaski's wide walls would keep it from serious harm by any bombardment from Tybee, nearly a mile away.

In January 1862 the Union commander in the district, General William T. Sherman, decided to take the fort by siege. He ordered troops to Tybee Island and constructed defenses on the smaller neighboring islands to cut the garrison from reinforcements. Sherman then placed Captain Quincy Gillmore of the Engineer Corps in charge of the siege preparations on Tybee, despite advice that "you might as well bombard the Rocky Mountains."

Gillmore ordered his engineers to construct a series of eleven artillery batteries along the north shore of Tybee Island. They worked mostly at night and camouflaged the work on the batteries to prevent the fort's garrison from discovering their plans. Once the batteries were built, the troops had to pull, by hand, artillery pieces weighing as much as 17,000 pounds through marshy land and into position.

By April 9, Gillmore had twenty cannons and fourteen mortars in position to bombard Fort Pulaski. Just after sunrise the next morning he demanded the surrender of the fort. Colonel Olmstead declined, stating he was there "to defend the fort, not to surrender it." The bombardment began at 8:15 a.m. with the Federal guns maintaining a slow, steady fire all day. By afternoon it became apparent that the heavy shells from the rifled cannons would be able to break through the walls of Pulaski. The guns from the fort returned fire but did no damage to the Union positions.

On April 11, the Union bombardment opened two thirty-foot holes in the southeast face of Pulaski. Soon, more shells were passing through the wall and striking the interior of the fort. Olmstead decided to surrender the garrison when the firing came perilously close to one of the main powder magazines. In less than thirty-six hours and with the loss of only one Union soldier, the new rifled cannons had brought the surrender of a fort that took eighteen years to build—a fort that some of the best engineers in both armies had said could not be reduced by such an artillery assault.

The reduction and capture of Fort Pulaski in 1862 not only deprived the Confederacy of a port it desperately needed but also signaled a major shift in the way future forts would be built as well as the way they would be attacked. Captain Gillmore took a risk when he decided to assault the fort with the new rifled cannons, but his gamble paid off and led to significant changes in military engineering.

Postwar

Following the surrender, Union troops garrisoned Fort Pulaski until the end of the war. During this period the fort served not only to bar Confederate shipping from Savannah but also to imprison captured Southern troops. After the Civil War, the U.S. Army Corps of Engineers began modernizing the fort but stopped before the project was completed. Pulaski remained virtually abandoned until 1924, when the government designated it a national monument. Nine years later it became a unit of the National Park Service, which continues to maintain it.

DAVID H. MCGEE

} Union Blockade and Coastal Occupation

The battle between ship and shore on the coast of Confederate Georgia was a pivotal part of the Union strategy to subdue the state during the Civil War. U.S. president Abraham Lincoln's call at the start of the war for a naval blockade of the entire Southern coastline took time to materialize, but by early 1862 the Union navy had positioned a serviceable fleet off the coast of the South's most prominent Confederate ports. In Georgia, Union strategy centered on Savannah, the state's most significant port city. Beyond Savannah, Union forces generally focused on securing bases of operation on outlying coastal islands to counter Confederate privateers.

Confederate defensive strategy, in turn, evolved with the Union blockade. After the fall of Port Royal, South Carolina, in November 1861, Confederate president Jefferson Davis appointed General Robert E. Lee to reorganize Confederate coastal defenses. Lee quickly realized the impossibility of defending the entire coastline and decided to consolidate limited Confederate forces and materiel at key strategic points. He countered Union naval superiority by ensuring easy reinforcement of Confederate coastal positions along railroad lines. In this way, Lee minimized reliance upon the fledgling Confederate navy and maximized the use of Confederate military forces in coastal areas, including both Georgia's Sea Islands and mainland ports with railroad connections.

Confederate Privateering and Naval Innovation

On the night of November 11, 1861, a daring Confederate blockade-runner, Edward C. Anderson, escaped under Union eyes and piloted his ship, the *Fingal*, into the port of Savannah. A native of Savannah, Anderson was the first of many who attempted to assist the Confederate cause by breaking through the Union's extensive coastal blockade, which stretched from Virginia to Florida. However, in Georgia none would match Anderson's success. The landing of Enfield rifles and cannons, as well as sabers and military uniforms, at the state's major port marked the high tide of the South's ability to penetrate the North's naval forces stationed along the Georgia shore.

But Anderson's remarkable feat also signaled to the Union that it needed to bolster its blockade and close off access to Savannah, which, like Charleston, South Carolina, to the north, offered an access point readily able to provide Confederate armies with necessary war materiel. If the Union hoped to wear the South down by cutting it off from the outside world, then it had to put a stop to incidents like the *Fingal*'s arrival at Savannah.

While smaller vessels than the *Fingal* sometimes did evade Northern capture, their modest hauls made for paltry victories. Because Union forces took control of the seas around Brunswick and St. Simons Island in the war's beginning stages, the virtual closing of Savannah's port to privateers like Anderson greatly contributed to eventual Union success in Georgia.

Confederate leadership and the people of Savannah came to pin their hopes of resisting Union occupation and breaking the blockade on a handful of gunboats. Three of these, the *Atlanta*, the *Georgia*, and later the *Savannah*, were ironclads patterned after the CSS *Virginia*, famous for its battle against the USS *Monitor* at Hampton Roads, Virginia, in 1862. The *Macon*, the *Sampson*, the *Resolute*, and the *Isondiga*, wooden gunboats of varying designs, constituted the remainder of the Confederate fleet in Savannah. In addition, Georgia's coastal defenses included innovative torpedoes, developed by Commodore Matthew Maury, which caused the Union navy periodic concern. Despite these innovations, the Confederate naval forces paled in comparison to Union naval strength. Despite fleeting successes by Southern naval forces, the increasingly potent Union navy ultimately enabled complete Union control of the Georgia coastline.

Fort Pulaski and Savannah Harbor

General Lee's decision to consolidate forces in 1862 began with the withdrawal of Confederate troops from St. Simons and Jekyll islands on the southeastern Georgia coast. On March 9, 1862, two Union gunboats arrived to find abandoned the earthwork batteries overlooking the channel between the islands. Sailing farther inland to the town of Brunswick, the ships found the town deserted and the wharf and depot ablaze.

Union naval forces took other Sea Islands with similar lack of resistance. Tybee, the northernmost of Georgia's islands and within easy range of Fort Pulaski, fell to Union forces without a fight. Along with Union gunboats, batteries erected on Tybee initiated the first major engagement in Savannah on April 10, 1862. Union forces under the command of Major General David Hunter and Captain Quincy A. Gillmore bombarded Fort Pulaski, which was commanded by Confederate colonel Charles H. Olmstead, overnight. The rifled cannons of the Union gunboat *Norwich*, as well as those from the land batteries, made short work of the masonry walls of Fort Pulaski. Fearing a complete breach in the walls and explosion of the fort's powder magazine, Olmstead surrendered. Union troops occupied Fort Pulaski for the remainder of the war.

Early in the war, 1,500 Confederate troops were ordered to St. Simons Island to defend it against the Union blockade. By the end of 1862

Robert E. Lee ordered those troops to move north to help defend Savannah, leaving St. Simons open to Union occupation. In June 1863 the Fifty-fourth Massachusetts regiment, one of the Union's first African American regiments, under commander Robert Gould Shaw, spent several weeks on the island and made an expedition up the Altamaha River. On June 11 they were ordered to attack the nearby port of Darien, which was thought to be a base for blockade-running activity. Despite objections from Shaw, his troops, along with the Second South Carolina Infantry, burned and looted the town, causing the greatest wartime destruction to civilian property along the Georgia coast. The film *Glory* (1989) recreates this incident along with the Fifty-fourth's suicidal assault on Fort Wagner, South Carolina, on July 18, 1863.

Fort McAllister and Savannah's Surrender

Two years passed before Union troops moved on Savannah itself, and contrary to Confederate expectations, the assault came from the west, not the east. Savannah's other protective bastion, Fort McAllister, to the city's south on the Ogeechee River, became its last remaining hope and a primary obstacle to Union forces.

Several naval sorties engaged Fort McAllister throughout 1862 and 1863. On July 29, 1862, four Union gunboats bombarded the fort for several hours, accomplishing little. Again, on November 19, three ships assailed the fort to little avail. On January 27, 1863, the Union ironclad *Montauk* and several wooden gunboats pounded the fort for several hours, again with little result. Similar engagements occurred on February 1, 27, and 28. In the last engagement, Union forces failed to drastically affect Fort McAllister but destroyed the Confederate privateer *Nashville*, which had grounded near the fort in seeking protection from Union ships. Another bombardment of the fort three days later again produced minimal results. These repeated repulsions of the Union navy by Confederate troops in Fort McAllister accomplished little for the Northern cause but heartened the Confederate troops, as well as the citizens of Savannah.

Drawing on this confidence, Confederate flag officer Josiah Tattnall sought to employ his ironclads to break through the Union blockade in Savannah's harbor. However, several ill-fated attempts to engage Union forces ultimately resulted in the loss of the ironclad *Atlanta* at the hands of the Union ironclad *Weehawken* on June 17, 1863. Though a new ironclad, the *Savannah*, became operational in July, along with two wooden gunboats, the *Macon* and *Sampson*, Confederate leadership in Savannah generally spurned offensive operations for the remainder of the war.

Nevertheless, in June 1864 Confederate naval troops managed a minor victory with the capture of the USS *Water Witch*. While anchored near Savannah, the *Water Witch* was captured by officers and crew members of the *Georgia, Savannah,* and *Sampson*. Ultimately, however, that small conquest did not improve the Confederacy's fortunes.

This increasingly defensive stance culminated in facing Union general William T. Sherman's troops on their 1864 March to the Sea. Fort McAllister formed the backbone of Savannah's remaining defensive line. Late in the afternoon of December 13, 1864, a Union division under Brigadier General William B. Hazen, part of Sherman's Fifteenth Corps, assaulted McAllister. Though slowed by obstacles and minefields, in addition to Confederate artillery fire, the Union troops overwhelmed the fort and forced its surrender.

Josiah Tattnall, born at Bonaventure Plantation, near Savannah, entered the U.S. Navy as a midshipman in 1812. Prior to the Civil War, Tattnall saw varied service around the world—he fought against Algerian pirates under Commodore Stephen Decatur and was wounded in action during the Mexican War.—From online entry "Josiah Tattnall"

WWW.GEORGIAENCYCLOPEDIA.ORG

With McAllister occupied, Sherman effectively linked with the Union navy, sounding the death knell for Confederate Savannah. The Confederate leadership realized the hopelessness of the situation following McAllister's capture and withdrew their remaining forces across the Savannah River into South Carolina. In retreat, the Confederates set fire to their surviving naval squadron, including the ironclad *Savannah*, effectively ending any resistance to Sherman's capture of the city. In a telegram dated December 22, 1864, General Sherman presented the city of Savannah as a Christmas gift to President Lincoln, ending both the March to the Sea and major military engagement on the Georgia coast.

JAMES H. WELBORN III
RICHARD HOUSTON

CSS *Savannah*

Over the course of the Civil War, three different fighting ships of the Confederate navy were given the name *Savannah*. All three ships saw only limited action along the Georgia coast during the war.

Privateer *Savannah*

The first ship to carry the name *Savannah*, this fifty-three-ton schooner was converted to an Atlantic Coast privateer after hostilities began in 1861. The ship was lightly armed with a single eighteen-pounder cannon, of War of 1812 vintage, that had been converted into a rifled gun. The privateer *Savannah* took one merchant ship as a prize of war before being captured by the brigadier USS *Perry* after two weeks of service.

CSS *Savannah* (Gunboat)

The second ship to carry the name, the gunboat *Savannah* (later called *Old Savannah*), was originally a side-wheel steamer named *Everglade*. It was built in 1856 at New York and purchased early in 1861 by the state of Georgia to be converted into a gunboat for coastal defense. With a moderate 406-ton displacement, the *Savannah* was armed with a single thirty-two-pounder cannon. Under the command of Lieutenant J. N. Maffitt, the *Savannah* was attached to the squadron of Flag Officer Josiah Tattnall, charged with the defense of Georgia and South Carolina. Tattnall's command of gunboats was so small that he dubbed it the "Mosquito Fleet." The tiny flotilla, which consisted of three converted tugs (the *Resolute*, *Sampson*, and *Lady Davis*) and a converted harbor craft (the *Savannah*) was no match for Union ships on the open sea, but the shallow draft of the small ships gave them a movement advantage in inland waters.

On November 5–6, 1861, the CSS *Savannah*, in company with the *Resolute*, *Sampson*, and *Lady Davis*, fought vessels from a much larger Union fleet of fifty-one ships under Flag Officer Samuel F. Du Pont. The fleet was preparing to attack Confederate positions at Port Royal Sound, South Carolina, between Savannah and Charleston. On November 7 the *Savannah* again briefly engaged with Union ships as they bombarded Fort Walker and Fort Beauregard. When this token defense was driven off by the Union fleet, Tattnall failed in his attempt to join the garrison at Fort Walker. The *Savannah* returned to the city of Savannah to repair damages, allowing the unopposed Union fleet to successfully take Port Royal and the town of Beaufort, South Carolina.

On November 26, 1861, Tattnall led the *Savannah, Resolute,* and *Sampson,* from Fort Pulaski to the mouth of the Savannah River, where the flotilla once again attacked the much larger force of Union vessels stationed there. The *Savannah*'s attack caused no damage but did force the Union fleet to operate with caution in the following months. On January 28, 1862, Tattnall ran his three ships through a "gauntlet" of thirteen Union gunboats to provision Fort Pulaski. Fortunately for the Confederates, Union batteries held their fire, hoping to bottle up the Confederate fleet and capture its ships. Tattnall managed to make the return trip safely through a hail of fire. Union forces subsequently constructed additional batteries on shore and further fortified their positions. Thereafter, the *Savannah* was no match for the combination of Union fleet and shore batteries.

Following the surrender of Fort Pulaski after a ferocious two-day shelling by Union guns on April 10–11, 1862, the gunboat *Savannah* served as a receiving ship at the city of Savannah. Its name was changed to the *Oconee* when the new Confederate ironclad css *Savannah* assumed the name in early 1863. In June 1863 the *Oconee* sailed toward England with a load of cotton to be exchanged for ammunition and other supplies but sank on August 18, 1863, before reaching its destination.

CSS *Savannah* (Ironclad)

The final ship to carry the name, the css *Savannah* was one of six ironclad rams built by the Confederacy. Although the ship saw limited action, its presence was a significant deterrent to Union plans to invade the coastal region of the Savannah River. The ironclad was constructed by F. Willink at the Savannah Shipyards. Its iron plates were manufactured in Atlanta, then transported to Savannah, where they were cut, drilled, and mounted. With a length of 172.5 feet, a 34-foot beam, and a 12.5-foot draft, the *Savannah* featured a conventional hull and casement with single screw, with 4 inches of iron armor over 22 inches of wood.

The *Savannah*'s armament included two 7-inch rifled cannons and two 6.4-inch Brooks guns. The engines, built in Columbus, were significantly underpowered. Although considered among the best ships built by the Confederacy, the *Savannah* boasted an estimated top speed of only six knots. It took almost thirty minutes to make a 180-degree turn. The crew consisted of 180 officers and men.

Launched on February 4, 1863, the ironclad *Savannah* was transferred in June to naval forces under Flag Officer William Hunter on the Savannah River. The ship remained on the river and did not engage in battle until

Union general William T. Sherman approached the city of Savannah in December 1864, at the end of his March to the Sea. Unable to prevent the city's capture, the *Savannah* remained on the river for two days to protect William J. Hardee's withdrawal across an improvised pontoon bridge, built with the help of the *Savannah*'s crew.

On December 20, 1864, the ironclad engaged in a spirited daylong artillery duel with Union guns, becoming the last ship of the Confederacy to fight in Georgia waters. When the *Savannah* attempted to escape, the ship was trapped by the South's own torpedo mines, leaving it a "trapped lion," in the words of General Sherman. On December 21 Tattnall ordered the *Savannah* to be burned to prevent capture. The ironclad was run aground on the South Carolina shore and set afire. The ensuing explosion was reported to have lit up the night sky for miles.

STEPHEN HUGGINS

USS *Water Witch*

The USS *Water Witch*, part of the Union fleet assigned to carry out a naval blockade of the Georgia coast during the Civil War, was captured by Confederate naval troops in 1864. This rare Confederate naval victory ultimately had minimal significance, however.

Constructed in 1852 in the Washington Navy Yard at Washington, D.C., the USS *Water Witch*, a wooden-hulled, side-wheel gunboat, spent years surveying South American rivers before being called to duty in 1861 for the Union blockade of the Confederacy. In 1863 the vessel joined the South Atlantic Blockading Squadron, which operated mostly in Georgia waters around Ossabaw Island.

In June 1864, while anchored in the placid waters south of Savannah, the *Water Witch* was surprised in the early morning hours by a Confederate raiding party comprising 11 or 12 officers and 115 men from the crews of the *Georgia*, *Savannah*, and *Sampson*. Led by Lieutenant Thomas Postell Pelot and Moses Dallas, an ex-slave paid a salary for his service as a ship pilot, the Confederates boarded and, after winning a pitched battle on deck, captured the Union ship. The Confederates lost both of their leaders, however, and without a pilot the surviving troops had difficulty navigating the *Water Witch* to shore.

During the attack, a former slave in the Union ranks leapt overboard, swam to shore, and warned other solitary blockaders that the *Water Witch* was no longer a friendly craft. Before the Confederates could pick off the ships one by one in the guise of a Union sloop, the Union mobilized its vessels and went on the offensive, forcing the Confederates to hide their new ship beneath a bluff on the Vernon River. In December 1864, as Union general William T. Sherman's troops bore down from the west on their March to the Sea, the Confederates cut their losses and burned the *Water Witch* so that it would not fall back into enemy hands.

In 2007 a team of researchers, led by the Georgia Department of Natural Resources, found what is believed to be the *Water Witch* shipwreck off the coast of Savannah beneath approximately fifteen feet of sediment. In 2009 the National Civil War Naval Museum at Port Columbus completed a full-scale replica of the *Water Witch*, which sits anchored in full view along Victory Drive in Columbus.

BRAD WOOD

} Naval War on the Chattahoochee River

As part of the Union naval strategy to blockade Southern ports during the Civil War, the U.S. Navy closed access to the Chattahoochee River system at Apalachicola, Florida, on June 11, 1861, and maintained its coastal presence there for the remainder of the war. In response, the Confederate navy built both a steam-powered gunship, the CSS *Chattahoochee*, and an ironclad, the CSS *Jackson* (also known as CSS *Muscogee*), to descend to open seas and break the blockade. However, the shallow coastline, the Chattahoochee's unpredictable flow, and a series of management and engineering mishaps prevented the enemies from engaging in battle throughout the course of the war.

Blockade's Impact

Within a year of the Union navy's arrival, military and civilian life on the lower Chattahoochee ground to a frustrating standstill while engineers, officers, politicians, and businessmen upriver struggled to convert industrial strength into naval might for the Confederacy. The strategic importance of the blockade was threefold: Columbus, Georgia, one of the most industrialized cities in the Deep South, sat at the head of the navigable portion of the Chattahoochee River; Apalachicola, a major shipping center, lay on the coast; and a fertile cotton-growing region, the lifeblood of the Southern economy, sprawled between the two.

The **Chattahoochee River** begins in the Blue Ridge Mountains of Georgia and flows southwest toward Alabama. It tumbles for twenty miles over the fall line— the region of transition between the foothills of the Piedmont and the flatter Coastal Plain. Below the fall line the river rambles south toward Florida, where its name changes to the Apalachicola.—From online entry "Chattahoochee River"

WWW.GEORGIAENCYCLOPEDIA.ORG

Apalachicola became a ghost of its antebellum self as farmers and industrialists to the north began using the railroad system to ship their goods. Columbus, meanwhile, expanded its industrial production and began manufacturing many of the Confederate navy's steam engines. The overall effect of the blockade was to swiftly shift economic and military importance elsewhere for the remainder of the war.

Although the U.S. Navy never ascended the Chattahoochee River to attack the Naval Iron Works at Columbus, it held the blockade of Apalachicola successfully, thereby circumscribing Confederate movement in and out of the port. Despite this success, seamen serving in the blockade experienced the desperate boredom of their duty and recognized the marginality of their contribution to the war effort. As the war dragged on, the Union ships stationed off Apalachicola became less likely to chase blockade runners and more likely to take on refugees, Confederate deserters, and runaway slaves looking for transport out of the area.

Construction on the Chattahoochee

While the Union navy blockaded the port of Apalachicola, rumors about the construction of a new Confederate gunboat began to filter downriver. In the fall of 1861, Confederate naval officers and the chief engineer of the Columbus Naval Iron Works contracted with a private firm based in Saffold, Georgia, 175 miles south of Columbus and 140 miles upriver from Apalachicola, to build a 130-foot-long gunboat in four months. In theory, the css *Chattahoochee* was to be both riverboat and ocean-sailing craft. Upon its completion, the Confederate navy hoped to steam it downriver, break the blockade, and open the port of Apalachicola for the return of supply ships and trade to the region.

However, disaster and mishap struck the construction and eventual launch of the gunboat at every turn, highlighting the strong disadvantages that the Confederacy held in building and managing a navy under wartime conditions and depletions. After many delays, the long-awaited launch of the *Chattahoochee* took place in February 1863, but the vessel ran aground on its first day on the river and seriously damaged its hull. By the time the steamer was again ready for service, the Confederate army, feeling impatient and vulnerable to attack, had sunk obstructions into the Apalachicola River, destroying any hopes that the *Chattahoochee*'s officers held of engaging the Union force at sea. By the spring of 1863 the Confederate navy had stationed the gunboat, now no more than a glorified floating battery, above the obstructions. On May 27, 1863, the boilers of the *Chattahoochee* exploded due to the crew's inexperience, killing several sailors, maiming others, and effectively destroying the ship for the remainder of the war.

During the war, the Columbus Naval Iron Works also supplied engine machinery for many of the Confederacy's ironclads. On the Chattahoochee River, the Confederacy commissioned the construction of the css *Jackson* in 1862. This ship also faced a series of setbacks and delays that prevented it from ever reaching the Union blockade. Despite a scarcity of resources, the *Jackson* was completed in less than a year. However, inconsistent river levels prevented its initial launch, and an ordered redesign of the paddle system cost the crew any opportunity to engage the blockaders at the mouth of the Apalachicola River.

Wilson's Raid and the Sack of Columbus

As the war's end approached, the Union command sent a cavalry unit of 13,500 men, under the command of Major General James H. Wilson, to capture and occupy the Chattahoochee River Valley of Alabama and Georgia.

Launching the campaign from Tennessee, Wilson's raiders swept swiftly through the poorly defended cities of Alabama, and on Easter Sunday, April 16, 1865, the cavalry crossed the Broadnax Street Bridge from Girard, Alabama, into Columbus, captured the city, and began laying waste to its industrial capabilities, including the Columbus Naval Iron Works. Wilson's men set the *Jackson* aflame and adrift on the river, where it burned for nearly two weeks before sinking; navy yard workers did the same to the *Chattahoochee* to prevent it from falling into enemy hands. In the early 1960s both ships were raised from the riverbed. Today, visitors to the National Civil War Naval Museum at Port Columbus can view what remains of both crafts.

LEVI COLLINS

 Guerrilla Warfare

Guerrilla warfare in Georgia during the Civil War often took place in sparsely populated regions where Unionist or anti-Confederate sentiment created divisions among the civilian population. In many cases Unionist and Confederate neighbors clashed for control of their communities. In other instances guerrillas operated against major field armies. Confederate guerrilla activities affected the policies of Union general William T. Sherman, pushing him to adopt harsh retaliatory measures to protect his railroad supply lines as he moved through Georgia in 1864. In the final stages of the Civil War, guerrilla activities became an acute problem for areas in which civil authority had broken down. Irregular bands terrorized and plundered farms and towns, killing or wounding large numbers of people.

According to historian Daniel Sutherland, Civil War guerrillas, regardless of what they called themselves or the side for which they fought, shared at least two characteristics. First, guerrillas utilized unconventional methods of warfare to harass and worry their foes, tactics that stood in marked contrast to those of conventional armies. Second, guerrillas saw their principal responsibility as defending their homes and communities from internal or external foes.

Guerrilla Activity in North Georgia

One of the earliest catalysts for guerrilla activity in Georgia was the Conscription Act, which was passed by the Confederate Congress in April

1862. Those men wishing to avoid the draft often formed armed bands, which were sometimes joined by Confederate army deserters. Such groups were particularly active in parts of north Georgia, where staunch Unionists and dissenting civilians who were disenchanted with Confederate government policies comprised a minority of the population. In July 1862, for example, a citizen in Gilmer County noted that a contingent of well-armed and mounted men, roaming the countryside to avoid conscription, were stealing, burning houses, killing livestock, and threatening the wives of Confederate soldiers.

In 1863 Governor Joseph E. Brown responded to such complaints by dispatching parties of state and Confederate soldiers into mountain counties to track down and arrest dozens of disloyal civilians. These same counties also responded to local disturbances by forming safety committees and home guard companies to protect them from "tories," or Unionists. Unionist guerrillas had their own support networks of civilians, particularly in such northern counties as Fannin, where anti-Confederate feelings were widespread.

In an effort to control guerrilla organizations and maintain order in north Georgia, Governor Brown granted commissions authorizing mounted commands to the region. Brown also attempted to address the problem of lawless bands of men stealing property from civilians around the state. The governor was careful not to accuse any of the bands raised under his authority with these crimes, noting that the lawless men often misidentified themselves as Confederate cavalrymen under General Joseph Wheeler.

John P. Gatewood and his murderous gang comprised probably the best-known guerrilla force operating in north Georgia. Gatewood never received official state sanction, but he might have operated periodically under Wheeler's authority. Although most of Gatewood's numerous victims were U.S. soldiers or Unionist civilians, his men sometimes brutalized even Confederate sympathizers.

Guerrilla Activity in South Georgia

The southern part of the state was also periodically plagued with guerrilla violence, and the swamps and pine barrens of south Georgia provided hiding places for deserters, draft evaders, and Unionists. In November 1863 an expedition involving state and Confederate troops passed through Wilcox, Ware, Coffee, and Clinch counties, arresting deserters and runaway slaves along the way. The Okefenokee Swamp was another refuge for individuals and small groups of men, although the number of draft evaders or deserters who hid there is impossible to determine.

Citizens in Worth County reported in October 1864 that lawless villains prowled over the county, stealing and committing depredations. Bands of deserters raided the town of Blackshear, in Pierce County, ransacking local stores seven times in February 1865. A Confederate inspector in Ware County reported that men seeking to evade conscription had banded together south of the Altamaha River to resist arrest.

Sherman's Response to Guerrillas

As Sherman's troops advanced into northwest Georgia during the 1864 Atlanta campaign, they encountered Confederate guerrillas intent on disrupting the Western and Atlantic Railroad, the Union's main supply line. Sherman declared that such activity was criminal and that guerrillas behaved like animals in their flouting of the conventions of war. Union general James B. Steedman, given responsibility for protecting the Western and Atlantic in late June 1864, attempted to fulfill his duty by issuing orders that any citizens found within three miles of the railroad be arrested and tried as spies. Despite such measures, Confederate partisans and guerrillas continually cut telegraph lines and partially disabled the railroad, although Union repair crews usually restored the lines in a timely fashion.

During the Atlanta campaign and the subsequent March to the Sea, Sherman employed a policy of punishing civilians for guerrilla activity. If guerrillas or bushwhackers struck at Union forces or attempted to impede their march by destroying bridges and obstructing roads, Sherman often ordered the destruction of houses in the vicinity. Some of the harshest reprisals for the attacks of guerrillas and Confederate cavalry scouts took place in the fall of 1864, when Union troops burned much of the town of Cassville, in Bartow County, and portions of other towns in northwest Georgia.

Surrender and Paroles

By the final months of the war, local legal systems no longer functioned in many parts of Georgia, and guerrilla activity increased accordingly.

Large numbers of Confederate army deserters in the Georgia mountains joined home guard, militia, or irregular organizations. Many of these deserters claimed that they had taken furloughs to protect their home communities from bushwhackers or robbers.

The presence of guerrilla and state-sanctioned irregular military organizations in north Georgia generated a passionate public debate over their activities and composition. Some citizens characterized these bands as fearless protectors of Southern citizens, while others claimed that the groups sheltered deserters and even men who had formerly served in Union home guard companies. A civilian writing to an Augusta newspaper in January 1865 noted that lawless parties were too large to capture and predicted that anarchy would result in north Georgia if the war did not end soon.

In early February 1865 Confederate general W. T. Wofford arrived in north Georgia, raising the hopes of civilians that law and order might be restored in their region. Wofford estimated that between 3,000 and 5,000 men in north Georgia belonged in the Confederate army, and he claimed that they would soon be organized not only to resist enemy raids but also to assume the offensive. Wofford's subsequent actions suggest that his primary goal was to restore law and order in his native region.

Wofford surrendered all Confederate forces in north Georgia at Kingston, in Bartow County, on May 12, 1865. In the preceding weeks, Wofford had attempted to meet with roughly 500 guerrillas who had refused to obey his orders to surrender. Union general Henry M. Judah, who had negotiated with Wofford, announced that anyone who did not surrender would be considered an outlaw. Judah believed that his ultimatum resulted in the capitulation of most guerrillas in north Georgia. The decision made in May 1865 by thousands of home guard soldiers to travel to Kingston to surrender and receive parole suggests some degree of continued affiliation with the Confederate army.

W. T. Wofford was a Confederate general during the war. He began his service as colonel of the Eighteenth Georgia Infantry, which was organized in 1861 at Camp Brown, in Cobb County. The regiment was later assigned to General John Bell Hood's Texas Brigade, which fought in the battles of Second Bull Run and Antietam.—From online entry "W. T. Wofford"

WWW.GEORGIAENCYCLOPEDIA.ORG

Guerrillas knew that their paroles would protect them from punishment at the hands of military authorities but not from local civil prosecution, leading Wofford to predict that most irregulars would move abroad. It is impossible to determine how many guerrillas actually migrated, but the notorious Gatewood and his gang were among those who departed the state, heading for Texas.

KEITH S. BOHANNON

 # Andrews Raid

The Andrews Raid of April 12, 1862, brought the first Union soldiers into north Georgia and led to an exciting locomotive chase, the only one of the Civil War. The adventure lasted just seven hours, involved about two dozen men, and as a military operation, ended in failure.

In early spring 1862 Northern forces advanced on Huntsville, Alabama, heading for Chattanooga, Tennessee. Union general Ormsby Mitchel accepted the offer of a civilian spy, James J. Andrews, a contraband merchant and trader between the lines, to lead a raiding party behind Confederate lines to Atlanta, steal a locomotive, and race northward, destroying track, telegraph lines, and maybe bridges toward Chattanooga. The raid thus aimed to knock out the Western and Atlantic Railroad, which supplied Confederate forces at Chattanooga, just as Mitchel's army advanced.

On April 7 Andrews chose twenty-two volunteers from three Ohio infantry regiments, plus one civilian. In plain clothes they slipped through the lines to Chattanooga and entrained to Marietta; two men were caught on the way. Two more overslept on the morning of April 12, when Andrews's party boarded the northbound train. They traveled eight miles to Big Shanty (present-day Kennesaw), chosen for the train jacking because it had no telegraph. While crew and passengers ate breakfast, the raiders uncoupled most of the cars. At about 6:00 a.m. they steamed out of Big Shanty aboard the locomotive *General,* a tender, and three empty boxcars.

Pursuit began immediately, when three railroad men ran after the locomotive, eventually commandeering a platform car. Two of them, Anthony Murphy and William Fuller, persisted in their chase for the next seven hours and over eighty-seven miles. First suspecting the train thieves to be Confederate deserters, the pursuers acquired a locomotive at Etowah Station. Aware they were being chased, Andrews's men cut the telegraph lines and pried up rails. Murphy and Fuller switched locomotives—they used three that day—picked up more men, and kept up the chase. The train thieves tried to burn the bridge at the Oostanaula River near Resaca, but the pursuers were too close behind, so close that at Tilton the *General* could take on only a little water and wood. At about 1:00 p.m. it ran out of steam two miles north of Ringgold, with the Southerners, aboard the *Texas*, fast upon them. The Confederates rounded up all the raiders. Only eight of the twenty (Andrews among them) were tried as spies and executed in Atlanta. The rest either escaped or were exchanged.

Though it created a sensation at the time, the Andrews Raid had no military effect. General Mitchel's forces captured Huntsville on April 11 but did not move on to Chattanooga. The cut telegraph lines and pried rails were quickly repaired. Nevertheless, the train thieves were hailed in the North as heroes. The soldier-raiders received the Medal of Honor; one, Jacob Parrott, was its very first recipient. Neither Andrews nor the other civilian was eligible.

In the postwar years several raiders, notably William Pittenger, published thrilling recollections of their adventures. In Atlanta, William Fuller testily challenged Anthony Murphy over who was in charge of the train pursuit. The escapade made its way into film with Buster Keaton's silent comedy *The General* (1927) and Walt Disney's *The Great Locomotive Chase* (1956).

STEPHEN DAVIS

A number of homes in **Ringgold** were used as hospitals for more than 20,000 Confederate soldiers in 1862 and 1863. During the Battle of Ringgold Gap in November 1863, Confederates held back advancing Union troops for hours. After the battle Union general Ulysses S. Grant set up his headquarters at the Whitman House on Tennessee Street in Ringgold.
—From online entry "Ringgold"

WWW.GEORGIAENCYCLOPEDIA.ORG

 # Black Troops

More than 3,500 black Georgians served in the Union army and navy between 1862 and 1865. Enlistment occurred in two distinct phases, beginning on the federally occupied Sea Islands of Georgia and South Carolina in 1862–63 and resuming in northwestern Georgia and southern Tennessee in mid-1864, during the latter stages of the Atlanta campaign.

Recruitment on the Sea Islands

The arrival of Union warships prompted Confederate forces to evacuate Georgia's coastal islands during February and March 1862. With the surrender of Fort Pulaski in the Savannah harbor on April 11, the state's coast fell under Northern control, and Georgia slaves began making their way to Union lines. On April 7, 1862, Abraham Murchison, an escaped slave preacher from Savannah, helped recruit 150 former slaves for a black regiment being organized by General David Hunter at Hilton Head, South Carolina. The regiment was later disbanded by presidential order, but a company of thirty-eight men was sent to St. Simons Island, Georgia, where they helped other black escapees defend themselves against Confederate attack.

In November 1862 Union authorities authorized black enlistment. The St. Simons detachment, together with a group of thirty to forty additional Georgia recruits, joined the army as Company A of the First South Carolina Volunteers. Former slaves from St. Simons also composed the bulk of Company E, and Georgia recruits could be found in smaller groups scattered throughout the regiment. In June 1863 a special draft for the Third South Carolina Volunteers was held on Ossabaw Island and at Fort Pulaski, Georgia, as well as at Fernandina Beach, Florida, near Georgia's southern border. This regiment, which was soon consolidated with the embryonic Fourth and Fifth South Carolina Volunteers to form the Twenty-first U.S. Colored Infantry (USCI), numbered slightly more than 300 men until December 1864, when its ranks were filled by former slaves who had followed General William T. Sherman to Savannah.

Enlistment in the Interior

During the Atlanta campaign of May–September 1864, General Sherman opposed black enlistment with word and deed. An avowed white supremacist and a reluctant liberator at best, Sherman made no effort to conceal his contempt for blacks or to disguise the racist dogma behind his opposition to black soldiers. Such phrases as "niggers and vagabonds," "niggers and bought recruits," and "niggers and the refuse of the South" filled his personal letters. Anxious to employ blacks as laborers, Sherman was determined that the forces under his command would remain exclusively white. On June 3, 1864, he issued Special Field Order No. 16 forbidding recruiting officers to enlist blacks who were employed by the army in any capacity.

Despite Sherman's opposition, black enlistment began in occupied areas of northwestern Georgia under authority granted to Colonel Ruben D. Mussey, the Nashville, Tennessee–based commissioner for the Organization of U.S. Colored Troops in the Department of the Cumberland. Most activity took place between July and September 1864, when the Forty-fourth U.S. Colored Infantry was stationed in Rome, Georgia, for recruiting purposes. By late summer the Forty-fourth USCI contained some 800 black enlisted men and was commanded by Colonel Lewis Johnson, who was white. Approximately three-fourths of these black soldiers were doing garrison duty in Dalton on the morning of October 13 when advance units of the 40,000-man Army of Tennessee, commanded by Confederate general John Bell Hood, converged unexpectedly upon the little village, cutting off all avenues of retreat. Initial skirmishing between black troops and Hood's men left several Confederates dead and their comrades "over anxious to move upon the 'niggers,'" as reported to Johnson. Hood vowed to take no prisoners if the Union defenses were carried by assault and later added that he "could not restrain his men and would not if he could."

Although Johnson claimed that his black troops displayed the "greatest anxiety to fight," he surrendered to Hood and quickly secured paroles for himself and the 150 or so other white troops attached to the garrison. The regiment's 600 African American enlisted men suffered a harsher fate. Some were reenslaved, while others were sent to work on fortification projects in Alabama and Mississippi. Many ended the war as prisoners in Columbus and Griffin, Georgia, where they were released during May 1865 in what one of them described as a "sick, broken down, naked, and starved" condition. Fearful of reprisals from embittered Confederates, the black veterans concealed their connection with the Union cause.

Additional black enlistment took place along the Georgia coast in

In June 1863 **Darien** was burned by Union forces composed of two African American units: the Fifty-fourth Massachusetts Volunteers, commanded by Colonel Robert G. Shaw; and the Second South Carolina Infantry, under Colonel James Montgomery. This incident caused considerable resentment among Southern sympathizers.

—From online entry "Darien"

WWW.GEORGIAENCYCLOPEDIA.ORG

1865 after the fall of Savannah and Sherman's departure into South Carolina. Many blacks from Georgia's coastal counties also saw service as pilots and seamen on Union vessels throughout the war.

CLARENCE L. MOHR

 # Battle of Chickamauga

The Battle of Chickamauga, the biggest battle fought in Georgia, took place September 18–20, 1863. With 34,000 casualties, it is generally accepted as the second bloodiest engagement of the war. The campaign that brought the Union and Confederate armies to Chickamauga began in late June 1863, when the Union Army of the Cumberland under Major General William S. Rosecrans advanced southeastward from Murfreesboro, Tennessee, against the Confederate Army of Tennessee, commanded by General Braxton Bragg. Rosecrans's goal was to capture the city of Chattanooga, Tennessee, an important rail junction and gateway to the Deep South. Through a series of successful and relatively bloodless turning movements, Rosecrans's army forced Bragg's troops to abandon middle Tennessee and fall back to Chattanooga.

Bragg subsequently deployed most of his troops at crossings of the Tennessee River northeast of Chattanooga, where he expected Rosecrans to attack. Instead, on August 29, 1863, the Union soldiers crossed the Tennessee River at several points west and southwest of Chattanooga. The Army of the Cumberland, numbering almost 60,000 men, then advanced southeastward in three widely separated columns over the rough mountain and valley terrain of northeast Alabama and northwest Georgia in an attempt to threaten Bragg's railroad supply line. When Bragg learned of the enemy threat to his rear, he abandoned Chattanooga on September 9 and retreated southward, even though Confederate reinforcements had arrived from Mississippi and East Tennessee.

As his army passed through LaFayette, Georgia, Bragg learned of the widely scattered condition of the Union army and planned an offensive movement against portions of the Union force. During the second week of September, he had several chances to destroy isolated portions of the Union army, but command dissension resulted in several bungled attempts to punish the enemy. At the same time, Rosecrans began ordering a concentration of his troops, realizing that the three isolated corps of his army were in danger.

By September 17, two of Rosecrans's corps were reunited and were moving north toward Lee and Gordon's Mill on Chickamauga Creek to join the third Union corps. Bragg believed that the Union troops at Lee and Gordon's Mill constituted the northernmost elements of Rosecrans's force. Thus he developed a battle plan to cross Chickamauga Creek north of the mill and drive the Union troops southwestward back against the mountains and away from Chattanooga.

September 18: The First Day of Fighting

The first day's fighting at the Battle of Chickamauga consisted of several Confederate attempts to seize crossing points on Chickamauga Creek. Union cavalrymen delayed the Confederates at Reed's Bridge, but eventually Southern forces seized the span and advanced southwestward toward Lee and Gordon's Mill. Union mounted infantrymen at Alexander's Bridge also fought a successful delaying action before being forced back. Southerners did get across the Chickamauga on September 18, but the delays prevented them from reaching the left flank of the main Union force.

September 19: The Second Day of Fighting

The actions on September 18 led Rosecrans to believe that Bragg might try to interpose the Confederate army between the Union forces and Chattanooga, so Rosecrans ordered one of his corps commanders, Major General George H. Thomas, to extend his lines northward from Lee and Gordon's Mill to the area of the Kelly farm. On the morning of September 19, Thomas sent troops eastward from the Kelly farm to destroy what he thought was a small and isolated enemy force. Instead, the Union soldiers encountered Confederate cavalrymen and ushered in a confused general engagement that lasted all day and spread southward for nearly four miles. Both Rosecrans and Bragg sent troops into the fighting, although the thick forests made it difficult for large bodies of troops to maneuver. At one point, a body of Confederates achieved a breakthrough and threatened to seize the LaFayette Road, but Northern reinforcements regained the lost ground. At the end of the day, the Union troops had withstood repeated attacks without losing their connection to Chattanooga. That night they pulled back to a defensive position along the LaFayette Road, which they strengthened by constructing log breastworks.

September 20: The Third Day of Fighting

During the night and early morning of September 19 and 20, Bragg divided his army into two wings, the right (or northern) wing under Lieutenant General Leonidas Polk and the left (or southern) wing under Lieutenant General James Longstreet, who had arrived from Virginia with additional Confederate reinforcements. Bragg's plans for September 20 called for an attack to begin at dawn on the Confederate right and continue southward, driving the Union troops away from Chattanooga. Ineptitude on the part of Polk and one of his subordinates caused the attacks to begin several hours late. Although a small force of Confederates briefly turned the enemy troops left, Union reinforcements drove back the Southerners. Union soldiers protected by breastworks bloodily repulsed the rest of the attacks launched by Polk's troops.

Shortly after 11:00 a.m. Rosecrans came to believe that a Union division in the center of his line had created a gap by moving out of position. In order to rectify the situation, Rosecrans ordered another division under Brigadier General Thomas J. Wood northward to fill the supposed hole. But a massive Confederate attack led by Longstreet began at this time, with thousands of Southerners charging into the real gap left by Wood's movement.

By noon, disaster had engulfed the center and right wings of the Union army, sending Rosecrans, several of his principal subordinates, and many of their men into a retreat northward to Chattanooga. Some Northern soldiers eventually formed a line on a series of steep, wooded knolls known as Snodgrass Hill or Horseshoe Ridge. Although the Confederates continued to attack Snodgrass throughout the afternoon, they were unable to capture the position. Late in the afternoon, Union general Thomas, who earned the name the "Rock of Chickamauga" for his outstanding performance that day, withdrew his forces from the

James Longstreet, a long-time resident of Georgia, rose to second-in-command of Robert E. Lee's Army of Northern Virginia, but in 1863 he became the scapegoat for that army's costly defeat at Gettysburg. Ten years after the war, Longstreet purchased a farm in Gainesville, which his neighbors derisively called Gettysburg.— From online entry "James Longstreet"

WWW.GEORGIAENCYCLOPEDIA.ORG

battlefield back toward Chickamauga to the safety of a gap in Missionary Ridge.

Chickamauga was an extremely costly battle for both armies. Rosecrans lost more than 16,000 men killed, wounded, and missing, while Bragg's army of roughly 68,000 men sustained more than 18,000 casualties. While the battle was considered a Confederate victory because it pushed the Union army back to Chattanooga rather than letting them proceed into Georgia (it would be the next year before the Union army tried again), Rosecrans achieved his objective for the campaign, the capture of Chattanooga. Union troops did have to be pulled from Virginia and Mississippi to reinforce Rosecrans's besieged army in Chattanooga, but otherwise the staggering losses sustained in both field armies produced few immediate tangible results.

KEITH S. BOHANNON

Atlanta Campaign

The "Atlanta campaign" is the name given by historians to military operations that took place in north Georgia during the Civil War in the spring and summer of 1864.

By early 1864 most Confederate Southerners had probably given up hopes of winning the Civil War by conquering Union armies. The Confederacy had a real chance, though, of winning the war simply by not being beaten. In spring 1864 this strategy required two things: first, Confederate general Robert E. Lee's army in Virginia had to defend its capital, Richmond, and keep Union general Ulysses S. Grant's forces at bay; and second, the South's other major army, led by Joseph E. Johnston in north Georgia, had to keep William T. Sherman's Union forces from driving south and capturing Atlanta, the Confederacy's second-most important city.

This win-by-not-losing strategy involved a time element as well. If Lee and Johnston could hold their respective fields through early November, then war-weary Northerners might vote U.S. president Abraham Lincoln out of office. The Democratic candidate, in turn, might seek an armistice with the Confederacy and end the war.

Synopsis of the Campaign

The stakes were high in early May when the campaign began with the skirmish at Tunnel Hill in north Georgia. Sherman had four reasons to be confident of success: first, numerical advantage (his troops outnumbered Confederate forces by roughly two to one); second, an efficient supply system to keep his armies fed, clothed, and armed; third, superior morale (the Confederate army had just been routed from Chattanooga, Tennessee, the previous November); and fourth, and probably most important, Johnston's record as an unaggressive, even timid army commander. Sherman, having faced and beaten Johnston in Mississippi the previous summer, was aware of this weakness in his adversary.

During the opening weeks of the campaign, Sherman seized the initiative and forced Johnston's army back from one position to another. By late May some Atlantans had begun to think that the fall of their city was inevitable. After Johnston had been pushed back nearly to Atlanta in late July, Confederate president Jefferson Davis feared that Atlanta would be given up without a fight. So he fired Johnston and replaced him with John B. Hood, an army corps commander who promised to attack Sherman and attempt to save the city.

Hood's chances of success, however, were virtually zero. Sherman's forces were five miles from Atlanta's outskirts when Hood took command of the Confederate army on July 18. Union strength stood at 80,000 to Hood's 50,000. Outnumbered and lacking strategic options, Hood nevertheless sought tactical opportunities. He launched three assaults around Atlanta between July 20 and 28 but was repulsed each time. Sherman spent the next month bombarding the city and its remaining residents, while cutting the three railroad lines that supplied Hood's armies. When the last of these lines, north of Jonesboro, was broken on August 31, Hood was forced to evacuate Atlanta. Sherman had won the campaign. Lincoln's reelection was assured, and the Confederacy was doomed.

The Union Advantage

After his appointment in March as general-in-chief of the Union armies, Lieutenant General Ulysses S. Grant placed Sherman, his trusted subordinate, in command of all three Union armies between the Appalachian Mountains and the Mississippi River: the Army of the Cumberland (Major General George H. Thomas), the Army of the Tennessee (Major General James B. McPherson), and the Army of the Ohio (Major General John M. Schofield). Sherman brought these armies together to form, by late April, a group of 110,000 men and some 250 cannons, all assembled around Chattanooga. Facing them near Dalton was the Confederate Army of Tennessee, which had been defeated and driven from Missionary Ridge the previous November and was now under a new commander, General Joseph E. Johnston. Numbering 54,500 officers and men on April 10, plus 154 artillery pieces, the army had been snapped back into shape during the winter by Johnston.

In the instructions given to them by their superiors, neither Johnston nor Sherman was informed about the taking of Atlanta as a military objective. Grant simply ordered Sherman to move against Johnston's army, "break it up," and get as far into the enemy's country as he could, wrecking their war resources along the way. As for the Confederate plans, President Davis wanted Johnston to advance back into Tennessee, but Johnston argued that, outnumbered and blocked at Chattanooga, he could assume no offensive. Davis reluctantly accepted Johnston's logic. The Confederates therefore stood on the defensive, aware that Sherman's thrust would be toward Atlanta, the occupation of which, as a pivotal industrial and railroad center, was key to the war's outcome.

Sensible of his troops' superior numbers and morale, and shrewdly anticipating his opponent's passive disposition, Sherman was supremely confident of success. On April 10 he outlined to Grant his plans for taking the city, once he had pushed Johnston back to it. First, he would maneuver around Atlanta and cut the railroads leading into the city, forcing the Confederate defenders to evacuate through want of supplies. Then he would push farther still into Georgia. In contrast to Sherman's confidence, Johnston was fearful and pessimistic at the start of the campaign. He called for reinforcements just to hold his lines and at times seemed doubtful of his ability to manage even that.

Sherman Flanking, Johnston Retreating

Sherman began marching his troops on May 5, and his opening maneuvers set the stage for the rest of the campaign. With Johnston's army formidably dug in along Rocky Face Ridge north of Dalton (and Johnston prepared to be attacked there), Sherman refused to launch a head-on assault against the Confederates. Instead he used Thomas's and Schofield's armies to demonstrate against Johnston's main position, while McPherson's column stealthily marched southward through undefended Snake Creek Gap, gained the enemy flank, and threatened, on May 9, the Western and Atlantic Railroad, the line running from Atlanta to Chattanooga that supplied the Confederate army. During the night of May 12–13, Johnston retreated to Resaca, a dozen miles south of Dalton, and dug into a new position. Sherman brought his forces up and repeated his previous maneuver, testing the Confederate lines with short, sharp attacks on May 14–15, while part of McPherson's army flanked to the south and crossed the Oostanaula River. Johnston ordered another retreat to take place the next night.

Sherman's troops, attracted by the cannons and other items manufactured for the Confederacy by the Noble Foundry in **Rome**, occupied the city from May to November 1864. On their way out of town the Union troops burned the Nobles' foundry as well as many downtown buildings.—From online entry "Rome"

WWW.GEORGIAENCYCLOPEDIA.ORG

The Southerners, clinging to the railroad, withdrew toward Cassville, just north of Cartersville. The Northerners followed in several widely separated columns. Johnston, seeing an opportunity to attack one of the Union columns, issued battle orders on the morning of May 19. He called it off, however, when enemy cavalry threatened his attacking column before the battle ever started. Johnston ordered another retreat, this time across the Etowah River to Allatoona. To his superiors in Richmond and to the Georgians increasingly alarmed at the Union advance, Johnston gave no assurances of any plan other than choosing successive defensive positions until he was flanked out of them. Moreover, even though the Confederate administration sent almost 20,000 reinforcements to his aid by late May, Johnston kept to his cautious, retrogressing strategy and allowed the enemy a leisurely, uncontested crossing of the Etowah on May 23.

Sharp Fighting Near Dallas and Kennesaw

Sherman maintained his initiative. Knowing the strength of the Confederate position at Allatoona, he bypassed it altogether and struck to the southwest, away from the railroad and toward Dallas. Johnston sidled west to confront him in a new line, which Sherman tested in severe fighting at New Hope Church on May 25 and Pickett's Mill on May

27. Standing on the defensive, the Confederates easily repulsed Sherman's attacks. Casualties for the four days from May 25 to 28 at the "Hell Hole" (the Northerners' name for the area), counting a costly Southern reconnaissance-in-force on May 28, were roughly 2,600 Union and 2,050 Confederate troops.

After his cavalry secured Allatoona Pass on June 3, Sherman moved his forces eastward, back to the railroad. Johnston stayed ahead of him, digging in around Kennesaw Mountain. Reinforced by a full infantry corps from Mississippi, the Union army still held a ten-to-six numerical edge in early June, an advantage of which Johnston was keenly aware and which fed his unaggressive posture. For several weeks Sherman was stymied in his maneuvers by almost daily rains, but he tried to force the issue with an attacking battle on June 27 against the Confederate lines at Kennesaw Mountain. Quickly repulsed, the Union army lost 2,000 troops, killed, wounded, and captured, to the Confederates' 400. Skirmishing and cannonading along the rest of the lines (an almost daily occurrence by this point in the Atlanta campaign) brought Union and Confederate casualties on that day to an estimated 3,000 and 1,000 respectively.

When the rains ended, Sherman returned to his flanking strategy on July 2–3 and forced Johnston to retreat about six miles from Kennesaw to a new line south of Marietta. Sherman's forces again pressed forward, skirmished, cannonaded, probed, and marched so that in forty-eight hours the Confederate army again withdrew, this time to fortifications on the very north bank of the Chattahoochee River.

Hood Replaces Johnston

Sherman's smart combination of numbers and flanking had brought his armies to the vicinity of Atlanta, and the city's residents were justifiably alarmed. Some had already fled. Johnston's orders in mid-May for the evacuation of Atlanta's army hospitals and munitions machinery heightened the public distress. When Sherman's probes up and down the Chattahoochee secured a crossing on July 8 at Roswell, the Southern army retreated across the river during the night of July 9–10 and took up a position south of Peachtree Creek.

Mirroring the alarm in Atlanta, President Davis feared that the city would be abandoned without a fight. On July 10 he began to consult with his cabinet and to inform Robert E. Lee and Georgia senator Ben-

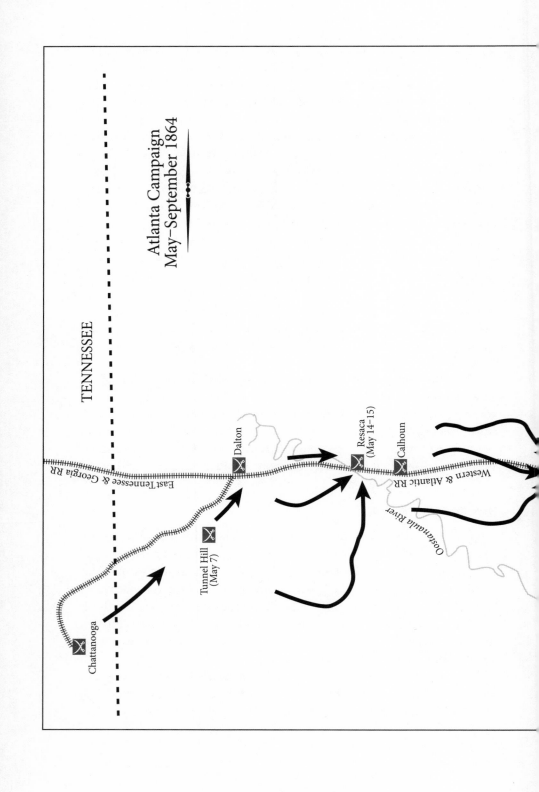

Atlanta Campaign
May–September 1864

TENNESSEE

Chattanooga

Tunnel Hill
(May 7)

Dalton

East Tennessee & Georgia RR

Resaca
(May 14–15)

Calhoun

Western & Atlantic RR

Oostanaula River

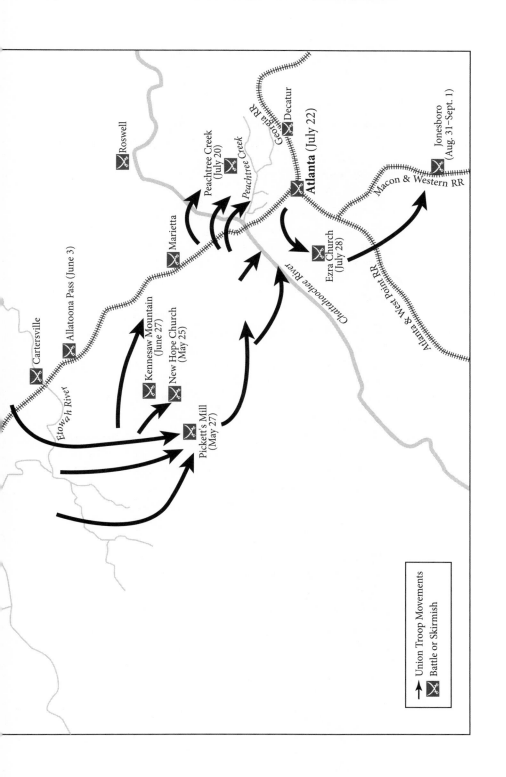

Roswell

Peachtree Creek
(July 20)

Peachtree Creek

Georgia RR

Decatur

Atlanta (July 22)

Jonesboro
(Aug. 31–Sept. 1)

Macon & Western RR

Marietta

Ezra Church
(July 28)

Chattahoochee River

Atlanta & West Point RR

Allatoona Pass (June 3)

Kennesaw Mountain
(June 27)

New Hope Church
(May 25)

Cartersville

Etowah River

Pickett's Mill
(May 27)

Union Troop Movements

Battle or Skirmish

jamin Hill of the need to replace Johnston, despite the fact that Sherman was looming at Atlanta's gates. A week of deliberations, including Davis's blunt telegraph to Johnston inquiring about his plans (answered quite evasively), led to the Confederate government's replacement of Johnston on July 17 with one of the army's corps commanders, General John B. Hood, who was well known for his pugnacity and willingness to attack.

Hood accepted command and, with it, the unfavorable odds. His army, about 50,000 strong, faced around 80,000 Union troops, whose advance was five miles from the city's outskirts. Working to Hood's advantage were the impregnable fortifications around the city, which had been in construction by the Confederates for more than a year. At the same time, Thomas's army was crossing Peachtree Creek; McPherson's army, having swung wide to the southeast, had struck the Georgia Railroad (Atlanta to Augusta) east of Decatur and was marching and destroying track westward toward the city; and Schofield's army was positioned northeast of Atlanta. Hood saw an opportunity to strike Thomas while the other two enemy armies were too far away to give support. Accordingly, he issued plans for an attack on the afternoon of July 20. In the resulting Battle of Peachtree Creek, the Confederates attacked, gaining minor tactical successes, but were ultimately repulsed. Casualties numbered 2,500 Southern, and 1,700 Northern.

As McPherson pushed closer to the city from the east, his army presented the next target for Hood. In a bold maneuver reminiscent of Stonewall Jackson's flanking assaults, Hood called for a third of his infantry to march south through the city, position on McPherson's left flank-rear, and attack. The Battle of Atlanta, on July 22, resulted in the Confederates' greatest success of the campaign, with approximately 3,600 casualties (including McPherson), 12 captured cannons, and a division-length of trenches rolled up. But here too the Confederates were ultimately repulsed and lost an estimated 5,500 men.

True to his plan of cutting Atlanta's railroads, and having already cut the lines heading east out of the city, Sherman swung the Army of Tennessee, now under Major General Oliver O. Howard, to the north of town and threatened the Confederate army's remaining rail lines to the south. Hood again ordered a flanking attack, scheduled for July 29, against Howard's army. The Confederate divisions marched out on July 28 to get into position, but the Union troops' unexpectedly quick advance led the Confederate officer in charge, Lieutenant General Stephen D. Lee, to order a premature frontal attack. The Battle of Ezra Church, on July 28, handed Hood a quick repulse and the loss of 4,600 killed, wounded, or captured troops, while Howard's losses of 700 men were considerably lighter.

The Fall of Atlanta

The Confederates quickly constructed a fortified railway defense line to East Point (six miles southwest of downtown Atlanta) that blocked the further advance of Union troops. Sherman, however, was determined to pound Hood out of the city. On July 20 he ordered that any artillery positioned within range begin a cannonading, not just of the Confederate lines but also of the city itself, which still held about 3,000 civilians (down from 20,000 earlier in the spring). The artillery barrage reached its height on August 9, when Union guns fired approximately 5,000 shells into town. Civilian casualties during the five-week bombardment were remarkably low; the townspeople who decided to remain in the city found shelter in basements or "bombproof" dugouts. During Sherman's barrage and semisiege of Atlanta (so called because at no point could the Union army completely invest the city's eleven-mile perimeter of works), about twenty civilians were killed. The number of wounded and maimed must be judged much higher, although Southern medical records offer no precise data.

Though his own headquarters came under shell fire, Hood refused to budge. Supplies continued to arrive into the city from Macon, even after the third railroad (to Montgomery) had been cut in mid-July by a Union cavalry raid in Alabama. Sherman tried twice to cut the last railroad, the Macon and Western, with cavalry raids in late July and mid-August. After these attempts failed (with a few miles of torn track quickly repaired), Sherman concluded that only a massive infantry sweep would cut the Macon Road. On August 25, with his forces withdrawn to guard the Chattahoochee bridgehead northwest of Atlanta and his siege lines abandoned, Sherman marched most of his army (six of seven corps) south and then southeast toward Jonesboro, fifteen miles from Atlanta.

Hood found that he could not stretch his outnumbered army far enough. With a third of his infantry and state militia forced to man the city defenses, he tried to send his troops down the railroad to meet the new threat. When Howard's army approached cannon range of Jonesboro and the railroad, Hood had no choice but to order an attack, which the entrenched Union troops handily repulsed on August 31. To the north on that same day, other Union troops actually reached the railroad and began wrecking the rails. Hood's attempt to send the army's reserve ordnance train southward failed as the engine, faced by enemy interdiction, had to chug back into the city. Hood was left with no option but to order the evacuation of Atlanta on September 1. Continued fighting at Jonesboro that day proved inconsequential—the fate of Atlanta was sealed when Sherman's troops cut the Macon and Western line. Union soldiers entered the city on September 2, thus concluding the Atlanta campaign.

Occupation and Destruction

Telegraphing Washington, D.C., General Sherman observed, "Atlanta is ours and fairly won." Battle casualties for the four-month campaign totaled 37,000 Union and about 32,000 Confederate soldiers killed, wounded, and missing. In both armies roughly seven out of ten soldiers fell sick at some time; their incapacitation for duty probably affected both sides in equal proportion.

Sherman's troops held Atlanta for two and a half months. Northern generals moved into the finer houses (Sherman occupied the John Neal home), while soldiers pitched camp in vacant lots or parks, such as those around City Hall, sometimes stripping buildings of wood to build shanties. In early November, with his plan set for a march to the sea, Sherman ordered his engineers to begin "the destruction in Atlanta of all depots, car-houses, shops, factories, foundries," and the like. Some structures had already been destroyed; in addition, retreating Confederates had detonated an ammunition train, which had leveled the big rolling mill. Sherman directed that the structures be knocked down by his engineers first "and that fire only be used toward the last moment."

The work began November 12, after Union troops had sent north their last train loaded with materials that the army would not use in its upcoming march. Captain Orlando Poe, Sherman's chief engineer, instructed his men to rip apart Atlanta's railroads, heating and bending each rail over the burning wooden ties. Not until November 15 did engineers begin torching designated sites, some with explosive shells placed inside. A hand-drawn map (now at the Peabody Essex Museum in Massachusetts) indicates the buildings that were destroyed, including a storehouse at Whitehall and Forsyth streets, a bank at the railroad and

Peachtree Street, the Trout and Washington hotels, and various other structures.

Four days earlier, on the night of November 11, Union soldiers milling about town began to torch private buildings, especially residences. Union officer David Conyngham related that about twenty houses were destroyed that night, ruefully and rather lamely attributed by Captain Poe later to "lawless persons, who, by sneaking around in blind alleys, succeeded in firing many houses which it was not intended to touch." Fires were set each night from November 11 to 15, although army officials tried to prevent them by guarding certain properties and catching or punishing the perpetrators. Churches were particularly kept under guard, resulting in five of them being spared from the flames that eventually consumed much of downtown.

On the final night of the Union occupation, November 15–16, Union troops, encouraged by the arson carried out by the engineers, committed unlicensed burnings that set much of downtown afire. Viewing from headquarters the fiery glow over much of the city that night, Major Henry Hitchcock of Sherman's staff predicted, "Gen. S. will hereafter be charged with indiscriminate burning." The Union army left Atlanta the next morning.

News of Sherman's capture of Atlanta provoked electric and tumultuous reactions in both the North and the South. The first significant Northern victory in 1864, the fall of Atlanta assured President Lincoln's reelection in November, as well as a pledged U.S. prosecution of the war to victory. With the loss of Atlanta, Confederate defeat was only a matter of time.

STEPHEN DAVIS

 # Battle of Resaca

Fought on May 14–15, 1864, the Battle of Resaca was the first major engagement of the Atlanta campaign. Situated on the north bank of the Oostanaula River approximately seventy-five miles northwest of Atlanta, Resaca was located on the strategically important Western and Atlantic Railroad. The fighting at Resaca demonstrated that the outnumbered Confederate army could only slow but not stop the advance of Union forces into Georgia.

Prelude to Resaca

Following its November 1863 defeat at Chattanooga, Tennessee, the Confederate Army of Tennessee retreated thirty miles to the southeast and encamped in Dalton, Georgia, for the winter. General Joseph E. Johnston assumed command of the demoralized Confederate troops and began preparations for a defensive struggle in the spring. Johnston entrenched his men in Dalton and along Rocky Face Ridge, a steep and rugged ridgeline on the outskirts of the town.

Completed in 1851, the Western and Atlantic (W&A) Railroad linked Atlanta with Chattanooga and, along with three other **railroads**, made Atlanta a rail hub for the entire South, as well as a key military target during the war. Many of the battles of the Atlanta Campaign were fought along the route of the W&A.—From online entry "Railroads"

WWW.GEORGIAENCYCLOPEDIA.ORG

In early May 1864 Union major general William T. Sherman opened the Atlanta campaign by moving south from Chattanooga with 110,000 troops. Confederate forces were outnumbered approximately two to one, but the last-minute arrival of reinforcements led by Major General Leonidas Polk increased Johnston's army to almost 70,000 men.

The first skirmish of the campaign occurred on May 7, when Union forces swept Confederate cavalry from Tunnel Hill, a small promontory in front of Rocky Face Ridge. Sherman then lined up his armies facing the ridgeline, and over the next two days he launched a number of small-scale attacks against the heavily fortified Confederate position. In the bloodiest of these encounters, Union soldiers fought their way up Rocky Face Ridge while Confederate defenders rolled large rocks down upon the attackers. The Confederate position proved impregnable.

However, the Union demonstrations against Rocky Face Ridge were merely a diversion, for Sherman had no intention of launching a full frontal assault against the well-entrenched Confederates. With General Johnston's attention focused on the Union forces to his front, Sherman sent McPherson's 25,000-man Army of the Tennessee on a covert march south to Snake Creek Gap. The unguarded road through Snake Creek Gap led a dozen miles south of Dalton to the village of Resaca. McPherson hoped to capture Resaca and then sever the Confederate supply line and trap Johnston's army. On the night of May 8–9, McPherson's army passed through the gap and emerged behind the Confederate front lines. Upon learning the news, a jubilant Sherman exclaimed, "I've got Joe Johnston dead!"

Sherman's elation proved premature, however, for McPherson proceeded with extreme caution and failed to seize Resaca. As Sherman sent more troops south to Snake Creek Gap, Johnston realized that he was being outflanked. On the night of May 12–13, he evacuated Rocky Face Ridge and the town of Dalton and marched his men south, where by the following morning they had taken up defensive positions along a four-mile front to the west and north of Resaca. The Confederates had shifted positions just in time to meet the arrival of Sherman's forces. Throughout the day on May 13, Union and Confederate troops fought a number of skirmishes, but the day ended before the Union armies were fully deployed for battle.

The Battle of Resaca

On Saturday, May 14, the fighting at Resaca escalated into a full-scale battle. Beginning at dawn, Union forces engaged the Confederates along the entire four-mile front. In the early afternoon John M. Schofield's Army of the Ohio attacked the sharply angled center of the Confederate line. The assault was badly managed and disorganized, in part because one of Schofield's division commanders was drunk. As the Union attack unraveled and became a fiasco, Johnston launched a counterattack on Sherman's left flank. The counterattack collapsed, however, in the face of a determined stand by a Union artillery battery. In the evening Union forces pushed forward and seized the high ground west of Resaca, which placed the bridges leading south from the town within artillery range and threatened Johnston's line of retreat.

The following day Sherman renewed his assault on the Confederate center. In order to fire on the advancing Union troops, Captain Max Van Den Corput's artillery battery assumed an advanced position some eighty yards in front of the main Confederate line. The four-gun Confederate battery, protected behind an earthen parapet, became the center of a furious struggle. Union troops massed in a ravine directly in front of the battery, and the Seventieth Indiana Regiment, led by Colonel Benjamin Harrison (the future U.S. president), swarmed over the parapet and overwhelmed the Confederate gunners. However, Harrison's men were exposed to withering fire from the main Confederate line and had to take cover. For the rest of the day the abandoned guns sat in a deadly no man's land. After the sun set, Union soldiers dug through the parapet, slipped ropes around the four cannons, and dragged them back to the Union lines.

As the fighting raged on May 15, Johnston learned that a division of Union troops had crossed the Oostanaula River southwest of Resaca. Sherman had once again taken advantage of his numeric superiority to outflank the entrenched Confederates. Johnston's position had thus become untenable, and during the night his troops abandoned their defenses and retreated farther south. The Battle of Resaca demonstrated that the Atlanta campaign would be hard fought and bloody. Johnston's army had suffered some 2,800 casualties, and Union losses were at least as high. But Sherman, with his superior forces, could continue pressing and outflanking the Confederate army, driving it farther south and ever closer to Atlanta.

State Historic Site

Resaca Confederate Cemetery, which contains the graves of more than 450 Confederates killed in the fighting at Resaca, was dedicated in 1866. For nearly a century the battlefield—an area of privately owned farms, pastures, and wooded hills—remained relatively undisturbed. In 1960 the construction of Interstate 75 significantly altered the local landscape, destroying approximately one-half mile of Confederate earthworks.

Beginning in 1994 the Friends of Resaca Battlefield—a nonprofit organization dedicated to battlefield preservation—began lobbying the state of Georgia to purchase and protect the remaining portions of the battlefield. In 2000 the Georgia Civil War Commission helped facilitate the state's purchase of a tract of farmland containing more than 500 acres, which included remnants of original entrenchments, in Gordon and Whitfield counties. In 2008 the Georgia Department of Natural Resources broke ground on the Resaca Battlefield State Historic Site, which is scheduled to include a museum, a welcome center, a theater showing an interpretive film, and marked trails.

KEVIN W. YOUNG

} Battle of Pickett's Mill

The Battle of Pickett's Mill was among the more decisive encounters of the Atlanta campaign during the Civil War. In May 1864 the Confederate army successfully prevented Union general William T. Sherman's troops from occupying Dallas, in Paulding County, which Sherman sought as a strategic base of operations as he moved toward Atlanta. The battle was the bloodiest to that point in the campaign and by all accounts delayed Sherman's eventual capture of Atlanta by at least a week.

Today, the Pickett's Mill Battlefield Historic Site is one of the most thoroughly preserved and interpreted Civil War battlefields in the nation.

The Battle

By May 23 Sherman's army had crossed the Etowah River in the move toward Atlanta. In order to skirt the Allatoona Pass, where Confederate general Joseph E. Johnston's forces defended the railroad, the Union forces crossed through the wilderness south to Marietta via Dallas, with more than 85,000 men and twenty days' worth of supplies. Searching for a route between Johnston's forces and the Chattahoochee River, Sherman drove his troops to the crossroads at New Hope Church, where they encountered Confederates under the command of Lieutenant General John Bell Hood on May 25. As Hood's Corps stood its ground on May 26, Sherman ordered Major Lieutenant General Oliver O. Howard to lead 14,000 Union troops to the left of the Union army and attack the Confederates on Hood's right.

The Battle of Pickett's Mill was fought in **Paulding County** on the grounds of a farm and gristmill owned by Benjamin and Malachi Pickett on Little Pumpkin-Vine Creek. Today the nearly 800-acre Pickett's Mill Battlefield Historic Site provides vivid evidence of the soldiers' battlements and a sense of how the area looked at the time of the battle.—From online entry "Paulding County"

WWW.GEORGIAENCYCLOPEDIA.ORG

Early in the morning of May 27, the artillery of the Union army began bombarding the Confederates at New Hope Church, and Howard ordered Brigadier General Thomas Wood to move his division toward the Confederates' right wing. Marching through rough and densely forested terrain, Howard and Wood had difficulty locating the Confederate right flank, allowing Johnston time to shift his armies in order to reinforce that endangered flank, under Major General Patrick R. Cleburne's command.

When Howard arrived at the west bank of Pickett's Mill Creek, he thought that his army had moved beyond the enemy's right and so ordered Wood to attack. Wood's first two battle lines composed Union brigadier general William B. Hazen's brigade. At 4:30 p.m. Hazen's troops advanced, only to encounter the fierce firepower of Brigadier General Hiram B. Granbury's Texans on the top of a rocky, tree-covered ridge. Soon after the battle began, the Texans were reinforced with Brigadier General Daniel Govan's Arkansas troops and Brigadier General Mark P. Lowrey's Alabama-Mississippi Brigade. After fifty minutes of bloody combat, Hazen's surviving troops began to fall back. At this moment Wood sent in Colonel William Gibson's brigade. This second attack also failed in the absence of sufficient support, and Gibson's men fell back an hour later.

Around 6:00 p.m. Sherman's troops received orders to end the attack. Howard immediately ordered Wood to send his remaining brigade, under Colonel Frederick Knefler, to the front with instructions to hold the Confederates in check until a regular defense line could be established around Pickett's Mill. At 6:30 p.m. Knefler's brigade encountered Confederates and pumped bullets at them until dark and then carried Hazen's and Gibson's wounded from the battlefield.

Knefler received an order to withdraw at 10:00 p.m. However, with the permission from Cleburne to clear his front, Granbury's Texans charged Knefler's brigade nearly at the same time. Surprised by the sudden onslaught, the Union forces fired a ragged, harmless volley and fled. The Texans took many of them prisoner.

Aftermath

The following morning, Johnston visited the battlefield, and Cleburne estimated the Union casualties to be 3,000, with 448 of them his own. In truth, Union casualties came to around 1,600. Nevertheless, the battle was a major victory for the Confederacy. Many of the dead were initially buried at the site, but in 1866 most were reinterred at the Marietta National Cemetery.

The Battle of Pickett's Mill delayed Sherman's progress; when his forces emerged from the wilderness, they were no closer to Atlanta than they had been almost two weeks earlier. The real significance of the battle was that it marked the beginning of trench warfare. Beginning at New Hope Church and continuing until September 2, much of the war around Atlanta was fought in trenches. Trench warfare cost Johnston his single important advantage of maneuver over Sherman's superior manpower and materiel, eventually leaving Johnston with no choice but to retreat or accept defeat.

Preservation and Excavation

The memory of the Battle of Pickett's Mill gradually faded. In the 1950s local historians Wilbur Kurtz and Beverly Dubose informally mapped the site of Pickett's Mill. Georgia Kraft Company owned the site, and interest remained minimal until the Civil War centennial of the early 1960s.

In 1971 a group of interested citizens, led by historian Philip Secrist, initiated the purchase of the battlefield, and the state of Georgia was persuaded to purchase it in 1973–74 and establish it as a state historic site. The state entered into negotiations with several other smaller landowners to purchase the last piece of the park in 1981.

The Pickett's Mill Battlefield Historic Site was officially opened to the public in 1990. It consists of 765 acres of nearly pristine wilderness, with evidence of trenches still apparent at various points on the battlefield. In addition to the remains of earthworks, parts of the old Pickett's Mill still stand. In 2010 the historic site received attention as one of the most endangered battlefields, due to state cutbacks in spending that affected maintenance of the site and its hours of accessibility to the public. It is currently the site of archaeological investigations.

JUN SUK HYUN

 # Battle of Kennesaw Mountain

On June 27, 1864, Kennesaw Mountain, located in Cobb County about twenty miles northwest of Atlanta, became the scene of one of the Atlanta campaign's major actions.

Beginning of the Atlanta Campaign

One month earlier, Union major general William T. Sherman led a force of three armies from Chattanooga into Georgia. His objective was the destruction of Confederate general Joseph E. Johnston's Army of Tennessee. Johnston hoped to prevent his army's annihilation while protecting his supply and communications center at Atlanta. He frustrated Sherman by conducting a masterful defensive strategy, entrenching his army across Sherman's path and forcing the Union armies into either a frontal assault or a flanking maneuver against well-prepared field troops. Johnston was ever alert for an opportunity to strike at isolated units of the Union army but was primarily concerned with keeping his own army together as a cohesive fighting force and blocking Sherman's push into Atlanta.

Even though Sherman continued to force the Confederates backward by skirting their positions, he worried that his inability to destroy Johnston's army would allow the Confederate government to transfer troops, bolstering Confederate general Robert E. Lee's Army of Northern Virginia against the Union's spring offensive in Virginia. These fears were allayed at Kennesaw Mountain in late June, where Sherman believed that his opponent had finally made a mistake and that a well-executed attack could crush the Army of Tennessee and open the way to Atlanta.

By June 19 Johnston had established a strong defensive line along Kennesaw Mountain. Sherman attempted to bypass the formidable position to the south, but a Confederate counterattack at Kolb's Farm on June 22 thwarted his move. Although the counterattack did not inflict serious casualties, it forced Sherman into either swinging his army wider to the south in order to bypass the Confederate position or attacking Confederate entrenchments. Surprisingly, Sherman chose to attack. He reasoned that by blocking the Union advance at Kolb's Farm, the Confederates had overextended their lines. Indeed, the Confederates were arranged in a large semicircle that stretched eight miles from Kolb's Farm in the south to Kennesaw Mountain in the north. Sherman concluded that a strike at the Confederate center would break its line and give him the advantage needed to destroy Johnston's entire army.

For Sherman's plan to succeed, the Union army would need to do three things: confuse Johnston by feigning attacks on each end of the Confederate line, forcing him to pull men away from the center; launch a diversionary attack at Kennesaw Mountain itself to probe for weaknesses and tie down the Confederates; and attack two key points in the

Confederate center to break the army's overextended line. The first would capture Pigeon Hill just south of Kennesaw Mountain, while a larger assault would overrun a wooded ridge further to the south (known today as Cheatham Hill in honor of Confederate major general Benjamin Franklin Cheatham, whose Tennesseans defended the hill).

Battle on Kennesaw Mountain

Sherman's troops bombarded the Confederate positions at nine o'clock on the morning of June 27 and then advanced along the base of Kennesaw Mountain. The Confederates easily repulsed this diversionary attack. Meanwhile, rough terrain and a stubborn defense stymied the Union assault at Pigeon Hill, which sputtered out after a couple of hours. At Cheatham Hill, the heaviest fighting occurred along a salient stretch in the Confederate line dubbed "Dead Angle" by Confederate defenders. Union troops made a desperate effort to storm the Confederate trenches. However, as elsewhere, the rough terrain and intense Confederate fire combined to defeat the Union army. Within hours, the Battle of Kennesaw Mountain was over. Union casualties numbered some 3,000 men while the Confederates lost 1,000, making it one of the bloodiest single days in the campaign for Atlanta.

Sherman hated to admit failure, and his pride led him to consider renewing the assault. However, his subordinates, especially General George H. Thomas, convinced him to reconsider such a hopeless endeavor. After several days of scouting and preparation, Sherman again flanked the Confederate lines. The ever-vigilant Johnston, however, abandoned his entrenchments on July 2 and deftly blocked the Union advance again at Smyrna. The war of maneuver continued. Although a tactical defeat for Sherman, the Battle of Kennesaw Mountain did not prevent his continued drive toward Atlanta. Strategically, Sherman still had the initiative, and more importantly, he had the men, the materiel, and the will to continue pressing Johnston's beleaguered force.

Kennesaw Mountain National Battlefield

Today visitors can explore this battlefield, thanks in part to the foresight of Lansing J. Dawdy, an Illinois veteran of the battle. In 1899 Dawdy purchased sixty acres of land near the Dead Angle. The property was transferred in 1904 to the Kennesaw Mountain Battlefield Association. In 1914, to commemorate the fiftieth anniversary of the battle, the organization erected a monument dedicated to the Illinois soldiers who fell in the assault on Cheatham Hill. However, unable to restore the battlefield as planned, the association transferred ownership of the property to the federal government in 1916, and the next year Congress authorized the Kennesaw Mountain National Battlefield site.

During the 1930s the battlefields at Chickamauga and Kennesaw Mountain were preserved through the efforts of the **Civilian Conservation Corps**, a federal employment program that carried out various projects, including flood prevention and parks development. Preservation of the battle sites included the construction of roads and trails and the restoration of historic fortifications.—From online entry "Civilian Conservation Corps"

WWW.GEORGIAENCYCLOPEDIA.ORG

The park itself was not formed until 1935. Since then, it has grown to nearly 3,000 acres. The first park facilities, roads, and trails were built during the 1930s and 1940s. The number of guests who visit the park each year has climbed steadily from around 4,700 in 1939 to 1.4 million in 2004. Part of the reason for this tremendous growth is that the park remains the largest wilderness area in the metropolitan Atlanta area.

Unfortunately, this heavy visitation comes with a cost. In 2005 the park was named one of the Civil War Preservation Trust's "Ten Most Endangered" battlefields, due primarily to the impact of urban sprawl and traffic congestion.

JOHN D. FOWLER

 Sherman's March to the Sea

The March to the Sea, the Civil War's most destructive campaign against a civilian population, began in Atlanta on November 15, 1864, and concluded in Savannah on December 21, 1864. General William T. Sherman abandoned his supply line and marched across Georgia to the Atlantic Ocean to prove to the Confederate population that its government could not protect the people from invaders. He practiced psychological warfare; he believed that by marching an army across the state he would demonstrate to the world that the Union had a power the Confederacy could not resist. "This may not be war," he said, "but rather statesmanship."

Preparation

After Sherman's forces captured Atlanta on September 2, 1864, Sherman spent several weeks making preparations for a change of base to the coast. He rejected the Union plan to move through Alabama to Mobile, pointing out that after Rear Admiral David G. Farragut closed Mobile Bay in August 1864, the Alabama port no longer held any military significance. Rather, he decided to proceed southeast toward Savannah or Charleston. He carefully studied census records to determine which route could provide food for his men and forage for his animals. Although U.S. president Abraham Lincoln was skeptical and did not want Sherman to move into enemy territory before the presidential election in November, Sherman persuaded his friend Lieutenant General Ulysses S. Grant that the campaign was possible in winter. Through Grant's intervention Sherman finally gained permission, although he had to delay until after election day.

Confederate Response

After General John Bell Hood abandoned Atlanta, he moved the Confederate Army of Tennessee outside the city to recuperate from the previous campaign. In early October he began a raid toward Chattanooga, Tennessee, in an effort to draw Sherman back over ground the two sides had fought for since May. But instead of tempting Sherman to battle, Hood turned his army west and marched into Alabama, abandoning Georgia to Union forces. Apparently, Hood hoped that if he invaded Tennessee, Sherman would be forced to follow. Sherman, however, had anticipated this strategy and had sent Major General George H. Thomas to Nashville to deal with Hood. With Georgia cleared of the Confederate army, Sherman, facing only scattered cavalry, was free to move south.

The March

Sherman divided his army into two wings. The right wing was under Oliver O. Howard. Peter J. Osterhaus commanded the Fifteenth Corps, and Francis P. Blair Jr. commanded the Seventeenth Corps. The left wing was commanded by Henry W. Slocum, with the Fourteenth Corps under Jefferson C. Davis and the Twentieth Corps under Alpheus S. Williams. Judson Kilpatrick led the cavalry. Sherman had about 2,500 supply wagons

Achieving the rank of lieutenant general in the Confederate army, Camden County native **William J. Hardee** was renowned for his understanding of tactical maneuvers in battle. His textbook, *Rifle and Light Infantry Tactics* (1855), was required reading for officers in both the Union and Confederate armies during the war.—From online entry "William J. Hardee"

WWW.GEORGIAENCYCLOPEDIA.ORG

and 600 ambulances. Before the army left Atlanta, the general issued an order outlining the rules of the march, but soldiers often ignored the restrictions on foraging.

The two wings advanced by separate routes, generally staying twenty miles to forty miles apart. The right wing headed for Macon, the left wing in the direction of Augusta, before the two commands turned and bypassed both cities. They now headed for the state capital at Milledgeville. Opposing Sherman's advance was Confederate cavalry, about 8,000 strong, under Major General Joseph Wheeler and various units of Georgia militia under Gustavus W. Smith. Although William J. Hardee had overall command in Georgia, with his headquarters at Savannah, neither he nor Governor Joseph E. Brown could do anything to stop Sherman's advance. Sherman's foragers quickly became known as "bummers" as they raided farms and plantations. On November 23 the state capital peacefully surrendered, and Sherman occupied the vacant governor's mansion and capitol building.

Military Encounters

There were a number of skirmishes between Wheeler's cavalry and Union troopers, but only two battles of any significance. The first came east of Macon at the factory town of Griswoldville on November 22, when Georgia militia faced Union infantry with disastrous results. The Confederates suffered 650 men killed or wounded in a one-sided battle that left about 62 casualties on the Union side. The second battle occurred on the Ogeechee River twelve miles below Savannah. Union infantry under William B. Hazen assaulted and captured Fort McAllister on December 13, thus opening the back door to the port city.

The most controversial event involved contrabands (escaped slaves) who followed the liberating armies. On December 9, Union commander Jefferson C. Davis removed a pontoon bridge at Ebenezer Creek, outside Savannah, before the slaves crossed. Frightened men, women, and children plunged into the deep water, and many drowned in an attempt to reach safety. After the march Davis was soundly criticized by the Northern press, but Sherman backed his commander by pointing out that Davis had done what was militarily necessary.

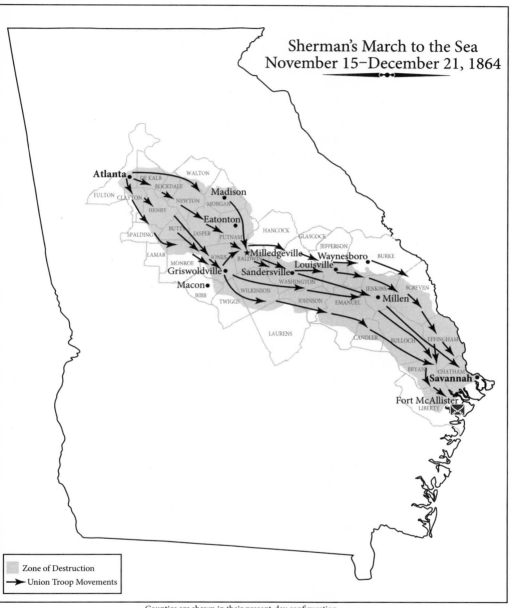

Sherman's March to the Sea
November 15–December 21, 1864

Zone of Destruction
Union Troop Movements

Counties are shown in their present-day configuration.

Sherman at Savannah

After Fort McAllister fell, Sherman made preparations for a siege of Savannah. Confederate lieutenant general Hardee, realizing his small army could not hold out long and not wanting the city leveled by artillery as had happened at Atlanta, ordered his men to abandon the trenches and retreat to South Carolina. Sherman, who was not with the Union army when Mayor Richard Arnold surrendered Savannah (he had gone to Hilton Head, South Carolina, to make preparations for a siege and was on his way back to Georgia), telegraphed President Lincoln on December 22 that the city had fallen. He offered Savannah and 25,000 bales of confiscated cotton to the president as a Christmas present.

Consequences of the March

Sherman's march frightened and appalled Southerners. It hurt morale, for civilians had believed the Confederacy could protect the home front. Sherman had terrorized the countryside; his men had destroyed all sources of food and forage and had left behind a hungry and demoralized people. Although he did not level any towns, he did destroy buildings in places where there was resistance. His men had shown little sympathy for Millen, the site of Camp Lawton, where Union prisoners of war were held. Physical attacks on white civilians were few, although it is not known how slave women fared at the hands of the invaders. Often male slaves posted guards outside the cabins of their women.

Confederate president Jefferson Davis had urged Georgians to undertake a scorched-earth policy of poisoning wells and burning fields, but civilians in the army's path had not done so. Sherman, however, burned or captured all the food stores that Georgians had saved for the winter months. As a result of the hardships on women and children, desertions increased in Robert E. Lee's army in Virginia. Sherman believed his campaign against civilians would shorten the war by breaking the Confederate will to fight, and he eventually received permission to carry this psychological warfare into South Carolina in early 1865. By marching through Georgia and South Carolina he became an arch-villain in the South and a hero in the North.

ANNE J. BAILEY

Griswoldville

Griswoldville, an industrial village on the Central of Georgia Railway in Jones County, produced cotton gins during the antebellum period and Confederate revolvers during the Civil War. The village was destroyed during Union general William T. Sherman's March to the Sea, and the only major infantry battle of that campaign was fought near its ruins.

Samuel Griswold, the village's founder, moved from Connecticut to Jones County in the late 1810s. Settling in Clinton, the county seat, he made a small start in the tinware trade before progressing to the much more lucrative business of producing cotton gins. By 1850 Griswold had moved his gin business to extensive acreage he had purchased in lower Jones County on the Central railroad and named his factory village for himself: Griswoldville. His complex included not only a steam-powered gin factory, with a lofty brick chimney, but also a gristmill, blacksmith and pattern shops, a soap and tallow factory, and a foundry. As the last station before Macon on the railroad from Savannah, Griswoldville boasted a depot, water tank, wood pile, and generous length of rail siding. Soon after the Civil War began, Griswold adapted his factory to produce weaponry and teamed with former employee A. N. Gunnison to manufacture firearms for the Confederacy styled after the Colt Navy revolver. On November 20, 1864, during Sherman's March to the Sea, the factory complex, along with much of the rest of Griswoldville, was burned by Captain Frederick S. Ladd of the Ninth Michigan Volunteer Cavalry and "one hundred picked men."

On November 22 a Confederate force, made up mainly of Georgia militia "on loan," attacked elements of Sherman's right wing at Duncan's Farm east of Griswoldville. The Confederate force was marching along the line of the Central railroad to meet a train sent to carry them to Augusta, thought to be Sherman's destination. In a tragedy of errors, the Union infantry was waiting for a Confederate cavalry attack that never came, while the Georgia infantry charged at them across an open field, thinking they were a small force of cavalry.

The Battle of Griswoldville lasted from mid-afternoon to dusk, with some 2,300 Confederates suffering about 650 casualties, a great number of them officers. Many of the wounded and dead were young boys and old men from the Georgia militia, leading one Union officer to remark, "I hope we will never have to shoot at such men again." The 1,500 Union troops lost about 62 men, but among the badly wounded was their commander, Brigadier General Charles C. Walcutt, who was carried from the field before battle's end.

Old and ailing, Griswold did not rebuild, though Griswoldville's crossroads location on a rail line would attract a population of around eighty by 1900, and the place would later be the site of a district school. By the mid-1950s the area had been bought by a Kraft conglomerate, and the site was once again given over to pine forests. The battlefield, however, is maintained as a Georgia state historic site.

WILLIAM HARRIS BRAGG

 # Wilson's Raid

In mid-March 1865, as the Confederate States of America struggled through its final days, Union major general James Harrison Wilson began a month-long cavalry raid that laid waste to much of the productive capacity of Alabama and Georgia.

In a war where cavalry troops were underutilized, frequently mixed with infantry troops, or simply relegated to hauling supplies and delivering mail, Wilson's approach to warfare was innovative: he used his 13,480 horsemen, without any infantry troops, in lightning quick raids against the productive centers of the Deep South. Much of the area from central Mississippi to central Georgia remained relatively unscathed, even in the late stages of the Civil War. Consequently, cities like Selma and Montgomery, Alabama, and Columbus, Georgia, survived as vital shipping points and major producers of Confederate war supplies. Wilson's aim was twofold: to destroy this critical supply link and to prevent the region from becoming the site of a Confederate last stand.

Wilson Begins His Raid

Wilson, the twenty-seven-year-old "boy-general," a native of Illinois, graduated from the U.S. Military Academy at West Point, New York, ranked sixth in his class in 1860. His star rose rapidly; he served under General William T. Sherman late in the war, after serving under General

Ulysses S. Grant at Vicksburg, Mississippi, and Chattanooga, Tennessee, and heading the Cavalry Bureau of the War Department. Wilson began organizing and training his cavalrymen in northwest Alabama in early 1865. Because Southern forces were preoccupied with stopping Sherman's March to the Sea, few Confederate troops were available to slow Wilson's progress. General Nathan Bedford Forrest, with about 5,000 men, only 3,000 of whom were well mounted, constituted the main Confederate force in the region, but his troops were widely scattered and heavily outnumbered and outgunned.

Alabama

By March 31, 1865, Wilson and the main body of his force had worked their way to Montevallo in central Alabama, the heart of the state's iron and coal district (just south of present-day Birmingham). Forrest's troops offered ineffective resistance to Wilson's men, who made quick work of the mills, coal mines, and foundries in the surrounding area, including facilities in Elyton (later Birmingham), Irondale, Oxmoor, and Brierfield.

Forrest then concentrated his troops outside Selma as Wilson's troops rapidly approached that city. The two sides clashed at Ebenezer Church some nineteen miles outside of Selma, with a decisive victory for the Union troops. Wilson lost only twelve men while inflicting considerably more damage on Forrest's troops, with Forrest himself sustaining a minor injury.

Significantly outnumbered, Forrest hastily organized a civilian defense of Selma. Wilson moved against the city on April 2. Casualties were significant on both sides, but Wilson's onslaught was too much. Forrest and his men fled the city in the middle of the night, putting the torch to the city's cotton stores as they scrambled out of town.

With the fall of Selma, Wilson inflicted a considerable loss on the Confederacy. Selma's arsenal contained, among other things, 15 siege guns, 60,000 rounds of artillery ammunition, and 1 million rounds of small arms ammunition. Wilson destroyed the city's eleven ironworks and foundries, which had produced war goods for the Confederacy, as well as locomotives and rail cars, thus depriving the Confederacy of one of its last reliable industrial centers. Moreover, Forrest's cavalry would harass Wilson's forces no more. In a meeting between Forrest and Wilson, Forrest reputedly said to Wilson, "Well, General, you have beaten me badly, and for the first time I am compelled to make such an acknowledgement."

As Wilson swung his troops eastward toward Montgomery, he faced increasingly diminished opposition. Like Selma, Montgomery was an important production center and a vital shipping point for distributing the region's agricultural goods. Moreover, as Montgomery was the capital of Alabama and a former capital of the Confederacy, its taking carried considerable symbolic weight. As Wilson's men approached Montgomery, Confederate general Dan Adams's troops, charged with defending the city, were ordered to Columbus to link up with Howell Cobb's Georgia State Troops. Montgomery was left defenseless, and Wilson's men entered the city facing no resistance. With the war winding down, Wilson stayed in Montgomery two days, sparing the city except for its arsenal and its railroad equipment and depots.

Following secession, **Howell Cobb** served as president of the Provisional Confederate Congress. At the conclusion of his term he entered the Confederate army and eventually rose to the rank of major general. In September 1863 he took command of Georgia state troops, which he later surrendered to Wilson's forces in Macon on April 20, 1865.—From online entry "Howell Cobb"

WWW.GEORGIAENCYCLOPEDIA.ORG

Georgia

Heading into Georgia, Wilson moved against Columbus on April 16, 1865. Columbus, too, was unprepared to defend itself. Many of those tapped to defend the city were taking part in their first combat. Wilson easily routed the Confederates there and took around 1,500 men prisoner. With the fall of Columbus, Wilson had taken "the last great Confederate storehouse." As Wilson headed for Macon, Confederate general Robert E. Lee had already surrendered at Appomattox, Virginia, and U.S. president Abraham Lincoln was dead. The war was effectively over.

Wilson organized cavalry patrols to capture fleeing Confederate leaders and to obtain the surrender of any bands of Confederates still roaming Alabama and Georgia. On May 10, 1865, a group of Wilson's men captured the former president of the Confederacy, Jefferson Davis, at Irwinville in south central Georgia. Groups of Wilson's men also captured or arrested former Confederate vice president Alexander Stephens, Georgia governor Joseph E. Brown, Georgia senator Benjamin Hill, and the infamous Henry Wirz, commandant of Andersonville prison. Wilson's forces were fully disbanded by early July.

Although no one denies the tremendous damage Wilson's men were able to inflict on the Confederacy's productive abilities, scholars debate just how much damage Wilson's troops inflicted on civilians and non-military targets. A group of more than 13,000 men and horses moving through an area, foraging for food and supplies, was bound to cause damage against civilian property, whether or not the intent was malicious. It is certain that some depredations against civilians and civilian property occurred. Wilson's Raid, however, should not be confused with Sherman's March to the Sea. As devastating as the raid was, its targets were largely military.

Historians have also debated the military necessity of Wilson's Raid. By the time Wilson took Montgomery and Columbus, the war was effectively over, possibly rendering the damage inflicted on those cities gratuitous. It also will never be known whether any rogue Confederates would have or could have used Georgia, Alabama, or points further west for a last stand had Wilson's Raid not occurred, although Wilson certainly made that possibility unlikely.

What is known is that in the course of a mere month, Wilson and his men covered hundreds of miles, took more than 6,000 men prisoner, and killed and wounded more than 1,000 Confederates, while having only 99 men killed and 598 wounded. Regardless of the timing that minimized the raid's significance, this surprisingly deft and mobile force of more than 13,000 cavalrymen effectively destroyed the rail centers, arsenals, mines, and factories at the heart of the Confederacy.

JASON MANTHORNE

 # Capture of Jefferson Davis

In early May 1865 the Confederate States of America was greatly disorganized, largely because of the frenetic events of the previous month. General Robert E. Lee had surrendered the Confederate armies at the Appomattox Courthouse in Virginia, and most Americans believed the Civil War was over. The assassination of U.S. president Abraham Lincoln in Washington, D.C., by John Wilkes Booth and other sympathizers with the Southern cause, cast suspicion over many in the Confederate government. Though still intact, the government was largely ineffective.

President Jefferson Davis still retained hopes for the future of the Confederacy. Privately, he harbored a desire to reinforce the armies and move the fighting to the western part of the Confederacy. Publicly, he was forced to flee the Confederate capital in Richmond, Virginia, with a cadre of trusted advisors, which in effect became a government in exile. Upon departing Richmond, Davis and his retinue established a temporary center of government at Danville, Virginia. They soon moved farther south, however, because Virginia was heavily saturated with Union troops.

Among Davis's advisors were John H. Reagan, Judah P. Benjamin, John Breckinridge, and Burton Harrison. A small but elite military escort was also in tow, and they all arrived in Washington, Georgia, on May 3. The next day Davis held a final meeting with his cabinet, and the group dispersed after the president authorized their belated compensation from the remaining Confederate treasury. Davis proceeded south to Sandersville, where on May 6 he oversaw the final dispersal of the Confederate government and on May 7 was reunited with his wife, Varina, and their children. Together they moved on through Abbeville on May 8, keenly aware that Union forces were close behind. The pursuit of Davis resulted largely from the U.S. War Department's false assumption that he was complicit in the assassination of Lincoln. A $100,000 reward was promised for anyone who could bring in the president and his aides.

Jefferson Davis held his last cabinet meeting at the State of Georgia Bank building in **Washington**. Traveling ahead of Davis, his wife and children stayed at the Holly Court residence in town. After his capture, the cache of Confederate gold traveling with him was stored in a basement vault on the south end of the town square.—From online entry "Washington"

WWW.GEORGIAENCYCLOPEDIA.ORG

Reaching the farming community of Irwinville in south central Georgia on the evening of May 9, the remaining hopefuls, still assuming that they were a step ahead of their pursuers, set up camp near a creek bed. Early the next morning the camp was awakened by a pop of gunfire and within minutes was surrounded by members of the First Wisconsin and Fourth Michigan cavalries. Not one shot was fired by the Confederates. Through some confusion President Davis made a quick dash toward the creek. He had thrown his wife's raglan, or overcoat, on his shoulders.

This led to the persistent rumor that he attempted to flee in women's clothes. A popular song of the era was "Jeff in Petticoats," and the major tabloids featured artists' renderings of the fallen leader dressed in everything from a wig to a hoop skirt. A zealous member of the Michigan detail quickly apprehended Davis, and he was transported to Fortress Monroe, Virginia, where he remained a prisoner for more than two years, though he was never put on trial. His poor treatment and its subsequent exposure in the press helped strengthen the cause of Southern nationalism.

A historic marker indicates the spot where he was arrested, and the surrounding area is now the Jefferson Davis Memorial Historic Site, a thirteen-acre park that features a museum, hiking trail, and picnic facilities.

BRIAN BROWN

Confederate Gold

The existence of caches of hidden or lost Confederate gold has been the source of numerous Georgia legends. These legends are fueled by the fact that the state was a hub of gold mining, minting, and trading and that, as Richmond fell to Union forces at the end of the war, the bulk of the Confederate treasury was brought to Georgia, where much of it disappeared.

The federal Branch Mint at Dahlonega had $23,716 in gold and silver when it was taken over by the Confederate States of America in 1861. During the autumn of 1862, the mint turned $40,000 in gold and silver from New Orleans into bars for shipment to Augusta. At the same time, Confederate officials seized from the Bank of Louisiana in Columbus $2.3 million in gold and $216,000 in silver specie that had traveled there after New Orleans fell to Union forces.

Other specie could be found in Civil War Georgia. Gold from civilians made Macon second only to Richmond as a Confederate depository. By the end of the war, Union general E. L. Molineux in Macon had charge of $275,000 in confiscated gold and silver. Molineux also seized $188,000 from the assets of the Central Railroad Bank of Savannah. However, he did not find $200,000 in gold coins from the Georgia State Bank of Savannah that were hidden in Macon. The federal government also confiscated more than $500,000 in assets from the Bank of Tennessee and its branches in Augusta.

The most famous Civil War treasure traveled by wagon to Georgia with Confederate president Jefferson Davis in the last days of the Civil War. This treasure train left Danville, Virginia, on April 6, 1865, with $327,022 in gold and silver coins, as well as bullion, donated jewelry, and even floor sweepings from the Dahlonega mint. Some $450,000 in coins and specie checks (paper money that could be redeemed for metallic coins) that originated with Richmond banks also traveled with the fleeing Confederate government.

Almost all of the Confederate assets were dispersed to pay soldiers returning home before the capture of Davis on May 10, 1865, near Irwinville. The remaining funds from the Richmond banks were left in Washington, Georgia. A detachment of Union soldiers set out to divert this specie to a railhead in South Carolina, but on May 24, 1865, bandits in Georgia attacked the wagons, which had stopped for the night at the Chennault Plantation in Lincoln County. Of the cache, $251,029 was lost, although bank officials eventually recovered some $111,000 of the stolen money.

The federal government seized the recaptured gold, and litigation over its ownership continued until June 22, 1893, when the U.S. Court of Claims decreed that the claimants on behalf of the by-then-defunct Richmond banks should receive $16,987. The other $78,276 remained the property of the United States.

ROBERT SCOTT DAVIS JR.

Civil War Photojournalist: George N. Barnard

A pioneer of nineteenth-century photography, George N. Barnard is best known for his work during the Civil War as the official army photographer for the Military Division of the Mississippi, commanded by Union general William T. Sherman. His images, first published in 1866 as a limited collector's edition entitled *Photographic Views of Sherman's Campaign* (and reproduced here courtesy of the Library of Congress, Prints and Photographs Division), record the destruction left in the wake of Sherman's Atlanta campaign and subsequent March to the Sea.

Barnard, a Connecticut native, began producing daguerreotypes (the first photographs commercially available to the public) around 1842, and for the next two decades he worked as a studio photographer and as one of the nation's first documentary news photographers. In 1861 Matthew Brady, a famous daguerreotypist, hired Barnard as a portrait photographer and sent him to Washington, D.C., to photograph Abraham Lincoln's 1861 inauguration as president of the United States.

When the Civil War broke out, Brady formed a crew of cameramen, "Brady's Photographic Corps," to document the conflict and the men who fought in it. In 1862, at the site of the Bull Run battle in Virginia, Barnard produced the earliest known collodion photographs using a "wet plate" process that allowed him to develop photographs in a darkroom on-site. In December 1863 he became the official photographer for the Military Division of the Mississippi, with headquarters in Nashville, Tennessee. During the early months of 1864 Barnard photographed the landscape of East Tennessee and then worked in Nashville to create detailed topographic maps, which Sherman utilized as his troops moved from Chattanooga to Atlanta.

Barnard traveled to the Atlanta front on September 11, 1864, after Sherman had captured the city. Over the next two months, he photographed Confederate fortifications, railroad yards, private homes, and city streets. Sherman's troops departed Atlanta in November and marched toward the coast. Barnard took no photographs during the march until he reached Fort McAllister, near Savannah, which Union forces captured in December. He remained in Savannah, duplicating maps of the march route, until late January.

After the war, Barnard revisited many of the key battle sites in Georgia, producing sixty-one finished prints that depict the state's ravaged landscapes and ruined cities. He also returned to the site where Union general James B. McPherson was shot and killed during the Battle of Atlanta, on July 22, 1864. Barnard found the death site largely preserved, and his resulting photograph highlights the bleached-out bones of a horse skeleton, suggesting the general's failed attempt to escape on horseback.

CINDY SCHMID

Barnard's photographic wagon and darkroom parked behind Confederate
fortifications on Marietta Street in Atlanta, circa 1864.

Union picket post pictured before the Battle of Atlanta, on July 22, 1864.

Union general William T. Sherman on horseback at Federal Fort No. 7 in
Atlanta, 1864.

View of the eastern portion of the battlefield after the Battle of Atlanta, 1864.

Union soldiers passing time at a captured Confederate fort in Atlanta, 1864.

Interior view, facing east, of a captured Confederate fort in Atlanta, circa 1864.

Railroad depot in Atlanta, 1864.

Union soldiers destroying railroad tracks in Atlanta, 1864.

Ruins of a railroad depot in Atlanta, circa 1864.

Union officers outside Confederate general John Bell Hood's former headquarters in Atlanta, 1864.

The Atlanta house of Ephraim Ponder, damaged by shells, circa 1864.

Sherman (front right, leaning on gun) with his staff at Federal Fort No. 7 in Atlanta, 1864.

Stereograph of Fort McAllister, on the Ogeechee River near Savannah, 1864.

Ruins of the Atlanta roundhouse, with steam engine and train cars, 1866.

View of a street corner in Atlanta, 1866.

The death site of Union general James B. McPherson near Atlanta, circa 1866.

MILITARY SUPPORT

Andersonville Prison in Macon County, circa 1865. Courtesy of Library of Congress, Prints and Photographs Division.

} Georgia Military Institute

Established in Marietta and opened to students in July 1851, the Georgia Military Institute (GMI) was the principal source of education for new engineers and teachers in the state during the decade prior to the Civil War. Originally funded by private subscription and donations, GMI began its official relationship with the state in 1852, when the legislature chartered the school and presented it with muskets, swords, and a battery of four cannons. Although GMI began with only three instructors and seven students, it quickly attracted a large number of cadets from Georgia's wealthiest families. Between 1853 and 1861, GMI's student body fluctuated between 150 and 200 cadets.

GMI's 110-acre campus included a parade ground, an academic building, four student barracks, and a residence for the school superintendent. Like most Southern military schools of the late antebellum period, GMI based its curriculum on the course of study at the U.S. Military Academy at West Point, New York. Discipline at the institution was strict, similar to that at the Virginia Military Institute in Lexington, Virginia, and the Citadel in Charleston, South Carolina. Between 50 and 75 percent of students left GMI each year because of the tough physical and academic standards.

Sometime during the 1850s the state legislature began subsidizing the education of ten cadets yearly as a way of providing qualified engineers and teachers for state projects. Upon graduation, those cadets were required to perform two years of service to the state.

GMI's existence was threatened in 1861, when Georgia seceded from the Union and Governor Joseph E. Brown called upon GMI superintendent Francis W. Capers to provide drill instructors for the new Georgia volunteers then flooding training camps in the state. Other GMI cadets left to serve in newly forming Southern armies in 1861 and 1862. The school survived by admitting more students, but the Confederate government's April 1862 Conscription Act left cadets susceptible to the draft, again threatening

The writer **Francis Fontaine** was a student at the Georgia Military Institute when the war began. He enlisted in the Confederate army and served throughout the war as a private and aide-de-camp, even after suffering serious hearing loss in the field. He distinguished himself in a number of battles, most notably at the Battle of Peachtree Creek.—From online entry "Francis Fontaine"

WWW.GEORGIAENCYCLOPEDIA.ORG

GMI's survival. Brown interceded on behalf of GMI and protected the institution by making it home to the state's engineer corps. Brown appointed Capers as chief engineer of Georgia with the military rank of major.

Although the cadet battalion spent most of the Civil War serving as funeral details, provost guards, prisoner escorts, and drill instructors, the arrival of Union general William T. Sherman's troops in spring 1864 forced Georgia officials to reassign every available man to the active defense of the state. Desiring to see his cadets enter service as a volunteer unit and not under the draft, Capers led them into the regular Confederate army in May. As Sherman's army approached Dalton, GMI cadets were assigned to active duty in the Confederate Army of Tennessee. Although Sherman's troops burned the GMI buildings in Marietta, the cadet battalion entered active service against the Union men and contested the Union invasion along the Chattahoochee River in July and during the siege of Atlanta in August.

During the late summer and fall of 1864 Brown reassigned the GMI cadets to protect the state capital at Milledgeville from Union cavalry raids. In mid-November 1864 the cadets left Milledgeville as part of a ragtag group of militia and convicts hoping to stop Sherman's March to the Sea. Despite their efforts Savannah fell in December, and the GMI battalion spent the remainder of the war acting as guards in Milledgeville and Augusta. The battalion officially disbanded on May 20, 1865.

After the war GMI alumni and Capers made several attempts to reopen the school, but all attempts failed to garner the needed financial support from the state. The Georgia legislature instead used the limited funds available during Reconstruction on public education at nonmilitary schools.

BARTON MYERS

 # Confederate Hospitals

During the Civil War, Confederate military medical authorities established general hospitals behind the lines in at least thirty-nine cities and towns in Georgia, though many of them remained at a particular location for only a short time.

There were two types of hospitals during the Civil War. Field hospitals accompanied the armies, treating the sick and wounded first before sending those needing lengthier care to the general hospitals behind the lines, often at some distance from the front. Each general hospital had a staff, preferably of a size appropriate to its bed capacity. This staff included surgeons and assistant surgeons, a steward (manager and pharmacist), ward masters (supervisors), nurses, female matrons (domestic supervisors), cooks, and laundresses. Many staff members were soldiers, with a few white civilians, numerous hired or impressed slaves, and a minority of women. One of the women who worked as a matron in several Georgia hospitals was Kate Cumming, who kept a journal of her experiences, which was later published.

Kate Cumming is best known for her dedicated service to sick and wounded Confederate soldiers. She served in numerous mobile field hospitals established throughout Georgia, spending considerable time in those at Americus, Cherokee Springs, Dalton, Newnan, and Ringgold. When the war ended in April 1865, she was working in southwest Georgia.—From online entry "Kate Cumming"

WWW.GEORGIAENCYCLOPEDIA.ORG

Savannah had a hospital early in the war, and general hospitals were established in Atlanta early in 1862, although little is known about the general hospitals in Georgia until they were incorporated into the Army of Tennessee system directed by Samuel H. Stout. A Tennessean and an excellent administrator, Stout had been in charge of the hospitals in Chattanooga. Beginning in August 1862, he became supervisor of the Army of Tennessee hospitals at Tunnel Hill, Ringgold, and Dalton, as well as those hospitals that would later be established between Chattanooga and Atlanta. By December 1862 the Atlanta hospitals were under Stout's control as well.

The hospitals in Georgia served sick and wounded soldiers who had fallen on battlefields outside the state. With the fall of Nashville, Tennessee, in February 1862, there were few "safe" places for hospitals behind the lines in Tennessee north of Chattanooga. (There were a couple of hospitals at various times in Knoxville.) Because they were accessible by railroad, the hospitals in Atlanta and northwest Georgia took in soldiers able to travel by train who had been evacuated from field hospitals to the north.

There was little military activity in Georgia until the late summer of 1863, when the Army of Tennessee under Braxton Bragg retreated through Tennessee to Chattanooga and then evacuated that city. Stout had to relocate his hospitals from Chattanooga, as well as from seven or eight vulnerable towns in north Georgia, to towns south and west of Atlanta. Stout had already developed a plan to mobilize his hospitals if needed. The patients would be transported to a hospital that was not moving. Then the staff would pack bedding, supplies, and other equipment and move to a preselected location, where they would set up the hospital again in local buildings or in tents.

Stout had established certain criteria for hospital sites. The town had to be on a railroad because trains were the quickest and most comfortable way to transport large numbers of patients. It also needed to have plenty of water and wood, appropriate buildings with empty land for hospital expansion, and adequate food available in the area. The town should also be some distance from battlefields and the risk of raids.

Unlike the general hospitals of Virginia, which stayed in one place, the Army of Tennessee hospitals went through waves of movement due to military conditions. Most hospital movements occurred in the summer of 1863, before the Battle of Chickamauga; around December 1863, after the Battle of Chattanooga; during the Atlanta campaign in the summer of 1864; and during and after John Bell Hood's Tennessee campaign in the fall and winter of 1864.

During the Atlanta campaign, especially, hospitals were continually relocating, even into Alabama, to avoid raiders from Union general William T. Sherman's army. At its peak during the summer of 1864, Stout's hospital system had at least fifty hospitals in nineteen Georgia towns, but locations changed frequently. In the fall of 1864 the hospitals tried to follow Hood into Tennessee, but due to deteriorating and indirect transportation routes, most were waylaid in Alabama or Mississippi and never provided any help to the sick and wounded.

After they returned from the Tennessee campaign, Stout's hospitals were reestablished in as many as ten Georgia locations, but they were very short on supplies. Although some of the hospitals were ordered to Charlotte, North Carolina, in April 1865, they were unable to go because of transportation collapse. Instead, most hospitals surrendered when captured by Union forces, though some continued to serve needy soldiers traveling home.

Army of Tennessee hospitals were located at one time or another in each of the following Georgia cities and towns: Adairsville, Albany, Americus, Athens, Atlanta, Augusta, Barnesville, Calhoun, Cassville, Catoosa Springs, Cherokee Springs, Columbus, Covington, Cuthbert,

Dalton, Eatonton, Forsyth, Fort Gaines, Fort Valley, Geneva, Greensboro, Griffin, Kingston, LaGrange, Macon, Madison, Marietta, Milledgeville, Milner, Newnan, Palmetto, Resaca, Ringgold, Rome, Thomaston, Tunnel Hill, Vineville, and West Point.

GLENNA R. SCHROEDER-LEIN

Industry and Manufacturing

The manufacturing might of the North during the Civil War often overshadowed that of the South, but the success of the Confederate war effort depended as much on the iron of its industry as the blood of its fighting men. Over the course of the war, Georgia, known as the antebellum "Empire State of the South," became an indispensable site for wartime manufacturing, combining a prewar industrial base with extensive transportation linkages and a geographic location secure for most of the war from the ravages of enemy armies. Manufacturing gunpowder, munitions, textiles, and a vast array of other essential materiel, Georgia's industry kept the Confederacy fighting, if never quite as well supplied as its Northern opponent.

Antebellum Industry

In the generation preceding the war, enterprising Georgians experimented with a variety of industries in an effort to lessen the state's dependence on cotton cultivation. Cotton farming dominated Georgia's antebellum economy, but by the mid-1830s declining prices fueled by overproduction led some to seek alternatives to agriculture's boom-and-bust cycles. Industrial development offered one such alternative, and a flurry of investment enabled a number of nascent industries to appear throughout the state. Primarily located in fall-line cities like Augusta, Columbus, and Macon, these early manufactories provided the foundation for later efforts to supply Confederate armies.

Two of Georgia's most important antebellum industries were textiles and railroads. Textile production was a logical extension of cotton farming, and Georgia was able to maintain a sizable industry, although it never effectively rivaled Northern output. Thirty-three mills were in operation on the eve of the war, producing the highest volume of textiles of any Southern state. At their peak during the war, these mills turned out more than 500,000 yards of cloth per week.

Railroad fever also swept Georgia in the 1830s, and though track mileage was slow to develop, by 1860 the state controlled 1,420 of the South's 9,182 miles of track, second only to Virginia. Railroads spurred a host of associated industries, including iron foundries, rolling mills, and machine shops, all of which shaped and prepared iron, steel, and other metals for the many demands of the railroad business. These manufactories also branched out to produce other metal goods; Macon's Findlay Iron Works, for example, built stationary steam engines for powering mills, cotton gins, and printing presses in the antebellum period. Railroads also effectively connected Georgia to the other states of the Confederacy, and by the beginning of the war, Georgia, and especially Atlanta, was the crucial nexus of Southern transportation and a heartland of Southern industry.

Powder and Munitions

In the spring of 1861 men throughout the Confederacy were ready to fight; Southern industry, though, was not ready to supply them. Gunpowder was especially scarce, and the Confederate states held stockpiles barely adequate to outfit their recently raised armies. With no domestic suppliers available, foreign sources offered, at best, only a temporary solution to the Southern states' dilemma. If the Confederacy was going to fight a protracted war, it would be necessary to manufacture powder domestically and in bulk.

Leading this effort was Colonel George W. Rains, who at the behest of the Confederate Ordnance Bureau selected Augusta in July 1861 as the site of a massive powder works sufficient to meet the needs of the Confederate forces. Georgia's prime geographic location made the state an ideal center for wartime munitions production; it was distant from the fighting fronts, and its extensive rail network allowed powder to be quickly moved wherever it was needed. Erected in a mere eight months, the works comprised a two-mile-long series of castellated Gothic revival buildings, straddling the Augusta Canal, that were designed to efficiently convert sulfur, niter (saltpeter), and charcoal into finished powder. At peak production, the Confederate Powder Works was capable of producing as much as 6,000 pounds of gunpowder per day, and by the end of the war, more than 3 million pounds had been produced.

Powder, though, does not constitute an effective weapon until it, along with a projectile, can be formed into a cartridge, loaded into a firearm, and detonated with a percussion cap, or otherwise ingeniously exploded. Arms and armament production, therefore, were also necessary for the Confederate war effort, and in Georgia these tasks were undertaken by a mix of public and private industry spread among the state's larger urban centers. In Atlanta, Augusta, Columbus, Macon, and Savannah the Confederate Ordnance Bureau maintained arsenals that manufactured such munitions as bullets, caps, cartridges, and friction primers, along with other military supplies like knapsacks and saddles. Many of these arsenals would occupy the iron foundries, rolling mills, and machine shops of the antebellum years, while many private firms also converted to wartime arms production.

Given its railroad ties throughout the Southern states, Atlanta was home to the largest of Georgia's arsenals, and the city also housed Confederate ironworks, which produced cannons, rails, and armor plate. Beginning operations in March 1862, the Atlanta Arsenal employed nearly 5,500 workers and acted as the primary ordnance supplier for the Army of Tennessee until its operations were removed farther south in July 1864. During its years of operation, the arsenal produced more than 46 million percussion caps, 9 million rounds of ammunition, and large quantities of other materiel. Further, companies like the Atlanta Machine Works manufactured forges for rifling muskets, and the Georgia Railroad's machine shops added several small cannons.

Griswoldville, a small industrial village in Jones County, produced cotton gins through much of the antebellum period and was transformed into a gun factory during the war. In the spring of 1862, Griswoldville's founder, Samuel Griswold, and his partner, A. N. Gunnison, began manufacturing revolvers modeled on the Colt Navy revolver and ultimately supplied the Confederate army with nearly 3,700 of these arms, more than any other firm in the South. Most of Griswold's workforce consisted of trained slave mechanics, who were paid regular wages for their work. This productivity made Griswoldville a target of attack by Union forces moving through the area as part of Sherman's March to the Sea in November 1864.

Other cities, too, served as critical sites for Confederate munitions manufacture. The Columbus Arsenal produced more than 10,000 rounds of small-arms ammunition daily, while the Columbus Naval Iron Works manufactured and assembled cannons and boilers for Confederate gunboats. The Savannah Arsenal was forced to relocate to Macon, owing to the capture of Fort Pulaski in April 1862, but once there fabricated a variety of supplies, including the famous Parrott rifled cannon. Finally, a number of smaller towns contributed weaponry, including swords from Dalton; cannons and batteries from Rome; and bayonets and rifles from Athens. (A two-barreled cannon was also produced in Athens but failed in testing and was never used in combat.)

Quartermasters and Profiteers

Armaments were essential to waging effective war, but the Confederacy's soldiers also needed to be clothed and shod. Georgia's textile mills took up the task of producing cloth for uniforms, blankets, tents, and other uses, while the state's 125 boot and shoe manufacturers turned out their wares as quickly as possible to keep the Confederate armies marching. Furthermore, in 1861 the Quartermaster Department constructed depots in both Atlanta and Columbus, representing the Confederacy's second- and third-largest depots (after the one in Richmond, Virginia). These facilities assembled jackets, shirts, shoes, and trousers on a massive scale. For instance, in 1863 the Atlanta depot contracted to produce 175,000 shirts, 130,000 jackets, and 130,000 pairs of shoes for the Confederate forces. However, production never quite kept up with the army's insatiable demand.

Textile and shoe manufacture showcased the persistent problem of scarcity plaguing Georgia's wartime manufacturers. As winter approached in 1861, wool was in high demand and low supply throughout the South, and the state's wool manufacturers were limited in their production by the unavailability of fibrous sheep fur. By 1863 the Confederate government had virtually monopolized the wool supply, forcing factories to produce only for government orders and leaving the civilian population with little access to woolen goods. Representing a broader trend, the Quartermaster Department's persistent purchases (or impressments) of the bulk of the state's textile and shoe manufactures left civilians facing intense scarcity and exorbitant prices. These conditions often led to accusations of profiteering, pressuring the Georgia legislature to pass a Monopoly and Extortion Bill as early as December 1861.

Industry was also hampered by a lack of consistent labor; the manpower requirements of the perpetually outnumbered Confederate armies worked against wartime manufacturers by drawing skilled labor to the front. In the place of these white male workers, both white women and slaves filled in to keep Georgia industry productive. At the start of the war, women in the textile industry were already doing a larger share of the unskilled, low-wage work than their male counterparts, with 1,682 women to only 1,131 men working in textile production in 1860. As the conflict progressed, more than 4,500 seamstresses would work in government depots in Augusta and Atlanta, while women were also instrumental in assembling small-arms munitions for the Augusta Armory.

The **Georgia penitentiary at Milledgeville** was used as an armory during the war. Prisoners manufactured rifles, bayonets, and other armaments to supply the Confederate armies. In 1864 Governor Joseph E. Brown pardoned almost all of the prisoners with the stipulation that they help defend Milledgeville from Union troops. Many of the prisoners deserted within the week.—From online entry "Georgia Penitentiary at Milledgeville"

WWW.GEORGIAENCYCLOPEDIA.ORG

Slaves, too, were used extensively in Georgia manufacturing, working in heavy industry primarily as common laborers. By 1863 around half the workforce at both the Macon Armory and the Augusta Powder Works were African American, and blacks also built and maintained the state's rail network by constructing bridges, grading, and laying new track. The state was so desperate for labor that, late in the war, convicts in the Milledgeville penitentiary were employed making shoes.

An End and a Beginning

Still, the lack of resources and manpower was far from the most destructive force facing Georgia industry; that honor goes to the army commanded by Union general William T. Sherman. Sherman's Atlanta campaign and later March to the Sea brought total war to Georgia and with it the destruction of much of the state's industrial capacity. The railroads that connected Georgia's industry to the rest of the Confederacy were a primary target for Sherman's forces, who followed the tracks from Tennessee to Savannah, ripping up rail as they went. Atlanta's factories were totally destroyed, and much of the city was burned. Cities like Augusta and Macon were spared, but without the rail connections through Atlanta, the products of their factories faced increasing difficulty in reaching the remaining Confederate forces.

The collapse of the Confederacy, though, did not presage the decline of Georgia's industry; in fact, the roots of Georgia's New South efforts can be distinctly traced to the state's manufacturing experiences during the Civil War. The stimulus of war expanded industry across the state, such that between 1860 and 1870 the number of establishments increased from 1,890 to 3,836, and the value of yearly product nearly doubled, from $16.9 million to $31.1 million.

Atlanta, once rebuilt, surged into the postbellum period intent on forging a new identity, one less reliant on Northern manufactures and more capable of producing needed goods at home. Industry continued to blossom across the state, and though cotton production still dominated, a more balanced economy emerged in the wake of Southern defeat. Yet, while the war lasted, Georgia remained a critical supplier of materiel and men, iron and blood, to the cause of Southern independence.

SEAN H. VANATTA
DAN DU

 # Atlanta as Confederate Hub

At the time of the Civil War, Atlanta boasted a population of almost 10,000 (one-fifth of whom were slaves), a substantial manufacturing and mercantile base, and four major railroads connecting the city with all points of the South. It was neither Georgia's capital nor the largest city in the state, but it was energetic and thriving.

Early War

After the outbreak of war in spring 1861, Atlantans volunteered and formed the bulk of the twelve companies of infantry from Georgia. Casualties soon occurred. The city's two main newspapers, the *Intelligencer* and the *Southern Confederacy*, honored nearly a dozen Atlantans who had been killed at the First Battle of Manassas, Virginia, on July 21. Soldiers' deaths left some families destitute; fund-raising groups formed to aid them, and physicians offered free care.

With the Confederate loss of middle Tennessee in early 1862, Atlanta became the military medical center. The Atlanta Medical College, which had already suspended classes, became a hospital, as did hotels and municipal buildings. Construction of a big hospital complex on the city fairgrounds eventually relieved the crowding of sick and wounded soldiers downtown. The railroad passenger depot in the center of town served as a busy receiving and distributing point for Southern servicemen. A convalescent camp was established in the northwest suburbs, near the home of Ephraim Ponder. The city cemetery, then twenty-five acres (today known as Oakland Cemetery and much larger), also had to be expanded; some 632 soldiers were buried during 1862 alone.

Advances of Union forces in Tennessee and Mississippi made Atlanta a city of refugees. Its population was estimated at 17,000 in mid-1862 and 20,000 a year later. Hotels and boardinghouses were overwhelmed as newcomers took over vacant lots and train cars. So many strangers milled about that the city council put up Atlanta's first street signs in May 1863.

Industrial Center

As a key railroad hub, Atlanta became an important military supply center. Commissary, quartermaster, and ordnance stores were warehoused throughout the town. More important were Atlanta's manufacturing facilities. Scofield and Markham's Atlanta Rolling Mill was one of only two in the South that could produce rails. The mill also turned out plating for such Confederate ironclad gunboats as the *Tennessee.* Smaller manufactories were more numerous and just as important, such as James L. Dunning's Atlanta Machine Works. After Dunning, who was a member of the city's small, secret circle of Union loyalists, refused to accept Confederate weapons contracts, the government took over the plant, which produced artillery shells and small arms. Other shops under government contract turned out swords, buttons, buckles, cartridge boxes, saddles, bridles, and other items.

The government also set up its own operations, such as the arsenal built at the racetrack outside the city's western limits; it produced percussion caps and artillery and small-arms ammunition, probably as many as 75,000 rounds per day by August 1862. In 1863–64 the Atlanta Arsenal employed nearly 5,500 men and women. In spring 1863 the Confederacy's Quartermaster Department had some 3,000 women in the city working as seamstresses and turning out thousands of wool jackets, pants, and cotton shirts. A government shoe factory produced 500 pairs a day, when leather supplies permitted. Bakeries and meatpacking plants made Atlanta a major army commissary as well.

Defending Atlanta

All these valuable shops and warehouses made Atlantans suspicious of spies and secret Union incendiaries in their midst. Martial law was declared for only a month in August 1862, but citizens suspected of having Union sympathies were always threatened with arrest. In the spring of 1863, when Union cavalry raided close to Rome (sixty miles northwest of Atlanta), Atlanta mayor James M. Calhoun and the city council called upon all able men to form volunteer militia companies. Policemen, firemen, railroaders, and ordnance workers all formed companies, ready for the next Union approach.

The city fathers resolved on May 22, 1863, that longtime Atlantan Lemuel P. Grant, captain of the Confederacy's Engineer Bureau and senior engineer with headquarters in the city, should survey along the Chattahoochee River for defensive earthworks to prevent enemy crossings of the river. Two months later the War Department Engineer Bureau in Richmond, Virginia, ordered further protection for Atlanta: preparation for a "proper system of defense," presumably a fortified perimeter around the city. That August, Captain Grant proposed his line of rifle pits and artillery forts, ten miles in circumference, averaging a mile outside the city. Thus after the fall of Chattanooga, Tennessee, in September 1863 and the Confederate army's retreat into north Georgia, but well before the onset of Union general William T. Sherman's campaign against Atlanta in the spring of 1864, the city had begun to ready itself.

A native of Maine, **Lemuel Grant** first came to the Atlanta area in 1849 to survey for the Atlanta and LaGrange railroad line. After the war he donated much of the land for the city's first park, which is named in his honor, and served the city in many official roles, including city councilman and water commissioner.—From online entry "Lemuel Grant"

WWW.GEORGIAENCYCLOPEDIA.ORG

Local Response to Sherman's Attack

The approach of Sherman's armies threw Atlantans into alarm. Newspaper editors urged calmness and chastised gloomy "croakers" who began to predict the city's fall. Increasing numbers of wounded soldiers arrived by train as the battles moved closer; the fall of Rome and other nearby towns poured more refugees into the city. Atlantans heard their first distant thud of cannon fire on May 25, 1864, when General Joseph E. Johnston's Confederate army held Sherman's forces near Dallas, Georgia. After the Battle of Kennesaw Mountain on June 27, a panic gripped many townspeople, who packed their families and belongings and fled. Even Mayor Calhoun sent his wife and two children away. Confederate officials began moving arsenal machinery to Macon and Augusta. On July 5 General Johnston ordered the military hospitals to pack up and leave. After Union troops got across the Chattahoochee River near Roswell, Johnston withdrew his army across the river in the night of July 9–10. The news heightened the public panic. Civilians vied with ordnance and medical officers for train and wagon space.

The Confederate government's replacement of Johnston with General John Bell Hood did little to bring calm. On July 20 the jarring sounds of battle at Peachtree Creek mixed with that of the first Union shells falling into the city—Sherman had ordered a bombardment of the downtown area to pressure Hood into evacuation. The thirty-six-day shelling drove more civilians to leave. Judging from newspaper reports, Sherman's artillery fire killed perhaps only a score of civilians but probably wounded hundreds more (medical records are nonexistent). The daily cannon fire intensified until August 9, when 3,000 to 5,000 exploding shells fell downtown, damaging and destroying countless buildings. Many townspeople, especially the poor, could not leave. Some simply chose to stay, seeking shelter in basements or specially dug "bombproofs." With stores and commerce closed, they fared on garden produce and rations distributed by the army.

From a population of about 22,000 in the spring of 1864, probably 3,000 civilians remained in the city when the Confederate army was forced out of Atlanta on September 1. Days later, Sherman ordered almost all noncombatants to leave town. With their exodus, Atlanta's significance as a Confederate military and industrial hub dissolved.

STEPHEN DAVIS

Roswell Mill Women

In July 1864 during the Atlanta campaign, General William T. Sherman ordered the approximately 400 Roswell mill workers, mostly women, arrested as traitors and shipped as prisoners to the North with their children. There is little evidence that more than a few of the women ever returned home.

As the Union forces approached Atlanta in the early summer of 1864, almost all the members of the founding families of Roswell—aristocrats from the Georgia coast, most of them owners and/or stockholders of the Roswell Manufacturing Company mills—had fled. The remaining residents were mostly the mill workers and their families. The two cotton mills and a woolen mill continued to operate, producing cloth for Confederate uniforms and other much-needed military supplies, such as rope, canvas, and tent cloth.

On July 5, seeking a way to cross the Chattahoochee River and gain access to Atlanta, Brigadier General Kenner Garrard's cavalry began the Union's twelve-day occupation of Roswell, which was undefended. The next day Garrard reported to Sherman that he had discovered the mills in full operation and that about 400 women were at work there. He ordered the mill destroyed, with Sherman's approval. Sherman also ordered that the owners and employees be arrested and charged with treason. The women, their children, and the few men, most either too young or too old to fight, were transported by wagon to Marietta and imprisoned in the Georgia Military Institute, by then abandoned. Then, with several days' rations, they were loaded into boxcars that proceeded through Chattanooga and Nashville en route to Louisville, Kentucky, the final destination for many of the mill workers. Others were sent across the Ohio River to Indiana.

First housed and fed in a Louisville refugee hospital, the women later took what menial jobs and living arrangements could be found. Those in Indiana struggled to survive, many settling near the river, where eventually mills provided employment. Unless husbands had been transported with the women or had been imprisoned nearby, there was little probability of a return to Roswell, so the remaining women began to marry and bear children.

The tragedy, widely publicized at the time, with outrage expressed in Northern as well as Southern presses, was virtually forgotten over the next century. Only in the 1980s did a few writers begin to research and tell the story. Even then, the individual identities and fates of the women remained unknown.

In 1998 the Roswell Mills Camp No. 1547, Sons of the Confederate Veterans, initiated a project to acknowledge and honor the deported mill workers. Through publicity, advertisements, and research, some of the descendants and other relatives were found; most of their deported ancestors had settled in the North. In July 2000 a monument commemorating the sacrifices of the mill workers was unveiled in Roswell's mill village park.

CAROLINE MATHENY DILLMAN

Prisons

Georgia was home to a number of Confederate prisons during the war years. Though dwarfed by the shadow of notorious Andersonville Prison, there were fifteen other facilities in the state. These ranged from well-constructed fortifications, such as county jails, to makeshift installations, such as wooded areas patrolled by armed guards surrounding prisoners. Prison sites were usually selected for their proximity to major transportation routes. Georgia was relatively distant from the battle lines for most of the war, which made it prime ground for incarcerating captured Union soldiers. Conditions at these prisons usually depended on the Confederacy's military fortunes. Toward the end of the war, as the tide turned against the Confederate army at the battlefront, the government's ability to supply and provision prisons in Georgia weakened. Conditions deteriorated to the point where prisoners were attempting to survive without the food, clothing, and shelter needed for sustenance.

One of Georgia's premier poets, **Sidney Lanier**, served in the Confederate army during the war. In 1864 he was captured and held as a prisoner of war for four months in Maryland, during which time he contracted the debilitating tuberculosis that plagued him for the rest of his life.—From online entry "Sidney Lanier"

WWW.GEORGIAENCYCLOPEDIA.ORG

Prison Sites

One of the first prisons to hold Union soldiers in Georgia was the Fulton County Jail in Atlanta. This facility, built before the war, was large enough to serve as a holding area for more than 150 prisoners in early 1862. The prisoners had been sent to Atlanta to relieve overcrowding at sites in Richmond, Virginia—the same reason such larger prisons as Andersonville later came into existence. On several occasions throughout the war, makeshift facilities were used in and around Atlanta before prisoners were transferred to other sites farther south. This was especially true as large campaigns in both Virginia and Georgia in 1864 swelled the numbers captured.

Also in 1862, a prison pen, known as Camp Oglethorpe, was opened in Macon. Wedged between railroad tracks and the Ocmulgee River, the site was enclosed by a rough stockade on fifteen to twenty acres. Nearly 1,000 prisoners arrived in May to find several buildings within, including one large enough to use as a hospital. The prisoners were a mixture of officers and enlisted men. Their living quarters consisted of sheds or stalls already on site or shelters constructed from materials found within the stockade. As a result of a formal exchange cartel agreed on by the combating powers, most of these prisoners gained their freedom, and by the beginning of 1863, Camp Oglethorpe was nearly abandoned.

The breakdown of prisoner exchanges, combined with General William T. Sherman's Georgia campaign, forced the Confederacy to reopen the facility as an officers' prison. By the summer of 1864, more than 2,300 Union officers were housed there. Shelter was barely adequate, and rations consisted of beans, cornmeal, and rice in meager amounts. The lack of sanitation, coupled with a dwindling diet, led to the usual litany of such diseases as chronic dysentery and scurvy. An official death total for the prison is unknown. Most of the prisoners were moved from the Macon facility by late July 1864 because of Union cavalry raids in the general vicinity, although some officers were held there until September.

The Shadow of Andersonville

When Sherman's Union army took Atlanta on September 2, 1864, Confederate prison authorities knew that Andersonville would be a prime target of any Union thrust into the heartland of Georgia, and they began moving Union prisoners of war to more secure locations. At Camp Davidson, constructed in July 1864 on the grounds of what had been the U.S. Marine Hospital in Savannah, prisoners were confined within a stockade that enclosed part of an orchard. The ample rations were a welcome respite from the horrors of Macon and Andersonville. The camp guards, the First Georgia Volunteers, had once been prisoners of war themselves. Because of overcrowding caused by the influx of Andersonville prisoners in September, a second Savannah prison, for officers, was set up on land adjacent to the city jail. Another stockade was hastily constructed for enlisted men. This structure, along with Camp Davidson, may have held more than 10,000 men, but both had to be abandoned after only a month and a half of use.

The most substantial prison holding former Andersonville captives was Camp Lawton in Millen, located in Jenkins County between Augusta and Savannah. Camp Lawton was a stockade structure enclosing forty-two acres, making it the largest Civil War prison in terms of area. Set only a mile off the Augusta Railroad, the pen was designed to hold up to 40,000 prisoners, although the population never grew to much beyond 10,000. By all accounts the prison at Millen was infinitely better than Andersonville. A generous spring ran north to south through the site, providing a fresh supply of drinking water. Rations were also more plentiful, since the countryside had yet to be scavenged of its food resources. Yet disease and death were not unknown because many of the prisoners were terribly debilitated from their incarceration at Andersonville. During the short time the prison was open, from late September to early November 1864, nearly 500 prisoners succumbed to disease.

As Sherman's troops approached Millen in the March to the Sea, the prisoners had to be moved yet again. Many of them were sent to South Carolina, and others were sent to Savannah. The exact site of Camp Lawton was not located until 2010, when its discovery by archaeology students at Georgia Southern University made national news. The find was significant because the site, previously unidentified and thus unplundered, yielded an unusually rich cache of artifacts left by prisoners and their guards. Researchers believe that many of the artifacts are possessions dropped by prisoners as they were forced onto trains during the camp's final evacuation.

From Savannah approximately 5,000 prisoners were transported down the Atlantic and Gulf Coast Railroad to Blackshear. This camp was basically a makeshift guard line with accompanying artillery pieces surrounding several thousand men in the piney woods of southeast Georgia. As might be expected, escapes were frequent, discipline lax, and resources scarce. The Blackshear area held prisoners for less than a month, from late November to early December. The collapse of the

Confederate infrastructure caused much confusion about what exactly to do with these prisoners. Some were shipped back to South Carolina, but the majority went southwest to Thomasville, where the Atlantic and Gulf rail line ended. Impressed slave labor from nearby plantations constructed yet another stockade.

The prison at Thomasville was located half a mile northwest of town, on a five-acre tract surrounded by a ditch six feet deep and ten feet wide. Planned as a temporary holding area, the site was occupied for only two weeks in December 1864. During that time approximately 5,000 Union prisoners were confined there. The men were allowed to construct their own shelters from existing timber within the site. Exposure to the elements and close quarters caused an outbreak of smallpox, which claimed the lives of hundreds of prisoners. Confederate authorities soon ordered the site to be abandoned, and the decision was made to send all of Thomasville's prisoners back to Andersonville. This meant a sixty-mile march north to Albany, where they reembarked on the Southwestern Railroad. This line took them back to Andersonville, where they arrived on Christmas Eve 1864.

Forgotten History

Though at present Andersonville is a National Historic Site, little has been done to commemorate other Civil War prison sites in Georgia. State historic markers have been erected at Blackshear and Thomasville. Magnolia Springs State Park now incorporates the area of Camp Lawton, including some historic earthworks. Other prison sites, such as those in Atlanta and Savannah, have been destroyed by development.

CHRIS WILKINSON

Andersonville Prison

In February 1864 a Confederate prison was established in Macon County, in southwest Georgia, to provide relief for the large number of Union prisoners concentrated in and around Richmond, Virginia. The new camp, officially named Camp Sumter, quickly became known as Andersonville, after the railroad station in neighboring Sumter County beside which the camp was located. By the summer of 1864, the camp held the largest prison population of its time, with numbers that would have made it the fifth-largest city in the Confederacy. By the time it closed in early May 1865, those numbers, along with the sanitation, health, and mortality problems stemming from its overcrowding, had earned Andersonville a reputation as the most notorious of Confederate atrocities inflicted on Union troops.

Prison Conditions

Andersonville station, the third of three sites considered by Confederate officials for the prison, lacked ready access to supplies. It was chosen, in fact, for its inland remoteness and safe distance from coastal raids and because there was little opposition from the inhabitants of this sparsely populated area. Local black labor—slave and free—was impressed into service to build the camp, which consisted of a stockade and trench enclosing more than sixteen acres. A small creek, Stockade Branch, ran through the middle of the enclosed area.

The camp was planned for a capacity of 10,000 prisoners, but with the breakdown in prisoner exchanges, which would have removed much of its prison population, its numbers swelled to more than 30,000. As the number of imprisoned men increased, it became increasingly hard for them to find space to lie down within the vast pen. The prisoners, nearly naked, suffered from swarms of insects, filth, and disease, much of which was generated by the contaminated water supply of the creek.

Andersonville had the highest mortality rate of any Civil War prison. Nearly 13,000 of the 45,000 men who entered the stockade died there, chiefly of malnutrition. Guards were also issued poor rations but had the option of foraging for food elsewhere. Critics charged that though the Confederate government could find the resources to move prisoners hundreds of miles and to build a facility in which to incarcerate them, it failed to provide adequate supplies or living conditions for the inmates or even for the staff.

In the summer of 1864 camp administrators, using the labor of Union prisoners and slaves, expanded the prison's size and facilities by constructing a hospital, a bakery, and some barracks. They also extended the stockade walls, adding an additional ten acres to the original site. Yet the overwhelming number of prisoners rendered their efforts hopelessly inadequate.

Prison Life

Prisoners did little to improve the miserable conditions under which they lived. Firewood details were curtailed when prisoners seized the opportunity to escape. The small stream that served as the camp's primary water supply, both for drinking and bathing, was polluted by the unsanitary habits of some inmates and by sewage and other garbage dumped into the swampy area that fed the stream. Wells were covered over and made inaccessible after prisoners used them to hide escape tunnels.

Camp inmates often preyed upon each other. Gambling tents and "stores," operated mainly by prisoners from Union general William T. Sherman's western troops, fleeced new arrivals. Roving gangs of raiders, chiefly from eastern regiments, robbed fellow inmates, despite efforts by guards to stop them. The prisoners hanged six of the raider leaders on July 11, 1864. After that, a new police force made up of prisoners sought to impose discipline on their fellow inmates. They tried to enforce sanitation practices, curtail robberies, and force captive officers to take care of the men under them. Their strong-arm tactics led some inmates to see these new "regulators" as no better than the raiders. Men detailed to take care of the sick often robbed the hospital of food and supplies.

The loyalty of many in the **Catholic Church** to the Confederacy helped to cement the religion's place in Georgia during and after the war. Catholic priests often were the only ministers at the Andersonville prison camp, and Catholic men served in Confederate units throughout the war. The Sisters of Mercy also played an important role as nurses in Confederate hospitals.—From online entry "Catholic Church"

WWW.GEORGIAENCYCLOPEDIA.ORG

In late March 1864 Captain Hartmann Heinrich "Henry" Wirz took charge of the prison. The Swiss-born commander, a physician in Louisiana when the war broke out, tried to impose order and security, but his lack of authority over the guards and supply officers limited his effectiveness. He quickly became the primary target of prisoners' resentment and hostility.

By August the prison population reached its greatest number, with more than 33,000 men incarcerated in the camp. But as Sherman's troops moved deeper into Georgia, the threat of attacks on Andersonville led to the transfer of most prisoners to other camps, particularly Camp Lawton, near Millen, and Camp Sorghum, in Columbia, South Carolina. By November the prison population was a mere 1,500 men. Transfers back to Andersonville in December brought the number back up to 5,000 prisoners, where it remained until the war's end five months later.

Prison Security

Andersonville's garrison consisted of troops from various units over the course of its fourteen months in operation. These included the Fifty-fifth Georgia Infantry, the Twenty-sixth Alabama Infantry, and a battery from Florida. As these troops were called away for combat duty elsewhere, Georgia state reserves and militia from Georgia and Florida replaced them. These grossly outnumbered and poorly armed guards, many of them old men and boys, kept their charges at bay with a "dead line." A feature of other prisons as well, North and South, this marked strip of ground bordering the stockade walls served as a killing zone for any prisoner who stepped into it. Cannons, guard towers, dog packs, and a second wall also served to foil escapes.

Most of the prisoners who did escape Andersonville fled from work details on duties that took them outside the camp walls. Inmates also attempted to dig at least eighty tunnels, nearly all of which were exposed by informants. Compared with other Confederate prisons, very few of those incarcerated at Andersonville made successful escapes. Those who did received help from sympathetic or war-weary white Southerners but found slaves to be their greatest allies. Winslow Homer's famous painting *Near Andersonville* portrays the irony of the imprisonment of Union soldiers who had come south to free slaves.

After the War

On May 7, 1865, just after the war's end, Captain Wirz and another officer, James W. Duncan, were arrested and tried separately for war crimes by federal military courts in Washington, D.C. Duncan received a fifteen-year sentence but escaped after serving only one year at Fort Pulaski. Wirz was sentenced to death. On November 10, 1865, he was hanged in the courtyard of the Old Capitol prison, just behind the Capitol in Washington. He was the only man executed for war crimes committed during the Civil War, and some Southerners soon came to see him as a martyr. The United Daughters of the Confederacy erected a monument to him in the town of Andersonville, and each year on the anniversary of his execution, local residents hold a ceremony paying tribute to him.

In the decades following the war Andersonville's notoriety was fueled by memoirs written by former prisoners, many of whom were inspired by public interest in the prison and by efforts to lobby Congress for special veterans' benefits for POWs. The propagandistic nature of these accounts perpetuated several myths and misconceptions about the prison and its officials. John McElroy's *Andersonville: A Story of Rebel Prisons*, published in 1879, typifies the tone and interpretation of the narratives of former prisoners writing about their experiences.

Writer MacKinlay Kantor drew on such memoirs for his best-selling novel *Andersonville*, which won the Pulitzer Prize for fiction in 1956 and was adapted as a television miniseries for Turner Network Television (TNT) in 1996. Another fictionalized account is found in Saul Levitt's 1959 play, *The Andersonville Trial*, which is based on the Henry Wirz case and serves as a morality tale about criminal acts committed under military orders. The play was adapted for television in 1970.

The prison site was preserved as a national cemetery soon after it closed, largely due to efforts by Clara Barton, founder of the American Red Cross, who worked to have all the graves identified and marked. Andersonville National Historic Site, which lies mostly in Macon County with a small portion in Sumter County, has long been a major tourist attraction. More recently, Southerners who felt that Andersonville had unfairly borne the brunt of horror stories of prison treatment campaigned for the creation of a museum at Andersonville to commemorate all American POWs. The National Prisoner of War Museum, which opened in 1998, documents the poor conditions not only at Andersonville but also at Northern camps during the Civil War, as well as those in World War II (1941–45), Korea (1950–53), and Vietnam (1964–73).

ROBERT SCOTT DAVIS JR.

HOME FRONT

DISTRIBUTING RATIONS.

"Distributing Rations," from J. T. Trowbridge's *The South* (1866). General Research & Reference Division, Schomburg Center for Research in Black Culture, The New York Public Library, Astor, Lenox, and Tilden Foundations.

} Newspapers

Georgia citizens in the nineteenth century relied on newspapers to keep them informed about what was happening outside their own towns and counties. The state could boast a few literary, religious, and agricultural magazines, but newspapers were by far the more important news source. They took on added significance during the Civil War, providing to Georgians not only information about the breakdown of the Union and the four-year conflict that followed but also a venue through which vital issues were debated before a broad reading public.

State Expansion and the Spread of Newspapers

As the nineteenth century began, Georgia had only five newspapers—two in Savannah, two in Augusta, and one in the state capital, Louisville—but soon newspapers appeared in several other towns. Georgia's expanding economy was the most important stimulant for newspaper growth. The state's first daily paper appeared in Savannah in 1817, when the *Columbian Museum* and the *Savannah Gazette* merged and began publishing six days a week. The *Augusta Constitutionalist* became a daily in 1834, followed in 1837 by the *Augusta Chronicle*. Newspapers did not appear in Atlanta until the 1840s. Cornelius R. Hanleiter put down the first permanent roots of Atlanta journalism when he moved his newspaper, the *Southern Miscellany*, there from Madison in 1847. Hanleiter moved because he believed the westward railroad expansion meant big things were in store for the hamlet, then called Marthasville.

By 1860 most of Georgia's major cities had two or more newspapers, mostly weekly, but several daily. Atlantans had access to five locally published newspapers during the war years, two of which were daily. Most households did not subscribe to these papers; rather they were available to be read at various public venues, such as post offices, courthouses, and taverns, where men gathered and often discussed or debated what they read. As such, newspapers served not only as the major sources of information but also as the impetus for discussion and debate.

Partisan Journalism

Georgia's antebellum newspapers were mostly political in nature and continued to be so through the war years. Editors were bombastic political impresarios who touted party lines and perhaps even held political office. A large portion of their papers' revenues came from political party patronage, even if the owners were not otherwise directly involved in the politics of the day. Editors commonly harassed and abused other journalists, politicians, and even private citizens who were of a different political persuasion. In the sectional conflicts of the late antebellum period, most Georgia newspapers leaned toward a Unionist position, though virtually all supported Southern rights. The issue was whether the South's rights could best be protected from inside or outside the Union.

The debates over nullification and secession were complicated by the issues of slavery and abolition. Most editors, themselves slave owners, opposed abolition and argued that vast social problems would arise should slaves be emancipated. Editors tried to downplay slave unrest. They said little in response to the Nat Turner revolt of August 1831, for example, though they increased the number of stern warnings they published about the possibility of further rebellion.

Secession and Civil War

By 1860 Georgia's editors were deeply divided on the issue of secession. Even most of the Unionist editors did not rule out secession entirely, but neither were they convinced that the election of U.S. president Abraham Lincoln was grounds for immediate secession. They preferred to take a wait-and-see attitude. As secession became a reality, however, editors promised unity and grew quite expansive in their approval of the move to divide the Union. This unity, however, was short-lived.

Once it became apparent that the war was not going to be short and that certain civil liberties would have to be suspended to support the war effort, some newspapers again began to question the wisdom of the war. A fairly widespread peace movement arose in Georgia to foster opposition to the war and to the freedom-limiting measures Confederate president Jefferson Davis and the Confederate Congress had adopted, such as conscription, the suspension of the writ of habeas corpus, and war taxes. One of the leading peace proponents was Alexander Stephens, the Confederate vice president and a Georgia native. Stephens, a master at managing relations with journalists, used his stable of press supporters, including the *Augusta Chronicle and Sentinel* and the *Southern Confederacy* of Atlanta, to spread his peace doctrine. By 1864, when the Georgia peace movement began to take hold, the state's citizens were war-weary and receptive to the idea that it was time for the war to end. However, no opposition newspaper was ever officially suppressed or harassed by mobs.

Toward the end of the war, newspaper editors engaged in an intense debate over whether the Confederacy should arm slaves as a means of coping with the military's manpower shortage and whether those slaves should be emancipated in return for their military service. The issue emerged in November 1864 when Confederate president Jefferson Davis proposed during his annual address to the Confederate Congress that slaves work in noncombatant jobs and eventually be granted emancipation. Soon thereafter, rival journalists at papers in Augusta, Macon, and other cities weighed in, as did readers whose letters to the editors were published. Both editors and readers were sharply divided, and both editorials and letters regarding this radical policy and its implications for the South's future fueled an ongoing debate that lasted through March 1865, when the proposal was abandoned.

In 1850 humorist **William Tappan Thompson** became the founding editor of the *Savannah Daily Morning News* (later the *Savannah Morning News*). He vigorously championed the Southern cause until he was forced to leave Savannah in 1864, as Union general William T. Sherman's army approached the city. He returned to Savannah and resumed his editorship of the paper in 1868.
—From online entry "William Tappan Thompson"

WWW.GEORGIAENCYCLOPEDIA.ORG

Difficulties in Publishing

Many obstacles existed to newspaper publishing in the nineteenth century. The difficulties were magnified by the Civil War and its attendant problems. Subscribers and advertisers were slow to pay their bills, and they were hard to find in adequate numbers in the small towns where most of Georgia's newspapers were located.

Actually acquiring news was often a problem during the war years. In March 1863 several newspapers throughout the South organized the Press Association of the Confederate States of America, a private organization that telegraphed war news to papers in all parts of the Confederacy, at least to those areas where communication lines had not been destroyed. Georgia papers often reprinted much material that appeared in Richmond papers as well as those in New York, Washington, D.C., and other major Northern cities, as was common practice throughout the nineteenth century.

Getting presses, type, and printing materials was another challenge. The closest suppliers were in Philadelphia and New York. Paper came primarily from Virginia, South Carolina, and North Carolina, though by 1808 at least one paper mill, Greene County's Scull Shoals Papermill, operated in Georgia, and a mill in Bath, South Carolina, just across the Savannah River from Augusta, supplied paper for many Georgia newspapers until it burned in 1862.

DEBRA REDDIN VAN TUYLL

The Countryman

The Countryman was a weekly newspaper published by Joseph Addison Turner on his Putnam County plantation during the Civil War. Despite his previous publishing failures, Turner's Countryman generated a wide Southern readership during its four-year existence.

Turner was born in 1826 on Turnwold, the family plantation near Eatonton. After a year of college education at Emory College in Oxford, Turner moved to Eatonton, where he taught for a year at the Phoenix Academy, then prepared for and passed the Georgia bar. In 1850 Turner married Louisa Jane Dennis. They had eight children.

Throughout the 1840s and 1850s, Turner pursued his literary passions. He published a wide array of poems, book reviews, articles, and essays under a variety of pseudonyms. He undertook several ventures at publishing monthly and weekly journals and magazines, none of which succeeded. He moved back to his plantation, Turnwold, in 1856, and there, only after the outbreak of the Civil War, did Turner achieve publishing success.

On March 4, 1862, Turner published his first issue of The Countryman, a unique venture that stands as probably the only newspaper ever published from a plantation. Declaring Turnwold's purpose to be the cultivation of "corn, cotton, and literature," Turner drew on the plantation's extensive library and built a full printing shop on the site. Despite difficulties created by shortages in ink, paper, and other materials over the course of the war,

The Countryman circulated throughout the Confederacy from its inception through its final issue in May 1866.

Turner was a staunch advocate for slavery and the Confederacy. The original motto for *The Countryman* read, "Brevity is the Soul of Wit," but by 1863 Turner had changed it to "Independent in Everything, Neutral in Nothing." He used *The Countryman* to voice his pro-Confederate views through articles and editorials. The venture was also distinguished for launching the journalistic career of yet another notable Georgian—Joel Chandler Harris. Turner hired the sixteen-year-old Harris, an Eatonton native, as an apprentice and typesetter for *The Countryman* in March 1862. Under Turner's guidance and stern editing, Harris remained with the paper for its duration. He developed into an excellent literary composer and contributed a number of essays, poems, and book reviews to the paper himself.

In June 1865 Union officials placed Turner under military arrest for "publishing disloyal articles," and publication of *The Countryman* was suspended for several months. Turner managed to revive *The Countryman* for four months before, exhausted, he shut down the operation for good in May 1866. He died two years later in Eatonton at forty-one years of age.

JARROD ATCHISON

 # Unionists

Historians of the Civil War have only recently begun serious study of Unionists, an often overlooked group of white Southerners who played a substantial part in sowing discontent and undermining the Confederate war effort. Unionists found themselves living in a new nation, the Confederacy, to which they chose not to give their allegiance. While their numbers in Georgia (or in any other Southern state) are uncertain, much about Unionist presence and activity in the state has come to light in recent years.

One of the challenges for historians of wartime Unionism in the South lies in the secrecy surrounding Unionist identities and activities. Many were careful not to leave paper trails that could fall into the wrong hands and serve as evidence with which Confederate neighbors could indict them. Nevertheless, scholars have found a number of ways to reconstruct the labors of this shadowy, often underground, movement in Georgia, as well as the lives of the men and women involved in it.

Another problem lies in defining the term *Unionist.* Many Southerners, simply apathetic about the war and the issues for which it was fought, sought to avoid any military involvement or dissented against the often intrusive Confederate policies toward civilians. But neither of these stances made one a true Unionist. Most scholars agree that sheer disaffection and neutrality toward the war are not characteristics of Unionism. Perhaps the best definition comes from William G. "Parson" Brownlow of East Tennessee, one of the most prominent Southern Unionists, who cited three essential traits of a true Unionist: an "uncompromising devotion" to the Union; an "unmitigated hostility" to the Confederacy; and a willingness to risk life and property "in defense of the Glorious Stars and Stripes."

Within Georgia, the Unionist experience offers stories as dramatic and varied as those in any other part of the Confederacy. From Atlanta to Savannah, from the northern mountains to the wiregrass and piney woods of south Georgia, these so-called enemies of the country survived, sometimes barely, as a small, secretive, and vulnerable minority in the midst of tremendous hostility, oppression, and danger.

Georgians in Blue

The geographical distribution of committed Southern Unionists is revealed in part by who joined the Union army. In his book *Lincoln's Loyalists*, historian Richard Current indicates that as many as 100,000 white Southerners became Union soldiers at some point over the course of the war, and that 70 percent of those came from Tennessee, Virginia, and West Virginia. Georgia supplied fewer Union troops than did any other Southern state except South Carolina. Approximately 400 Georgians enlisted in Union military units, compared with around 5,000 in North Carolina, more than 3,000 in Alabama, and a remarkable 42,000 in Tennessee.

Of the few Georgians who chose to join Union forces, most were from the mountains and had to cross state lines to enlist. As many as 270 Georgians enlisted in the First Alabama Cavalry, organized near Huntsville in mid-1862. Nearly half the Fifth Tennessee Mounted Infantry consisted of exiled Georgia Unionists. In November 1864 eight men from Fannin, Towns, and Union counties, all poor farmers who had deserted the Confederate army, were on their way to join the Fifth Tennessee in Cleveland, Tennessee, when they encountered John P. Gatewood's notorious Confederate guerrilla force near the state line. In what came to be known as the Madden Branch Massacre, Gatewood's men captured six of the eight, lined them up, and gunned them down at close range.

The First Georgia State Troops Volunteers, organized in the spring of 1864 during Union general William T. Sherman's Atlanta campaign, was the only official Union force established within the state. Its approximately 200 enlistees were motivated as much by the defense of their homes against Confederate raids into the mountains as by any loyalty to the Union. Given this priority, many of its troops chose to flee back home rather than stay put and hold Dalton when it came under Confederate attack in October 1864. The First Georgia's commander, Union general James Steedman, called the battalion "utterly worthless" and ensured that it was disbanded a month later.

Home-Front Activity

Although few Georgians ever wore Union uniforms during the war, significant numbers of Unionist civilians, either on their own or in small, often secret communities, made concerted efforts on behalf of the Union and against the Confederacy over the course of the war. Much of that activity was concentrated in north Georgia, where the relative lack of slavery or a slave-based economy, along with the region's social and commercial isolation, gave many mountain residents little reason to support the Southern cause. Such sentiments were never universal, and the divisions among Georgia's highland residents often led to violent and vicious guerrilla warfare, as exemplified by the Madden Branch Massacre.

Given that highland Unionists often enjoyed a critical mass not apparent in other parts of the state, they formed small independent and irregular bands that waged localized campaigns to defend their families and property from Confederate forces, which were often guerrilla bands themselves. As tensions escalated in the war's latter half, many of these same "Tory" bands, made up of true Unionists as well as deserters and other dissenters, resorted to more aggressive actions, including brutal vendettas against Confederate neighbors, home guard units, or conscription officials.

Pockets of Unionists, often working even further underground than the rural highlanders, appeared in Georgia cities as well. Researchers have gathered information (much of it anecdotal) about these urban Unionists from their journals and diaries, several of which have been discovered in recent years. An anonymous document, long known as "Miss Abby's Diary," proved to be a major source of information on a small, but fully engaged, Unionist community in Atlanta. Historian Thomas G. Dyer decoded the diary and discovered that its author, Vermont native Cyrena Stone, had moved to Fayetteville, Georgia, with her husband in 1850 and then to Atlanta around 1853. When the war broke out, they found themselves, along with other so-called secret Yankees, faced with constant surveillance, social ostracism, and persecution from local law enforcement.

This group of no more than 100 families found various means not only to survive but also to subvert Confederate war efforts. They helped Union prisoners of war and wounded soldiers brought into the city for either incarceration or treatment and provided information to Union forces as they approached Atlanta. Once Sherman's troops occupied the city, its Unionist residents were allowed to remain for several weeks after the rest of the populace was forced to evacuate. The Unionists eventually left the city as well, and many returned to the North.

Horace King, born into slavery, became one of the most respected bridge builders in the Deep South. From the 1830s until the 1880s, he constructed bridges over most of the major rivers in the region. After the war he claimed that the federal government owed him, as a Unionist, for the confiscation or plundering of his property by Union troops.—From online entry "Horace King"

WWW.GEORGIAENCYCLOPEDIA.ORG

Other accounts by Unionist women suggest that they lived in isolated situations, lacking even the small network of fellow loyalists found in Atlanta. Dix and Louisa Fletcher, also New England transplants, operated a hotel on the square in Marietta. In her journal, Louisa Fletcher recounts considerable harassment by local residents suspicious of the couple's loyalties, and ostracism that continued well after the war's end. The war even alienated the Fletchers from their adult daughters, who cast their lot with the Southern cause. Nellie Kinzie Gordon, a native of Chicago, felt even more isolated as the wife of prominent Savannahian William Washington Gordon II. Living with her in-laws in Savannah, and under constant scrutiny by local residents, she was far more guarded, and even ambivalent, in her professions of Union loyalty. Her situation was further complicated by the fact that her uncle,

Union general David Hunter, had enraged Savannah residents by capturing and occupying nearby Fort Pulaski.

These stories, and others like them, suggest that the experiences of Georgia Unionists varied greatly. The degree of activity, sentiment, and commitment to the Union cause was often dictated by setting and circumstance, and no two of these cases are alike in terms of what factors determined loyalty to the Union or how that loyalty was expressed. Much depended on where one happened to be and what opportunities presented themselves.

JOHN C. INSCOE

 # Desertion

Desertion plagued Georgia regiments during the Civil War and, along with other factors, debilitated the Confederate effort. Deserters were not merely cowards or ne'er-do-wells; some were seasoned veterans from battle-hardened regiments.

The most significant wave of desertion among Georgia soldiers occurred from late 1863 through 1864 in the wake of the Battle of Chickamauga and Union general William T. Sherman's Atlanta campaign. The proximity of the army to soldiers' homes following those battles, Sherman's advance through the state, and Georgians' sense of duty to alleviate the social and economic hardships endured by their families and communities encouraged Confederates to abandon the ranks and return home. According to historian Ella Lonn, of the approximately 103,400 enlisted men who deserted the Confederacy by war's end, 6,797 were from Georgia. Among the eleven Confederate states with significant (defined as more than 3,500) numbers of deserters, Georgia ranked sixth—behind North Carolina (23,694), Tennessee (12,155), Virginia (12,071), Mississippi (11,604), and Arkansas (10,029). The bulk of Georgia deserters belonged to the Army of Tennessee and hailed from the north Georgia mountains and upper Piedmont region.

Desertion Legislation

As neither Confederate nor Union forces initially possessed a formal policy regarding deserters, individual officers adopted impromptu regulations. It was not until 1863, when the U.S. War Department approved General Orders No. 286 and U.S. president Abraham Lincoln launched his Proclamation of Amnesty and Reconstruction, that Union forces established a formal policy on desertion. Federal policies encouraged Confederate desertion and attempted to shorten the war not only by pardoning and restoring citizenship rights to deserters who took a loyalty oath to the Union but also by allowing former Confederates to return to their homes. In August 1864 Union general Ulysses S. Grant issued Circular No. 31, which rewarded Confederate deserters with monetary incentives and transport home.

In response to these Union policies, the Confederate Congress passed legislation in an attempt to stifle desertion and maintain Confederate armies. In December 1863 Confederate authorities passed an act that made it illegal for civilians to transport, feed, or shelter deserters. This act also made it a crime for family members to encourage soldiers to return home. On August 10, 1864, Confederate general Robert E. Lee also attempted to sustain his fighting force by issuing General Orders No. 64, which offered amnesty to any deserter who returned to Confederate service.

Patterns of Desertion

In his study of desertion patterns in Georgia, historian Mark Weitz estimates that 3,368 Georgians deserted and hid behind Union lines. Desertion was most common among enlisted soldiers and low-ranking officers. Nearly 93 percent of Georgia deserters were privates or noncommissioned officers. In contrast to traditional patterns of Confederate desertion, which peaked in the fall and winter of 1864, Georgia's wave of desertion had subsided by late 1864. Of the Georgians who fled to Union lines and took the oath of allegiance to the Union, more than 90 percent fled between December 1, 1863, and December 31, 1864.

Roughly 400 Georgians had enlisted in the Union army by the end of the war, but it remains unclear how many of these loyalists had deserted Confederate armies. Although communities in the Georgia mountains provided only 114 Confederate companies, or 14 percent of the total number of Georgia units, the majority of deserters hailed from that region. They accounted for approximately 2,058, or 61 percent, of the soldiers who abandoned the Confederacy for Union lines.

Motivations for Desertion

Various factors influenced the increased desertion rates among Georgia highlanders. Because of Sherman's advance on Atlanta, those Georgians in Confederate units along his route were in close proximity to their homes in the mountains and upper Piedmont, which made returning to their communities more feasible. As the Union army upheld lenient desertion policies, its presence throughout north Georgia encouraged desertion. Soldiers also deserted in an attempt to alleviate the hardships endured by their families and communities. Enlistment in the army kept men away from their homes for extended periods and destroyed the economic foundation of semi-subsistent mountain families. Crop failures, as well as salt shortages and guerrilla raids, plagued north Georgia communities. Deteriorating home-front conditions compelled many families to write soldiers and urge them to desert and return home. Despite Governor Joseph E. Brown's attempts to maintain order and relieve shortages of food and other supplies, many soldiers lost faith in the state's ability to do so and chose family loyalty over allegiance to the Confederate army.

During the war, infantry companies from the **wiregrass Georgia** region, with names like the Irwin County Cowboys and the Forest Rangers, were shipped off to the front. But as the war wore on, anti-Confederate sentiment raised its head among the region's Unionists, and pockets of deserters found refuge in the woods.
—From online entry "Wiregrass Georgia"

WWW.GEORGIAENCYCLOPEDIA.ORG

Whereas the sixty-three plantation-belt counties in the lowlands provided more than 50 percent of the volunteer infantry companies, desertion rates among soldiers hailing from this region were among the lowest in the state. This phenomenon may be partially accounted for by the fact that Confederate social and military authority remained reasonably intact in the lowlands for most of the war, making it perilous for would-be deserters from the area to flee home.

Although Sherman's March to the Sea from Atlanta to Savannah was brutal, Union forces advanced rapidly, were largely unopposed, and did not occupy any place along the route long enough for deserters to flee to their lines. Also, because the majority of regiments from central and south Georgia belonged to the Army of Northern Virginia and engaged in battles far from their homes, potential deserters found it much less practical to return home than did those serving in the Army of Tennessee. It was also difficult for the lowland Georgians in the Army of Tennessee to flee home because the army returned to Tennessee instead of pursuing Sherman through southeast Georgia.

The economic structure of the plantation belt and the widespread use of slave labor also allowed lowland Georgians to remain in the Confederate army without worries for the safety of their homes and families. Whereas the 1864 Confederate Conscription Act depleted north Georgia of its male population, wealthy plantation owners in the lowlands were able to apply for exemptions. While 3,368 Georgians deserted to Union lines throughout the war, approximately 11,000 affluent Georgia men received exemptions and were able to remain in their communities and maintain social and economic stability. When Union and Confederate armies left the state in early 1865, desertions among Georgia troops persisted but at a greatly reduced rate until the war's end.

SAMUEL B. MCGUIRE

 # Dissent

The Civil War home front in Georgia, far from reflecting unity in a common cause, was rife with conflict and dissent. Though the state was largely spared the impact of invading armies until late in the war, social and economic divisions set Georgians against one another in ever worsening internal conflicts that undermined support for the Confederacy well before the war's end.

Secession and War

Southerners, including Georgians, were not united in their support for secession. Although, according to historian Michael P. Johnson, more than half the popular vote for delegates to the Georgia Secession Convention of 1861 went to candidates who initially opposed secession, enough delegates shifted their votes to give secessionists a 166 to 130 majority in the first vote at the convention. The remaining antisecession delegates urged that the secession ordinance be put to the people for a vote. Fearing the outcome of such a move, secessionist delegates refused. Georgia, like the other seceding states, left the Union without submitting the issue to a direct popular vote.

With Georgia out of the Union, opposition to secession continued. Officials in Pickens County flew the U.S. flag over the courthouse for weeks after secession, and some private citizens did the same. One Unionist, James Aiken, informed Georgia governor Joseph E. Brown by letter in February 1861 that he and other residents of Dade and Walker counties adamantly opposed secession. Aiken wrote that secession benefited only "those that owns lands and Negroes!" and threatened that 2,500 volunteers in northwest Georgia would secede from the state if the governor did not put the issue to a popular vote.

Opposition to secession waned after the Confederacy fired on Fort Sumter, in the harbor of Charleston, South Carolina, in April 1861. By the following month approximately 18,000 Georgians had joined the Confederate army, ready to defend the South against Union forces. The most pressing problem for the new recruits was a shortage of food, due in part to the lack of railroads throughout the South but mainly to agricultural practices that favored the cultivation of cotton over food crops.

Cotton and Starvation

Food shortages led to class tensions and to some of the earliest internal opposition to the war. According to one resident of southwest Georgia, writing to Governor Brown in the spring of 1862, cotton planters amounted to "internal enemies of the country, for they will whip us sooner than all Lincolndom combined could do it." Despite legal restrictions on the amount of cotton to be grown and exported, cultivation and shipment of the lucrative crop continued. Planters smuggled tons of cotton out of the South, reaping extravagant profits throughout the war. Even Confederate brigadier general Robert Toombs, of Wilkes County, ignored the restrictions, despite protests from his neighbors in Randolph County. The resulting food shortages created extreme hardship throughout Georgia, affecting in particular the women and children of Confederate soldiers. Despite their obligation to provide food for the home front, the state's planters failed to do so. Moreover, those who did raise food crops often sold their harvest to speculators, who in turn charged more than most yeoman farmers and poor whites could afford.

On the brink of starvation, women around the state began rioting for food in early 1863. In Columbus a mob of about 65 armed women raided the stores of speculators on Broad Street. Such "bread riots," as they were known, also occurred that spring in Atlanta, Augusta, Macon, and Milledgeville, and the following year in Savannah nearly 100 women raided stores on Whitaker Street. Women in the rural communities of Blackshear, Cartersville, Colquitt, Forsyth, Hartwell, Marietta, Stockton, Thomasville, and Valdosta also participated in bread riots.

Thousands of petitions describing this desperate situation and begging for relief flooded into Richmond, Virginia, the capital of the Confederacy, from women all across the South. A letter dated September 8, 1863, from soldiers' wives in Miller County, is typical of these pleas: "Our crops is limited and so short. . . . We can seldom find [bacon] for none has got but those that are exempt from service . . . and they have no humane feeling nor patriotic principles. . . . I tell you that without some great and speedy alterating in the conducting of affairs in this our little nation God will frown on it and that speedily."

Desertion, Draft, and Resistance

Soldiers' wives wrote of their distress to their husbands as well, and before the first year of the war had ended thousands of Georgia troops abandoned ranks in answer to their families' calls. Replacing these deserters was difficult, and attempts by the Confederate Congress to institute a military draft met with much resistance, especially among the working class who did not qualify for exemption by owning twenty or more slaves. Governor Brown, though opposed to the Confederate draft, created his own conscription in order to build up the Georgia militia, but again the wealthy were easily able to avoid service, creating animosity among the poorer classes.

Although many deserters returned home to help their families, others took refuge in the mountains of north Georgia and the wiregrass region of south Georgia. One officer called the state's southern region "one of the greatest dens for Tories and deserters from our army in the world." These "tory" (anti-Confederate) or "layout" gangs engaged in raids and battles in order to survive and resist arrest. One such group formed a battalion called the Volunteer Force of the United States Army from

Georgia. In early 1863 Governor Brown sent the state militia to put down deserter gangs around Dahlonega with little success, and a year later he sent an expedition against anti-Confederate gangs to southeast Georgia. Such efforts had little effect.

African Americans in Georgia also found means of resistance, particularly in their attempts to secure freedom from enslavement. Rebellion attempts involving both black and white Georgians were put down in Calhoun County in 1862 and in Brooks County in 1865. Thousands of blacks joined the forces of Union general William T. Sherman during the March to the Sea in 1864, and many found refuge on the state's coastal islands.

During the war white Georgians feared that slaves might rebel. As a result, the movement and behavior of slaves became more strictly regulated through such strategies as **slave patrols**, especially after the Emancipation Proclamation of 1863. Authorities in Atlanta, for example, arrested blacks found on the streets at night and prevented social gatherings of African Americans unless patrollers or policemen were present.—From online entry "Slave Patrols"

WWW.GEORGIAENCYCLOPEDIA.ORG

A Rich Man's War

On April 5, 1865, only days before the Confederacy's collapse, an Early County newspaper, the *Early County News*, published an editorial that reflected a common feeling on the Georgia home front. "This has been 'a rich man's war and a poor man's fight.' It is true that there are a few wealthy men in the army, but nine tenths of them hold positions, always get out of the way when they think a fight is coming on, and treat the privates like dogs. . . . There seems to be no chance to get this class to carry muskets." Such attitudes had long since undermined support for the Confederacy and have led many scholars to conclude that internal dissent, as much as the invading armies, was a significant, perhaps decisive, factor in the war's outcome.

DAVID WILLIAMS

} Women

During the Civil War, women across the South took on new roles to support their families and the Confederacy. Women in Georgia proved no exception. The war provided elite white women with opportunities to take part in the public sphere. They often voiced their opinions about events, and they filled roles previously held by men. For poor white women, the war proved less liberating, as the demands of the war and economic hardship created major challenges in supporting themselves and their families. By 1865 the war and emancipation had also transformed the lives of African American women.

Elite White Women

The interest in the sectional crisis for many white Georgia women began prior to the outbreak of hostilities. After the election of U.S. president Abraham Lincoln in 1860, slaveholding women across Georgia pushed the men of their families to support secession by appealing to their sense of familial duty. The enthusiasm of many did not wane upon the vote for secession on January 19, 1861. Planters' wives and other elite women often rejoiced that their state had finally broken from what they saw as the Union's oppressive hold. Although the horrors of war would later dampen much of this initial enthusiasm, many white Georgia women took an active and educated part in the movement to separate the South from the North.

When the hostilities began, many women encouraged their husbands to enlist by appealing to their manhood and sense of honor. Women throughout the Confederacy treated shirkers with scorn, often shaming them into service. Single women publicly declared that they would date or marry only those who volunteered to serve, and kinswomen urged their loved ones to fight for the Southern cause.

As they encouraged men to enlist, white women revealed their confidence in their own abilities on the Georgia home front. With the men gone, their wives, mothers, sisters, and daughters assumed the management of their homes, farms, plantations, and businesses. By working their own fields, as well as taking jobs in local industries, Georgia women provided Confederate troops with food, uniforms, and other necessities.

More affluent women also engaged in voluntary activities on the home front that proved vital to the Confederacy. Like women throughout the South, they formed aid societies to provide soldiers with socks, undergarments, shirts, gloves, blankets, shoes, comforters, handkerchiefs, scarves, bandages, and food. In more isolated areas, women worked as individuals to send supplies to the soldiers. They also planned and attended bazaars, fairs, concerts, raffles, and dances to raise money for army supplies and even sponsored specific Confederate gunboats through fund-raising drives.

In addition, white women took on the traditionally male occupation of nursing during the Civil War, taking care of the Confederacy's wounded as best they could. Because many Georgia towns became battlefields during the war, local women often inadvertently became frontline nurses. Hospitals were set up anywhere—homes, churches, town halls, and streets. Other women left their homes to care for wounded troops on the front lines, seeing battle and its ravages firsthand.

Class Distinctions

Poorer women were often far more vulnerable to the war's devastation than were elite slaveholding women. The wives and children of yeomen farmers had far fewer resources to draw on when left to their own devices, and many experienced food shortages as early as 1862. Governor Joseph E. Brown's papers are filled with letters from indigent women seeking relief, in terms of either food and farm supplies or exemptions for their husbands and other male relatives from military service. Neither sort of request met with much response from the state government until the war's midpoint, when it implemented sporadic efforts at relief for soldiers' wives and widows through the distribution of corn or grain, and sometimes money. Wives of deserters or Unionists were usually denied any share in such relief.

In such urban areas as Macon, Augusta, and Columbus, poor women sometimes found work in factories or arsenals, though those operations often closed well before the war's end. In Savannah "needle women" were hired by the state to sew uniforms and tents for the Confederate cause, but only until the Union blockade forced that enterprise to fold and move elsewhere in the state.

Many Georgia women grew desperate by the war's midpoint. This desperation led to the widespread looting of stores and raids on warehouses by groups of destitute women, often driven by hunger. Such riots occurred in major cities and small towns. In April 1863, for example, sixty-five women, some armed with pistols and knives, moved down Broad Street in Columbus, looting several stores before police were able to restore order. Dozens of such incidents throughout the state served to undermine support for the war and led many soldiers to desert the army and return home to take care of their families.

Sherman's March

Georgia's civilian population faced its greatest trial during Sherman's 1864 campaign. After a four-month campaign for Atlanta, Union general William T. Sherman and his troops took control of Atlanta on September 2. Once in command of the city, Sherman issued Special Field Order No. 67, which forced the evacuation of the city's more than 1,500 civilians. When confronted with vehement protests from Confederate officials and civilians, Sherman asserted that a hostile civilian population would not only impede military activities but also unnecessarily burden the Union army.

Sherman and his troops left Atlanta on November 15, burning many homes on their March to the Sea. As the soldiers made their way southeastward toward Savannah, they terrorized the white women in their path. The Union assault on the home front, however, did not necessarily deter elite Georgia women from their dedication to the Southern cause. Instead, the invasion served as impetus for some women to increase their support of the Confederacy, continuing to send items to the soldiers on the front lines. For other women, Sherman's march merely intensified the pleas for their men to abandon the military and return home.

The Civil War also created opportunities that allowed slave women to make the war their own. For most, this meant escaping from bondage, protecting children, and reuniting with family members whenever possible. Some slaves took advantage of lessened oversight on their plantations and fled. More frequently, slaves capitalized on the approach of invading Union troops. During Sherman's march, for example, so many slave women escaped to Union lines that soldiers complained of the "helpless women and children" who followed them and ate their rations.

Individual Portraits of Women at War

The most familiar portraits of women in wartime Georgia are fictional, most notably in three popular novels from three different eras. Augusta Jane Evans's *Macaria; or Altars of Sacrifice* was published in 1864 and became a best seller throughout the Confederacy, with 20,000 copies sold before the war ended. The novel tells the story of two young women's thwarted romances over the course of the war and their commitment to the Confederate cause, which was meant to inspire Southern women readers to make similar sacrifices. Margaret Mitchell's *Gone With the Wind* (1936) and Margaret Walker's *Jubilee* (1966) portray two very different Georgia women and their contrasting plights over the course of the war. Mitchell's novel centers on Scarlett O'Hara, the daughter of an upcountry planter, while Walker's novel follows Vyry, a slave woman on a southwest Georgia plantation for whom the war takes on very different meanings, including her emancipation at its end.

A number of Georgia women left vivid autobiographical accounts of their wartime experiences. The narrative of Eliza Frances Andrews, published in 1908 as *The War-Time Journal of a Georgia Girl, 1864–1865*, was one of the best known. In it Andrews recounts her flight from her home in Washington, Georgia, across the state to take refuge from Sherman's troops at her sister's plantation in southwest Georgia, south of Albany. Susie King Taylor's *Reminiscences of My Life in Camp with the 33d United States Colored Troops*, published in 1902, is the sole wartime narrative by an African American woman and recounts her experience as a teacher of both freed slaves and black troops on St. Simons Island during the Union occupation there in 1862.

In 1862 **Susie King Taylor** became the first black teacher to work in a freely operating freedmen's school in Georgia. She taught both children and adults on St. Simons Island, where she married Edward King, a black noncommissioned officer in the Union forces. For the next three years she moved with his regiment, teaching many soldiers to read and write.—From online entry "Susie King Taylor"

WWW.GEORGIAENCYCLOPEDIA.ORG

Two women in the Atlanta area provided detailed accounts of civilian life there through the upheaval and dislocation brought on by Union forces in 1864: Mary Harris Gay of Decatur in *Life in Dixie during the War* (1892) and Sallie Clayton, an adolescent at the time, whose memories of her own and her family's ordeal, recorded just after the turn of the century, were published in 1999 as *Requiem for a Lost City*.

Not all Georgia women supported the Confederacy. Several non-Southerners moved to Georgia not long before the war broke out and left records of their efforts to maintain their loyalties to the Union. Cyrena Stone, a Vermont native living in Atlanta, kept a diary of her experiences as a secret sympathizer of the Union and of her interactions with other Unionists in the city, which historian Thomas G. Dyer has chronicled in *Secret Yankees* (1999). Chicago native Eleanor "Nellie" Kenzie Gordon, later the mother of Juliette Gordon Low, had married William Washington Gordon II, a Savannah native and Confederate captain. Gordon found herself a newlywed living in Savannah with her Confederate in-laws during the war and had to suppress her own Northern loyalties, even as her uncle, Union general David Hunter, led the forces that captured Fort Pulaski in 1862.

LISA TENDRICH FRANK

Nancy Harts Militia

The Nancy Harts militia, formed in LaGrange during the first weeks of the Civil War, was a female military unit organized by the wives of Confederate soldiers to protect the home front.

On April 26, 1861, the LaGrange Light Guards of the Fourth Georgia Infantry, comprising men mostly from LaGrange, in Troup County, left home to fight for the Confederacy. In that year alone, 1,300 men left LaGrange, making the town particularly vulnerable to Union attack because of its location midway between Atlanta and the Confederacy's first capital at Montgomery, Alabama. Soon after the men departed, two of their wives, Nancy Hill Morgan and Mary Alford Heard, decided to form a female military company. The two women called a preliminary meeting at a schoolhouse on the grounds of U.S. senator Benjamin Hill's home. Almost forty women attended, ready to do their part to defend their homes and families.

Inexperienced with firearms and unfamiliar with military matters, the women turned to A. C. Ware, a physician who remained in town due to a physical disability, for assistance in their training. The members initially elected Ware as captain but soon thereafter chose Nancy Morgan as captain and Mary Heard as first lieutenant. The regiment leaders were assisted by elected sergeants, corporals, and a treasurer. The group called themselves the "Nancy Harts," or "Nancies," in honor of Nancy Hart, a Patriot spy who outwitted and killed a group of Tories at her northeast Georgia cabin during the Revolutionary War (1775–83).

The women began their military training using William J. Hardee's *Rifle and Light Infantry Tactics* (1861) and met twice a week for drilling and target practice. The leaders offered prizes to the best markswomen, and after several mishaps, including shooting a hornet's nest and a cow, the women became expert shots.

Although the Nancy Harts organized as a military unit, they served primarily as nurses. During the latter half of the war, LaGrange became a medical and refugee center because of its proximity to key battlegrounds and its intact rail line. LaGrange's four hospitals were often full, and a number of residents, including nearly all the Nancy Harts, took patients into their homes for individualized care.

Although it was not the only female military unit organized during the Civil War, the Nancy Harts militia was unique in several respects. First, the women drilled and continued target practice until the end of the war. (Most other such groups existed only fleetingly.) Second, unlike other female militias, the women faced Union troops as a regiment. In mid-April 1865 Major General James H. Wilson led a Union raid on west Georgia. As the Union troops approached LaGrange from West Point, the local Confederate cavalrymen fled, and the Nancy Harts stepped in to protect the town.

On April 17 the Nancy Harts marched to the campus of LaGrange Female College (later LaGrange College) on the edge of town to meet the enemy forces. When the Union cavalry arrived in LaGrange, the women peacefully surrendered the town to Union colonel Oscar H. LaGrange (coincidentally named) and organized an effort to feed both the Union and Confederate soldiers. In return, the Union troops destroyed facilities in LaGrange that were helpful to the Confederate war effort, including factories, stores, and railroad tracks, but spared most private homes and property.

After the war the Nancy Harts members returned to their prewar duties, though many were forced to make difficult adjustments since more than a quarter of LaGrange's enlisted men did not return home. Many women joined the LaGrange chapter of the United Daughters of the Confederacy (UDC), formed by a former Nancy Harts member. In December 1896 Leila Pullen Morris, who had been eighteen years old at the time of the town's surrender in 1865, gave the only recorded firsthand account of the Nancy Harts at an Atlanta UDC meeting.

The Nancy Harts have been a point of pride for residents of LaGrange over the decades. In 1904 the *Ladies Home Journal* published an article on the Nancy Harts, giving the militia national attention. In 1957 the Georgia Historical Commission placed a historical marker commemorating the women's service in front of the LaGrange courthouse, and four years later a group of LaGrange women staged a reenactment of the Nancy Harts' activity for the Civil War centennial, complete with officer elections. In 2009 the UDC planted a tree in Griffin at the Stonewall Confederate Cemetery in honor of the Nancy Harts.

KATHERINE BRACKETT

Welfare and Poverty

Georgia's civilian population felt the effects of the Civil War nearly as soon as soldiers left home to fight. As the war progressed, those on the home front faced growing shortages of food, salt, cloth, and cash. Governor Joseph E. Brown and the state's legislators were acutely aware of increasing deprivation, and they responded with a series of measures designed to prevent starvation and suffering. The nineteenth-century attitude toward welfare was that it should be provided as needed but should not be excessive, for fear of encouraging "idleness" and dependence upon the government. Georgia's wartime welfare expenditures, however, contrasted with that attitude.

Before the war, Georgia's government played no significant role in providing welfare, but the shortages associated with the conflict forced the state to undertake new welfare measures. Several factors combined to create the shortages in the state, but as the war dragged into its second year, the scarcity of supplies became more widespread as available materials were allocated to the military.

Wartime Needs

In 1863 the state experienced a serious drought and an early frost, and Governor Brown announced to the legislature that the "bread question" was crucial to Georgia's success. Dissent among citizens on the home front, particularly women, resulted in bread riots around the state early in 1863. In September of that year Union and Confederate armies fought in the Battle of Chickamauga in northwest Georgia, and by early

May 1864 the Atlanta campaign was under way. Both armies foraged the countryside, impressing food, fuel, and livestock, and Georgia faced an increasing refugee problem with people fleeing both to and from the Union army as the lines of battle advanced.

The state legislature responded to food shortages in 1863 and 1864 by approving three separate corn appropriation acts, totaling $1.89 million. The first provided corn to north Georgia, the area hardest hit by the drought and the war. Inferior-court justices in each county were responsible for its distribution. The families of Confederate soldiers, the first priority, received corn at no charge. Others who could pay shipping costs were expected to do so. The second appropriation act provided aid specifically to Habersham County, though any county's inferior-court justice could apply for assistance by a direct appeal to the governor. By November 1864, the date of the last appropriation, any corn that the state could procure was free to anyone who needed it, with the exception of Unionists, who were denied aid from both the Confederate and state governments throughout the war.

As chief supply officer for Confederate general James Longstreet, **Raphael Moses** was responsible for feeding and supplying up to 54,000 Confederate troops and personnel. Forbidden by General Robert E. Lee to enter private homes in search of supplies during raids into Union territory, Moses always paid for what he took from farms and businesses, albeit in Confederate tender.— From online entry "Raphael Moses"

WWW.GEORGIAENCYCLOPEDIA.ORG

Also in short supply was salt, necessary for curing meat, tanning leather, dyeing fabric, and supplementing the diets of horses and livestock. Lacking a substantial salt industry, Georgia obtained its wartime supply from Virginia and Louisiana, with the state's railroads providing free shipping. Over the course of the war, the state spent more than $1 million to procure and distribute salt to needy Georgians. Salt, provided free to the indigent, was sold at reduced rates to soldiers' families and at low prices to those who could afford it.

Home production of cloth became an important activity during the war, as many textile mills closed throughout the state. In 1862 the legislature addressed the scarcity of cotton cards (wire brushes with wooden backings and handles used to process raw cotton into thread), and throughout the war it appropriated approximately $1.3 million to purchase or produce the cards. As with corn and salt, soldiers' families and the destitute were top priority and received the cards for free. Those who could pay did so. Inferior-court justices again oversaw distribution.

To address the cash shortage that plagued the entire Confederacy, Georgia established the Indigent Soldiers' Families Fund to provide financial assistance, which was also distributed through the inferior courts. The initial appropriation for 1863 was for $2.5 million. The legislature made another $6 million available for 1864, and an additional $8 million for 1865, although most disbursements ended in late April or early May 1865, as the war ended. The funds were in highly inflated Confederate currency, which may explain the need for such large increases.

Expenditures

Georgia's wartime welfare programs peaked in the fiscal year 1863–64. Total state expenditures for that period were $13,288,435. One-third of this amount was disbursed through the Indigent Soldiers' Families Fund. Including expenditures for salt, cotton cards, and corn (more than $6.5 million), the state spent 50.6 percent of all appropriated funds on these welfare measures.

The state also made other welfare-related expenditures. The Educational Fund, the Small Pox Fund, the state Academy for the Blind, the Georgia Lunatic Asylum (later Central State Hospital), and the Georgia Relief and Hospital Association all received assistance, though on a much smaller scale. Altogether the government spent $7,587,947, or more than 57 percent of its funds, on direct and indirect welfare support during the 1863–64 fiscal year.

Welfare programs were established to assist Confederate soldiers' families and thus were intended for white Georgians only. No provisions were made in the legislation for slaves, who were expected to depend upon their masters. Nor did the legislation mention any allocations of aid for Georgia's free black population, who did not receive rations from the federal Freedmen's Bureau until after the war ended.

DENISE WRIGHT

｝ Emancipation

Emancipation did not come suddenly or easily to Georgia. The liberation of the state's more than 400,000 slaves began during the chaos of the Civil War and continued well into 1865. Emancipation also demanded the reconfiguration of the full range of social and economic relations. What would replace slavery was unclear. Former slaves, ex-slaveholders, and the Northerners responsible for enforcing freedom had their own ideas about what the future should bring. Struggles between those competing visions punctuated emancipation in Georgia. In waging those battles, however, black people and white laid the foundations for a new social order. Though fragile and incomplete, it rested on assumptions of universal freedom and civil rights.

Breaking the Chains

The liberation of Georgia's slaves started piecemeal soon after the Civil War broke out in 1861 and then accelerated with the Confederate surrender in April 1865. During the war, emancipation came largely at the hands of slaves determined to secure their own freedom. Some historians believe that 10,000 to 20,000 slaves took advantage of the disruption caused by General William T. Sherman's troops in their March to the Sea and joined their columns; historical records indicate that as many as 7,000 of those may have still been with the Union forces as they arrived in Savannah.

After the war vastly more people played roles in emancipation. Union soldiers, most notably those of Sherman's army in its march from Atlanta to the sea, liberated slaves as they crossed the state. Slaveholders unintentionally spread the news by talking too freely of their nation's loss in the presence of their servants. Slaves were always alert for the quietest whisper of freedom and eagerly shared whatever they learned, spreading word from quarter to quarter. But despite the efforts of slaves and soldiers alike, weeks passed before the revolution penetrated the farthest corners of the state. Many slave owners sought to maintain the old system, and often only the threat of military force impelled them to release their slaves. Bondage lingered into the summer months of 1865, particularly in the more remote neighborhoods of southwest Georgia.

Imagining Freedom

However and whenever freedom arrived, black Georgians rejoiced in the opportunity to remake their lives. Some started small, with simple experiments to test their new status. They took a few hours off work to visit with friends, or they wore their finest clothes to promenade through city streets.

Others, determined to refashion their lives altogether, took bolder steps. They fled to the nearest military post or city (more than 6,000 fled to Atlanta and even more to Savannah), determined to escape forever the brutality that had scarred them in bondage. They struck out in search of family members scattered first by slavery and then by war and in search of new economic opportunities offered by cities and towns. A study of Dougherty County in southwest Georgia shows that the black population of Albany, the county seat, grew by more than 75 percent between 1860 and 1870.

Freedmen's education during Reconstruction commenced when Georgia's emancipated slaves demanded formal schooling. Legislation passed in 1829 had made it a crime to teach slaves to read, and literacy was discouraged within Georgia's small free black community. When schools for freedpeople opened in early 1865, they were crowded with both children and adults.—From online entry "Freedmen's Education during Reconstruction"

WWW.GEORGIAENCYCLOPEDIA.ORG

These new freedmen and freedwomen looked to the future as well, organizing schools for themselves and their children and asserting authority over their churches and liturgy. Sometimes freedpeople combined those goals, as did a black Baptist minister who, having learned to read in slavery, opened a school in Wilkes County.

Most especially, freedpeople refused to work like slaves. Ideally, they hoped to separate themselves completely from their old masters by becoming landowners themselves. That independence was nearly achieved by a few, primarily those who settled on the coastal reserve set aside for their exclusive use by Sherman in January 1865 under his Field Order No. 15. Most could not. Slavery had left the majority of black Georgians bereft of the resources necessary to farm independently, and necessity compelled them to seek employment on white-owned farms and plantations.

That requirement brought Georgia's freedpeople into conflict with former slaveholders, who envisioned a very different emancipation. In their minds the best freedom resembled slavery. They preferred that black people remain in their old homes, accept the same clothing and food provided in slavery, and observe the same rules of etiquette they had as slaves. Ex-slaveholders saw no reason to foster the education of freedpeople or to permit them to congregate without white supervision. Indeed, for many former owners, such aspirations posed a threat to good order.

Former slave owners especially rejected freedpeople's desire for economic independence. Dependent on black labor for their own prosperity, they expected agricultural work to remain unchanged. Black laborers would continue to perform accustomed work in accustomed ways, under the watchful eyes of whip-wielding overseers. Ex–slave owners resisted allowing former slaves a say in the conditions of work or extending to them the legal and political rights enjoyed by free workers in the North. In the lexicon of the day, liberated slaves would live and "work as heretofore."

That sentiment did not please the Northerners responsible for enforcing emancipation. Believing that victory on the battlefield had awarded them the right to reshape the South to their own liking, Northern officials such as John Emory Bryant, one of the first Freedmen's Bureau agents to assume duty in Georgia, anticipated modeling the South after their native society. Former slaves would assume roles as employees, and ex-slaveholders would become employers. Freely and fairly negotiated contracts would compensate industrious workers with material and moral rewards and would ensure landowners of the labor necessary to bring the South back to economic prosperity.

Northerners' vision left no room for those who yearned for the command of slavery or those who preferred to seek their livelihoods outside wage work. Disputes between employees and employers had to be settled by courts of law, not by recourse to whips. Workers had to be protected in their right to seek out the most favorable and lucrative employment. Promptly paid wages would finance black people's pursuit of moral, educational, and economic advancement, especially since the federal officials' vision of freedom precluded the independence that would have resulted from giving land to former slaves.

Defining Freedom

Disputes erupted across Georgia as former slaves, former slaveholders, and Northern victors struggled to enforce their individual visions of freedom. Freedpeople acquiesced to Northern insistence that they return to work, especially since they realized their own well-being depended on seeing the year's crops to harvest. But they refused to "work as heretofore." Black Georgians riled ex–slave owners by shortening their work days, demanding payment for services rendered, and exercising their new legal rights to bring charges against employers who attempted to whip them as of old. Most black parents resisted efforts by Georgia planters to "apprentice" their children to uncompensated farm labor until they reached the age of twenty-one, though some gave in to pressures to do so.

Freedpeople discovered that Northerners were allies in their quest for education and independent churches, whether through government agents, Union troops, or teachers and preachers sponsored by the American Missionary Association and other such organizations. But they also confronted Northerners who seemingly sided with former slaveholders when they impeded black people's efforts to seek livings outside wage work or punished those who failed to meet the exact terms of their labor agreements.

No single group achieved its vision of freedom by the end of 1865 and the legal abolition of slavery. But in the struggles of emancipation, Georgians—black and white—hammered out a compromised freedom. For better or worse, most freedpeople henceforth sought their living through paid labor, usually on white-owned plantations. The conditions of that work and life outside of work reflected black people's visions of freedom more than their former masters' memories of slavery. Black children and some adults attended schools in Savannah, Augusta, Albany, Atlanta, and elsewhere. Black congregations listened to black ministers preaching a gospel of their own. Families reunited, often with the assistance of Northern officials. And although white Georgians would continue for some time to monopolize political office, former slaves had issued calls for their first convention and had begun planning for the day when they too would exercise the full range of civil and legal rights. Emancipation did not complete the transformation of Georgia society, but it had certainly started that process.

SUSAN E. O'DONOVAN

} Sherman's Field Order No. 15

On January 16, 1865, Union general William T. Sherman issued his Special Field Order No. 15, which confiscated as Federal property a strip of coastline stretching from Charleston, South Carolina, to the St. John's River in Florida, including Georgia's Sea Islands and the mainland thirty miles in from the coast. The order redistributed the roughly 400,000 acres of land to newly freed black families in forty-acre segments.

Sherman's order came on the heels of his successful March to the Sea from Atlanta to Savannah and just prior to his march northward into South Carolina. Radical Republicans in the U.S. Congress, like Charles Sumner and Thaddeus Stevens, for some time had pushed for land redistribution in order to break the back of Southern slaveholders' power. Feeling pressure from within his own party, U.S. president Abraham Lincoln sent his secretary of war, Edwin M. Stanton, to Savannah in order to facilitate a conversation with Sherman over what to do with Southern planters' lands.

On January 12 Sherman and Stanton met with twenty black leaders of the Savannah community, mostly Baptist and Methodist ministers, to discuss the question of emancipation. Lincoln approved Field Order No. 15 before Sherman issued it just four days after meeting with the black leaders. From Sherman's perspective the most important priority in issuing the directive was military expediency. It served as a means of providing for the thousands of black refugees who had been following his army since its invasion of Georgia. He could not afford to support or protect these refugees while on campaign.

The order explicitly called for the settlement of black families on confiscated land, encouraged freedmen to join the Union army to help sustain their newly won liberty, and designated a general officer to act as inspector of settlements. Inspector General Rufus Saxton would police the land and work to ensure legal title of the property for the black settlers. In a later order, Sherman also authorized the army to loan mules to the newly settled farmers.

Sherman's radical plan for land redistribution in the South was actually a practical response to several issues. Although Sherman had never been a racial egalitarian, his land-redistribution order served the military purpose of punishing Confederate planters along the rice coast of the

South for their role in starting the Civil War, while simultaneously solving what he and Radical Republicans viewed as a major new American problem: what to do with a new class of free Southern laborers. Congressional leaders convinced President Lincoln to establish the Bureau of Refugees, Freedmen, and Abandoned Lands on March 3, 1865, shortly after Sherman issued his order. The Freedmen's Bureau, as it came to be called, was authorized to give legal title for forty-acre plots of land to freedmen and white Southern Unionists.

The immediate effect of Sherman's order provided for the settlement of roughly 40,000 blacks (both refugees and local slaves who had been under Union army administration in the Sea Islands since 1861). This lifted the burden of supporting the freedpeople from Sherman's army as it turned north into South Carolina. But the order was a short-lived promise for blacks. Despite the objections of General Oliver O. Howard, the Freedmen's Bureau chief, U.S. president Andrew Johnson overturned Sherman's directive in the fall of 1865, after the war had ended, and returned the land along the South Carolina, Georgia, and Florida coasts to the planters who had originally owned it.

Although Sherman's Special Field Order No. 15 had no tangible benefit for blacks after President Johnson's revocation, the present-day movement supporting slave reparations has pointed to it as the U.S. government's promise to make restitution to African Americans for enslavement. The order is also the likely origin of the phrase "forty acres and a mule," which spread throughout the South in the weeks and months following Sherman's march.

BARTON MYERS

Seabrook Village, a **living history museum** in Liberty County, portrays life between 1865 and 1930 in a coastal African American community through authentic structures, exhibits, demonstrations, and oral history. After Sherman issued Field Order No. 15, freedmen and women forged new communities anchored by their culture, including the Geechee dialect and a common history of bondage.—From online entry "Living History Museums"

WWW.GEORGIAENCYCLOPEDIA.ORG

SECTION 3 }} The War's Legacy

Officials of the Stone Mountain Confederate Monumental Association and the Eighth District Chairmen, Special Guests, and Speakers at the Eighth District Children's Founders Roll Campaign Conference and Luncheon, February 12, circa 1925. Stone Mountain Collection, Manuscript, Archives, and Rare Book Library, Emory University.

"IT SOMETIMES SEEMS that the Confederacy is more alive today than it was in the 1800s," observed historian Anne Sarah Rubin in her book *A Shattered Nation* (2005). To be sure, since the end of the Civil War, Georgians have commemorated the conflict profusely and pervasively, with the literary and cinematic phenomenon of *Gone With the Wind* and the carvings on Stone Mountain being merely the most conspicuous reminders. This final section on Georgia's postwar legacy echoes, in many ways, the preceding section on the war years and demonstrates how the state's memory and commemoration activities are based as fully on its home-front experiences as on its military campaigns and incidents.

The attitudes and identities of white Southerners in the wake of the Civil War were shaped as much by the experience of Reconstruction as by the war itself. The first part of this section opens with an overview of that pivotal era, during which time the ideology of the "Lost Cause" began to develop across the South. By the late nineteenth century, many white Georgians, both individually and collectively, chose to understand and commemorate the war through the tenets of the Lost Cause, which provided a means of shaping both their personal identities and the identity of their region.

Physical sites, covered in the second part of the section, have provided more tangible and, perhaps, enduring means through which the war has been remembered by and interpreted to Georgia's residents and visitors. Cemeteries, monuments, and archaeological sites related to the war appear throughout the state, as they do throughout the South, but Georgia also lays claim to two of the nation's most striking Civil War memorials: the Cyclorama mural in Atlanta and the carvings of Confederate leaders on Stone Mountain. Other forms of commemoration, including historic preservation and reenactment events, are documented in this section as well.

Finally, the perspectives provided by writers and filmmakers, both Georgian and non-Georgian, have added much to our understanding of the Civil War within the state. Indeed, the drama of Sherman's Atlanta campaign and March to the Sea has inspired numerous novels, films, and memoirs, as has the infamous Andersonville prison camp. The final part of this section highlights the variety of fictional, nonfictional, musical, and cinematic works that draw upon these and other experiences to tell the story of the war in Georgia, from the myriad viewpoints of soldiers and civilians, masters and slaves, and men and women, sometimes all within the confines of a single work. Well before the scholarship on the war began to focus on the home-front experience, such imaginative portrayals explored what women, families, and African Americans, both slave and free, endured and, in some cases, gained over the course of the war.

POSTWAR IDENTITY

African American schoolchildren in Liberty County, circa 1890. Courtesy of
Hargrett Rare Book and Manuscript Library / University of Georgia Libraries.

} Reconstruction

As a defeated Confederate state, Georgia underwent Reconstruction from the aftermath of the Civil War in 1865 until 1871, when Republican government and military occupation in the state ended. Though relatively brief, Reconstruction transformed the state politically, socially, and economically.

War's Aftermath

As the Civil War ended in early May 1865, Georgia's Confederate governor, Joseph E. Brown, surrendered to Union authorities and was paroled. After attempting to convene the Georgia General Assembly, however, he was arrested and briefly imprisoned in the District of Columbia.

Brown left behind a war-ravaged state, devoid of civil order and fast approaching chaos. Politically rudderless and economically destitute, Georgia faced the future with a white population, which had numbered more than 590,000 in 1860, depleted by some 40,000 Georgians who had been killed or permanently dispersed by the conflict. The state's black population, principally more than 460,000 newly freed slaves, confronted a new world with hope and uncertainty.

In late June 1865 the Military Department of Georgia was established. For the state's whites and blacks, the U.S. Army provided a measure of stability, as well as much-needed food rations in some portions of the state. The soldiers' numbers during the period from 1865 to 1871 fluctuated greatly, from around 9,000 (June 1865) to more than 15,000 (September 1865), but for most of the period their numbers totaled less than 1,000.

Presidential Reconstruction, 1865–1866

In mid-June 1865 U.S. president Andrew Johnson appointed as provisional governor of Georgia James Johnson, a Columbus Unionist who had "sat out" the war. Following Governor Johnson's directive (and President Johnson's Reconstruction plan), elections were held for delegates to a constitutional convention that met in late October 1865 in the capital at Milledgeville. Voters—restricted to white adult males who would take a loyalty oath—numbered only some 50,000 in a state in which 107,000 had cast votes in the prewar presidential election of 1860.

Under the leadership of original antisecessionist Herschel Johnson, the convention's delegates framed a state constitution that repealed the Ordinance of Secession, abolished slavery, and repudiated the Confederate debt. Otherwise, the framers made few changes to the constitution of 1861. Major alterations included a prohibition of interracial marriage and a limit on the term of governorship to two two-year terms.

Charles Jones Jenkins, most noted for his defiance of military authority while governor of Reconstruction Georgia from 1865 to 1868, was also a prominent political figure in the Whig Party during the antebellum period and a justice of the state supreme court during the war.—From online entry "Charles Jones Jenkins"

WWW.GEORGIAENCYCLOPEDIA.ORG

On November 15, 1865, Georgians elected a new governor, congressmen, and state legislators. The balloting, though not subject to the restrictions of the earlier vote for convention delegates, yielded a dismal turnout of only 38,000 voters. Voters repudiated most Unionist candidates and elected to office many ex-Confederates, though several of these—including the new governor, old-line Whig Charles Jones Jenkins—had originally opposed secession, had sought and secured pardons at war's end, and had sworn allegiance to the United States.

In early December 1865 the Georgia General Assembly ratified the Thirteenth Amendment to the U.S. Constitution, which ended slavery. The Union's war aims of unification and emancipation having been met, President Johnson returned the government of Georgia to its elected officials on December 20. The legislature selected the state's two U.S. senators in January 1866, paving the way for Georgia's participation in national deliberations for the first time since 1861. The legislators' choices—Alexander Stephens and Herschel Johnson—created a political firestorm in Washington, D.C., however. Undeniably ex-Confederates (vice president and senator of the Confederacy, respectively), both were also popular, seasoned, and moderate statesmen. The North singled out Stephens as the most flagrant example of the defiance and recalcitrance of Georgia and the South. Neither he nor Johnson nor any of Georgia's House delegation were allowed to take their seats.

Georgia's Freed Populace

At the time, politics seemed a luxury few Georgians could afford. Along with its crippled agrarian economy, Reconstruction Georgia faced daunting challenges relating to labor. During harvest time in 1865, many of the emancipated slaves tested the limits of their freedom. Flocking to towns, where they encountered overcrowding and a shortage of food, large numbers of blacks fell prey to epidemic diseases. Meanwhile, on farms and plantations that had depended on slave labor, harvests were small, with poor planning and miserable weather further diminishing them. Corn and wheat were scarce in late 1865. The state's traditional money crop, cotton, plummeted in 1865 to around 50,000 bales from a high in 1860 of more than 700,000 bales.

Complicating the situation, rumors suggested that the freed slaves would soon be given freeholds and plowing animals. The widely anticipated "forty acres and a mule" for former slaves stemmed from Union general William T. Sherman's Special Field Order No. 15, issued from Savannah in January 1865. Under that order, federal authorities confiscated "abandoned lands" along the coast and distributed them to freed slaves. This distribution proved temporary, however, as most of the land was soon restored to its original owners. Nonetheless, some black families were able to buy or lease land from the government.

In the fall of 1865 the Freedmen's Bureau became active in administering the land program in Georgia and returned much black labor to the fields, mediating a contract-labor system between white landowners and their black workers, many of whom were their former slaves. Labor would never be the same, however. Field work—once the province of entire black families—was transformed as the freedwomen withdrew their labor and their children's labor to the household. Both children and adults began to take advantage of educational opportunities, usually offered by teachers from the North. Often education was associated with the burgeoning number of all-black churches that also characterized Reconstruction.

White Georgians looked askance at many of these changes. Many interpreted emancipation in antebellum terms, assuming that the freed slaves would enjoy only the limited freedom of the prewar period's "free persons of color." With assumptions of white supremacy still prevalent, there was little talk of the freedpeople as fellow citizens, much less as voters.

Nonetheless, the Georgia General Assembly of 1865–66 treated the black population as more than a labor source. Among the ex-Confederate states, Georgia stood alone in not creating a harsh Black Code. Though labor problems were partially addressed by controversial but color-blind laws relating to vagrancy, enticement, and apprenticeship, the freed slaves were also afforded what has been described as "practical civil equality." They had access to the courts in being able to make and enforce contracts, to sue and to be sued. They also gained property rights, which meant they could buy, sell, inherit, and lease both land and personal property. They were not to be subjected to any punishment or penalty that did not apply to whites as well. Their marriages and children were legitimized. Nonetheless, important rights were also denied, particularly some that Republicans argued endangered the freedpeople's security: they had no right to serve as jurors or to vote, and they could not testify against whites in court.

The End of Presidential Reconstruction

President Johnson's Reconstruction program had begun during a lengthy congressional adjournment that extended from March to December 1865. When the Thirty-ninth Congress convened at the end of the year, the Radical Republicans argued that Johnson had exceeded his power in restoring the former Confederate states, all of which but Tennessee they considered unworthy of restoration. Determining to start Reconstruction anew, the Republican majority in Congress created a Joint Committee on Reconstruction that held hearings from January to June 1866 on conditions in the former Confederacy.

The committee reported two portentous pieces of legislation. One—the proposed Fourteenth Amendment to the U.S. Constitution—in its most concise form made the freed slaves citizens. But it also contained numerous other provisions. These included office-holding disabilities and disenfranchisement for many white Southerners, along with incentives for states either to grant black voting rights or proportionally lose representation in Congress. The other bill, the First Reconstruction Act, called for placing the South under military occupation.

Since this legislation appeared several months before the off-year elections, President Johnson's supporters and opponents campaigned vigorously in late summer 1866. In August 1866, Georgia's white conservatives sent Alexander Stephens, Confederate general John B. Gordon, and other delegates to the National Union Convention in Philadelphia. The convention assailed the Fourteenth Amendment and the Reconstruction Act and championed Johnson's policies, hoping to turn the Radicals out of Congress in 1866 and return Johnson to office in 1868.

In response, the Southern Loyalists' Convention assembled in Philadelphia in September, with delegates including Georgia Radical George

Ashburn of Columbus. The convention supported the Fourteenth Amendment and argued for the continuation of Reconstruction in the South. Both conventions did agree on one issue: neither favored black suffrage. Johnson's own campaigning failed disastrously. The Republicans swept the November elections, and the president's power was permanently broken.

Congressional Reconstruction, 1867–1868

When the Georgia legislature met after the election in November 1866, it almost unanimously rejected the Fourteenth Amendment. The negative report of the joint legislative committee argued that if Georgia was not a state, its legislature had no role in ratifying amendments, and that if Georgia was a state the amendment had not been placed before it constitutionally. After its Christmas adjournment, this assembly never reconvened, and in March 1867 the First Reconstruction Act passed Congress. Georgia, together with Alabama and Florida, became part of the Third Military District, supervised by General John Pope.

As directed by Congress, General Pope registered Georgia's eligible white and black voters, 95,214 and 93,457 respectively. From October 29 through November 2, 1867, an election was held for delegates to another constitutional convention, which would meet from December 1867 into March 1868. General Pope directed the convention to meet at the Atlanta City Hall, which was convenient to his headquarters, since Milledgeville was considered less accessible, and its press was thoroughly anti-Republican. As the Atlanta convention met, a two-day Conservative Convention assembled in Macon to attack Radical policies and to decry black political participation.

In January 1868 Governor Jenkins, having reestablished state credit and stabilized Georgia's finances, protested as illegal and unconstitutional General Pope's $40,000 draft on the state treasury to pay convention expenses. Removed by Pope's successor, General George G. Meade, Jenkins was replaced by a military governor, General Thomas Ruger. Simultaneous with Ruger's administration (January–July 1868), the impeachment, trial, and near-conviction of President Andrew Johnson took place in Washington.

By March the 169 convention delegates in Atlanta, including 37 blacks, had framed a new state constitution that fulfilled the demands of the First Reconstruction Act, including a provision for black voting.

The constitution also called for the establishment of a free public school system, provided for debt relief, gave wives control of their property, increased the governor's term to four years, and moved the seat of state government from Milledgeville to Atlanta.

A vote on ratification of the constitution and for state officers and U.S. congressmen was held in April, following the sensational murder of Ashburn after he returned home to Columbus. In the gubernatorial race, the Republican candidate, Rufus Bullock, defeated the Democratic candidate John B. Gordon (83,527 to 76,356), with the new constitution approved by a vote of 88,172 to 70,200. In the elections for the General Assembly, 84 Republicans (29 of them black) fell 3 seats short of a majority of the 172 House seats. In the state senate, however, the Republicans (3 of them black) took control, with 27 seats to the Democrats' 17 seats.

Carpetbaggers and Scalawags

In 1868 the terms *carpetbagger* and *scalawag* became preeminent in Georgia politics. Coined by white conservatives, the terms were used to describe the two major groups of white Republicans allied with the far more numerous black Republicans. Carpetbaggers were Northerners who came south after the war to seek their fortune through politics, under a system in which a one-year residence in any Southern state brought voting and office-holding rights. Scalawags were Southern-born white Republicans or, by a broader definition, any white Republicans who had lived in the South before the war.

By these definitions, Georgia's Republican government was more scalawag than carpetbagger, particularly since it sent scalawags, rather than carpetbaggers, to Congress. Governor Bullock, though a New York native, was not a carpetbagger, having moved to Augusta in 1859 and having served as a Confederate quartermaster officer. The murdered Ashburn had also been a scalawag. The state's arch-scalawag, former Democratic governor Joseph E. Brown, became a Republican in 1868 and exercised much power in his new party. Georgia's major carpetbagger, Union veteran John Emory Bryant of Maine, had come south as a Freedmen's Bureau official and newspaper publisher.

The term Ku Klux Klan also gained currency in 1868 to describe what the Republicans considered to be the terrorist wing of the Democratic Party: night riders who acted to suppress Republicans of all races and origins. According to most historians, the Klan's debut in Georgia had been the Ashburn killing in Columbus, and its "Grand Dragon" was none other than Gordon.

Black Republicans, particularly their leaders, served as the principal target of the Klan. Arguably foremost among these targets were Henry McNeal Turner and Tunis Campbell. Turner was a Union chaplain during the war and a minister in the African Methodist Episcopal (AME) Church. Working first among the freed slaves as a minister, he soon became their political leader, promoting the Republican Party, as did many other AME preachers. Campbell, a New Jersey native, settled in McIntosh County after the war, organized an association of black landholders along the coast, and registered black voters. Both men served as delegates to the constitutional convention in 1867 and were elected to the Georgia legislature in July 1868.

That month proved momentous in Georgia Reconstruction: the newly elected General Assembly ratified the Fourteenth Amendment, Republican governor Bullock was inaugurated to a four-year term, and Georgia was readmitted to the Union. But during late July, the Democrats convened in Atlanta to ratify the nomination of the anti-Reconstruction candidacy of Horatio Seymour. At the city's Bush Arbor Rally, "the largest political mass meeting ever held in Georgia," prominent Georgia Democrats—including Robert Toombs and Howell Cobb—attacked Congressional Reconstruction in a series of passionate speeches. They reserved special contempt for newly converted Republican Joseph E. Brown, lately a delegate to the Chicago convention that had nominated Union general Ulysses S. Grant for president.

During the April 1868 campaign, Brown had argued that the new constitution did not confer office-holding rights on blacks. Consequently, in July, the General Assembly's Democrats and their white Republican allies began a campaign to expel the black legislators. Although Turner, Campbell, and other black colleagues in the House and Senate had argued against purging obvious ex-Confederates from the General Assembly, they nonetheless were removed from the body themselves in September 1868. A week later in the south Georgia town of Camilla, in an incident known today as the Camilla Massacre, a confrontation preceding a black Republican rally ended in violence and death, with some twelve blacks killed and several whites wounded.

These developments led to calls for Georgia's return to military rule, which increased when Georgia became one of only two ex-Confederate states to vote against Grant in the presidential election of 1868. In March 1869 Governor Bullock, seeking to prolong Reconstruction, "engineered" the defeat of the Fifteenth Amendment. That same month the U.S. Congress once again barred Georgia's representatives from their seats. Military rule resumed throughout the state in December 1869.

The Bullock Administration

From the beginning, white conservatives tarred the Bullock regime with charges of fraud, corruption, and general malfeasance. Many of these charges revolved around Bullock's friend Hannibal I. Kimball, whose Atlanta opera house was converted into the new state capitol building and whose railroad activities drew scrutiny. Other accusations involved Foster Blodgett, Bullock's political ally and fellow member of the "Augusta Ring," who was pilloried for alleged plundering as superintendent of the state's Western and Atlantic Railroad.

The Republican Party in Georgia encountered other difficulties in attempting to create lasting power. The Republicans themselves were split by discord, breaking into pro-administration and anti-Bullock camps, the latter prominently including such leaders as Bryant and Amos T. Akerman, who became U.S. attorney general in 1870. Bullock's calls for continued military occupation formed a major point of disagreement. Additionally, a permanent working majority, white and black, never emerged, and black politicians never felt that they were given a fair share of power or patronage. Nonetheless, Georgia's lone black congressman of the era, Jefferson Franklin Long of Macon, served a brief term in 1870–71 and gave the first speech by a black representative ever presented before Congress. He spoke against removing restrictions on ex-Confederates holding office.

The End of Congressional Reconstruction, 1869–1871

In June 1869 in *White v. Clements*, the Supreme Court of Georgia ruled two-to-one that blacks did indeed have a constitutional right to hold office in Georgia. Ironically, one of the two deciding justices was Chief Justice Joseph E. Brown, appointed by Bullock in July 1868. In January 1870, Alfred H. Terry, the third and final commanding general of the District of Georgia, conducted "Terry's Purge." He removed the General Assembly's ex-Confederates, replaced them with the Republican runners-up, and then reinstated the expelled black legislators, thus creating a heavy Republican majority in the legislature. In February 1870 the newly constituted legislature ratified the Fifteenth Amendment and chose new senators to send to Washington. The following July, Georgia was again readmitted to the Union.

In December 1870 an election was held for the next General Assembly, to convene in November 1871. The Democrats won commanding majorities in both houses. Bullock's chances of completing his term now depended on his once again having Georgia remanded to military rule. He failed, and in late October 1871 he fled the state to escape impeachment. In a special election held in December, Democrat and ex-Confederate colonel James M. Smith was elected to complete Bullock's term. Consequently, as of January 1872 Georgia was fully under the control of the Redeemers, as the state's resurgent white conservative Democrats came to be known.

The Legacy of Georgia Reconstruction

By 1877, when the final remnants of Reconstruction ended elsewhere in the South as a consequence of the disputed presidential election of 1876 and the removal of federal troops, much had changed in Georgia. Joseph E. Brown, Democrat again and soon-to-be U.S. senator, was increasing the profits of his northwest Georgia coal mines by using the convict lease system, one of the least humane innovations of Reconstruction. Brown's sometime ally and business partner, Bullock, had recently been tried and acquitted and had embarked on a new Atlanta career that would include the presidency of the Chamber of Commerce. Charges against him and his administration, however, would lead the Democratic Redeemers to draft a new state constitution in 1877 that restricted legislative and gubernatorial power and instituted severe financial retrenchment. Democratic strength in Georgia would increase with time, making the state a reliable component of the Solid South. No Republican would again occupy the Georgia governor's chair until 2003, when Sonny Perdue took office.

Black Georgia voters, first manipulated, were ultimately disfranchised, beginning in the 1890s. The last black member of the General Assembly, W. H. Rogers, resigned in 1907 as the final representative of the Reconstruction-era coastal Georgia political machine created by Campbell. Not until 1963, during the civil rights movement (also called

"Second Reconstruction" by some scholars), would another black politician, Leroy Johnson (a Democrat), enter the General Assembly, with a black Republican, Willie Talton of Warner Robins, not following until 2005.

In large part, for the masses of Georgians, black and white, the major legacy of Reconstruction would be a sharecropping life. Property taxes, which had previously fallen most heavily on slave owners, now fell on landowners, and during Reconstruction tax rates increased as well. For this and other reasons, a transformation took place. While the majority of Southern whites had owned land during the antebellum period, the majority had become landless sharecroppers by the early 1900s. Though landownership by Georgia's black farmers had grown to 13 percent by 1900, most remained sharecroppers. White and black Georgians awaited another transformation of the economy; it would take World War II (1941–45) to bring it about. Where black political rights were concerned, another Reconstruction would be necessary.

WILLIAM HARRIS BRAGG

 # Lost Cause Religion

Near the end of the Civil War, women from Columbus began to care for soldiers' graves. One of them, Lizzie Rutherford, proposed an annual observance to decorate graves, inaugurating Confederate Memorial Day. Thirty years later one of the Columbus women compared their work to that of Mary Magdalene and the other women who came to Christ's grave. This seems overblown but is really apt, for what the women in Columbus were engaged in was no less than a new form of Southern religion. Historians refer to this as Lost Cause religion, which was interdenominational and functioned as a culture religion.

The term *Lost Cause* is not a modern invention but was used by Southerners immediately after the war. Many scholars attribute the term to the Virginia journalist Edward A. Pollard and his postwar books, including *The Lost Cause: A New Southern History of the War of the Confederates* (1866). The Lost Cause concept supplied a heroic interpretation of the war so that Southerners could maintain their sense of honor. As Georgian Clement Evans, a war veteran, put it, "If we cannot justify the South in the act of Secession, we will go down in History solely as a brave, impulsive but rash people who attempted in an illegal manner to overthrow the Union of our Country." The assertion of the Lost Cause was the solution.

The argument of the Lost Cause insists that the South fought nobly and against all odds not to preserve slavery but entirely for other reasons, such as the rights of states to govern themselves, and that Southerners were forced to defend themselves against Northern aggression. When the idea of a Southern nation was defeated on the battlefield, the vision of a separate Southern people, with a distinct and noble cultural character, remained. The term *culture religion* refers to ideals that a given group of people desire to strengthen or restore, and Lost Cause religion sought to maintain the concept of a distinct, and superior, white Southern culture against perceived attacks. Major components of religion include myth, symbol, and their expressions through rituals. The Lost Cause culture religion manifested all three.

When scholars of religion refer to myth, they do not mean to imply a falsehood. Rather, in the context of religious studies, a myth is a foundational or sacred story, a story that explains. Lost Cause proponents knew well the power of myth. The main components of the Lost Cause myth, repeated in writings, sermons, lectures, and speeches by scores of postwar Southern figures, are easily identified. First, the prewar South—the Old South—was a place of nobility and chivalry. (There is no better capsule description of the Old South of the Lost Cause myth than the opening words of the movie version of *Gone With the Wind*, with its elegiac reference to the now-vanished pretty world "of Cavaliers and Cotton Fields," where gallantry "took its last bow.")

In a second component of Lost Cause dogma, the Civil War was recast as a defense of the South against aggressive, money-grubbing Northerners. In Lost Cause mythmaking, the "War of the Rebellion" (as the federal government called it) became the "War of Northern Aggression." While Southerners were a people of honor and purity, Northerners were invaders, a people consumed by lust for power.

Finally, Lost Cause proponents preached the message that adherence to the civility of the prewar South meant that the Cause was not truly lost. Victory would come if white Southerners maintained their superior and pure culture. The South need not be separate politically to rise again spiritually. This message was spread far and wide by agents of the Lost Cause, but perhaps no voice was as persistent and vocal as that of Georgian Mildred Lewis Rutherford, the longtime historian general of

Lizzie Rutherford is credited as the originator of Confederate Memorial Day. Her idea that a special day should be set aside in order to decorate Confederate soldiers' graves and thereby honor them in perpetuity was inspired by *The Initials*, a novel by Baroness von Tautphoeus that mentions the custom of caring for the graves of dead heroes.—From online entry "Lizzie Rutherford"

WWW.GEORGIAENCYCLOPEDIA.ORG

the United Daughters of the Confederacy, who tirelessly proclaimed the glories of the Old South. Her 1920 book, *Truths of History*, promotes a Lost Cause interpretation of the Civil War in opposition to what Rutherford viewed as the false claims of Northern historians.

Some of the major symbols of the Lost Cause are conveniently laid out in a Memorial Day address given in 1896 by north Georgian Clement Evans, who, in addition to being a veteran, was also a Methodist minister and onetime commander of the United Confederate Veterans. Evans referred to "a deep and honorable respect for some things which we call our mementoes"; they are, he said, "sacred." Limiting himself to "only three, each of which deserves our perpetual commemorations," he listed the song "Dixie," the Confederate battle flag, and the gray uniform of the South.

To Evans's list may be added the living symbols of the Lost Cause, the Confederate soldiers themselves and their heroic leaders. Jefferson Davis, Robert E. Lee, and Thomas J. "Stonewall" Jackson each played a major role in the hagiography of the Lost Cause and provided Moses and Christ figures. (These three figures are carved into Stone Mountain.) There was also a figure of evil in Lost Cause religion. Several Lost Cause proponents accused Georgian James Longstreet of losing the war by his actions at Gettysburg. In the process Longstreet became identified as a Judas-like figure (and, therefore, though he had been Lee's senior subordinate officer, numerous United Confederate Veterans groups refused to acknowledge his death with the customary wreaths or statements).

In addition to Confederate Memorial Day, "the Sabbath of the South," additional rituals honored Confederate veterans, especially the erection of Confederate monuments, which served as reminders of the Lost Cause throughout the year and as focal points for cultural memory. The historian Gaines M. Foster has identified 94 Confederate monuments that were erected in the South by 1885 (a further 406 were added by 1912). Some of the oldest of these monuments are in Georgia, such as the pillar in downtown Athens, which was erected in 1872. Perhaps the most storied Confederate monuments in the state are in Savannah, Atlanta, and Augusta. The Augusta monument contains what may be the most common inscription on Georgia's Confederate monuments: "No nation rose so white and fair: None fell so pure of crime"—a Lost Cause sentiment to be sure.

Such, then, are the major components of Lost Cause myth, symbols, and rituals. In 1900 J. William Jones, a Baptist minister known as the "Evangelist of the Lost Cause," gave a sermon to a veteran group in which he asked those assembled if "when the roll is called up yonder," they would be prepared to "'cross over the river and rest under the shade of the trees' with Davis and Lee and Jackson and other Christian comrades who wait and watch for your coming?" In Jones's mind, to be a Confederate hero and pious was a guaranteed combination.

DAVID S. WILLIAMS

Confederate Veteran Organizations

Confederate veteran organizations were formed to alleviate and address many of the challenges facing former soldiers and their communities in the aftermath of the Civil War. The objectives of these organizations included burying and commemorating dead soldiers; caring for cemeteries; providing aid to widows, orphans, and indigent veterans; and preserving the Confederate interpretation of the war's history (often referred to as Lost Cause ideology).

These organizations later served an important social function by helping veterans maintain ties to those with whom they had served, both through reunions and through such magazines as *Confederate Veteran*, which was founded in Nashville, Tennessee, in 1893 and published until 1932.

Early Organizations

Founded in 1865, the Oglethorpe Light Infantry Association in Savannah was one of Georgia's earliest military veteran organizations. Organized by "company," "regiment," or "brigade," military-type organizations served as one of the best ways to reunite men who had served together in the war.

A number of local organizations were established in the late 1870s and throughout the 1880s. In 1878 Augusta-area veterans formed the Confederate Survivors' Association (CSA), under the leadership of Stewart County native Clement Evans. Like many of the other early veteran groups, the CSA sought to encourage friendship among veterans, to protect memories of the past, to promote the practice of "manly virtues," and to provide for sick and indigent veterans. Despite these broadly defined objectives, the CSA functioned primarily as a memorial society in its early years.

In 1861 **Clement Evans** resigned as state senator and joined the Confederate army as a private. Wounded five times (twice severely), he rose to command the Thirty-first Georgia Infantry (Bartow Guards) and fought in the Shenandoah campaign and in nearly every major battle of the Army of Northern Virginia. In 1864 Evans was promoted to brigadier general.—From online entry "Clement Evans"

WWW.GEORGIAENCYCLOPEDIA.ORG

The Fulton County Confederate Veterans' Association formed on April 20, 1886, at the Fulton County courthouse in Atlanta. Originally consisting of 182 members, the organization was led by a mission similar to that of the Augusta association and in addition sought to compile a "true" history of the war as its members had known it. The association's earliest members included such "first citizens" of Georgia as Samuel Inman, reputedly one of the richest men in the state, and W. Lowndes Calhoun, a former mayor of Atlanta. Though not a veteran himself, Henry W. Grady, the acclaimed journalist and managing editor of the *Atlanta Constitution*, held an honorary membership.

In addition to his affiliation with the Fulton County Confederate Veterans' Association, Grady was heavily involved in the early stages of developing a Confederate soldiers' home for veterans. Grady's sudden death in 1889 and the subsequent political controversy over the site of the home led to a decade-long struggle to secure legislative approval for the project, which had by then been embraced by other veterans' and women's organizations. The home finally opened in Atlanta on June 3, 1901, the birthday of Confederate president Jefferson Davis, with forty "gray hair remnants" from twenty-six Georgia counties moving in. Though the building was destroyed by fire three months later, a new home was built and opened a year later. It remained standing until 1967 and ultimately housed around 1,200 Georgia veterans over the course of its existence.

The United Confederate Veterans

By far the largest and most influential Confederate veteran organization was the United Confederate Veterans (UCV). Founded in New Orleans, Louisiana, in 1889, the UCV was created for mostly social, charitable, and memorial functions. However, it also sought to unify the many separate organizations scattered across the former Confederate states into one larger regional body. The UCV conducted much of its activity through committees on history, relief, finance, and monuments, and it was organized hierarchically along military lines with a commander in chief, officers who held rank, and local associations known as "camps."

Georgia native John B. Gordon, former Confederate general and head of the Georgia Veterans' Association, was elected the UCV's first commander in chief. In addition to his administrative duties as commander, Gordon presided over the conventions, oversaw the formation of new member groups, and served as the spokesman for the organization. Many saw Gordon's leadership of the UCV as representing a significant shift away from the Virginia-dominated leadership and agendas of the early postwar years. Some Southerners found Gordon's priorities too slanted toward reconciliation efforts with the North, but he remained very popular with the rank and file and maintained his position as commander in chief until his death in 1904. Clement Evans, a UCV founder, headed the Georgia chapter for twelve years and served as commander in chief from 1908 to 1910.

Auxiliary Groups

By 1890 Georgians made up nearly 11 percent of living Confederate veterans, with only Virginians and Texans registering higher numbers, and 88 percent of Georgia counties had individual UCV "camps," one of the highest rates in the South. Many of these camps formed auxiliary groups that included other members of veterans' families. Katharine Du Pre Lumpkin, whose father was an early leader in Georgia's veteran activities, describes such roles in her autobiography, *The Making of a Southerner* (1947): "My mother and older sister were 'Daughters of the Confederacy'; my brothers, as each grew old enough, [were] 'Sons of Confederate Veterans'; we who were the youngest [were] 'Children of the Confederacy.'"

In 1896 male descendants of veterans organized their own association independent of the UCV. The organization was originally called the

United Sons of Confederate Veterans, but concern that it might be confused with the United States Colored Volunteers, which shared the acronym USCV, led its members to drop "United" to become the Sons of Confederate Veterans (SCV).

Reunions

The earliest veteran reunions tended to be local. Lumpkin claimed that the first regimental reunion of Confederates in the South was an 1874 gathering of Third Georgia Regiment veterans in Union Point, in Greene County. The reunion was organized by her father, who had served with that unit.

Over the history of the UCV, annual national reunions were held in nearly thirty cities, almost all in the South. In addition, "Blue-Gray," or combined, reunions of Confederate and Union veterans were held several times. These were encouraged by John B. Gordon and others as an effective means of demonstrating reconciliation between the North and the South. Individual states also held their own UCV division reunions, at which delegates to the national reunions were elected. While Chattanooga, Tennessee, and Richmond, Virginia, hosted the greatest number of national reunions, Atlanta hosted them in 1898, 1919, and 1941, with an additional Blue-Gray reunion there in 1900. Macon, the only other city in Georgia to host a national reunion, held the 1912 event.

The reunions came to have such a strong religious tone, opening with prayers and usually including a memorial service for the deceased, that the Chaplains' Association was made an official auxiliary group at the 1898 meeting in Atlanta, which had more than 60,000 in attendance.

Attendance at Confederate reunions began to diminish by the early twentieth century. The last national UCV reunion was held in 1951 in Norfolk, Virginia. At the time, only twelve Confederate veterans were known to be living. Three attended the reunion, including William Joshua Bush from Fitzgerald.

Historical Mission

One particular area in which the UCV took great interest was the remembrance and interpretation of the war. Members of the UCV's history committee sought to recognize those books that they believed treated the Confederacy fairly and to condemn those that did not. In 1892, for example, the UCV approved only nine texts, all written by Southerners, as appropriate for use in Southern classrooms. The UCV denounced history books that depicted Confederates as rebels or traitors and lobbied text-book companies to use the phrase "Civil War between the states" instead of "war of rebellion."

Equally as strong a priority was the collection and preservation of soldiers' own memories of their war experience. The Southern Historical Society (SHS) was founded in New Orleans in 1869 primarily as a means of collecting firsthand testimonials by former Confederates. Even earlier, Charles C. Jones Jr. of Savannah began collecting Confederate service records and reminiscences of former soldiers, and he continued to do so until the 1880s. Though he never wrote a history of the Confederacy, as was his original intention, he often drew on his collection of testimonials for the frequent speeches he made to veteran groups throughout the state. His efforts prompted many veterans to write book-length memoirs and reminiscences of their war years.

FRANKLIN C. SAMMONS JR.

 # United Daughters of the Confederacy

The Georgia division of the United Daughters of the Confederacy (UDC) was formed on November 8, 1895. Initially, the UDC worked both to maintain the beliefs of the Lost Cause, a heroic interpretation of the Civil War that allowed Southerners to maintain their sense of honor, and to build monuments in honor of Confederate heroes. Its members also aimed to preserve Southern culture. The organization rapidly grew to include chapters in almost every town across the state, and it connected many middle- and upper-class white women across the South with one another.

Origins

On September 10, 1894, Caroline Meriwether Goodlett, from Nashville, Tennessee, and Anna Davenport Raines, from Savannah, founded the

National Association of the Daughters of the Confederacy. As a national federation of Confederate women's organizations, the group brought together numerous women's associations working to memorialize the Confederacy. At its second meeting, held in Atlanta, the group renamed itself the United Daughters of the Confederacy and revised its constitution. In 1895 the four chapters of Savannah, Augusta, Atlanta, and Covington united to form the Georgia Division of the UDC.

Positions within the national organization of the UDC included a president general, vice president general, recording secretary general, and historian general and were filled with women from various states. With its tight connections to powerful Southern politicians, the UDC attracted a sizable and influential membership. Women who could prove they were blood descendants of those who honorably served the Confederacy were eligible to join.

The UDC established five objectives delineating their memorial, historical, educational, benevolent, and patriotic responsibilities. Among other goals, UDC members strove to present what they considered to be a truthful history of the Civil War, to honor the Confederate dead, and to preserve historic Confederate sites.

Georgia's UDC in Action

Prominent women have been affiliated with the Georgia Division of the UDC since its founding. Although Lizzie Rutherford did not live long enough to be part of the UDC, she is nonetheless closely associated with the organization. In 1898 the Lizzie Rutherford Chapter of Columbus took the name of the local citizen who had pioneered the practice of decorating Confederate soldiers' graves in the years immediately after the war. This annual event became known as Confederate Memorial Day, and UDC members joined thousands of people all across the South to visit graves, decorate headstones with flowers, and hold eulogy services.

Rebecca Latimer Felton, from Cartersville, spoke to UDC chapters throughout Georgia on a crusade to educate farm women in 1897. Aiming to empower poor whites as well as sustain

Rebecca Latimer Felton was the first woman sworn into the U.S. Senate. Appointed in 1922 to fill a vacant seat, she did not actually "serve," because a special election was held to fill the seat before the next session opened. Felton is also the South's best-known and most effective champion of woman suffrage in the early twentieth century.—From online entry "Rebecca Latimer Felton"

WWW.GEORGIAENCYCLOPEDIA.ORG

notions of white supremacy, Felton argued that although farm women were not cultured like members of the UDC, they too were the descendents of Confederate veterans. She believed that rural girls, as future mothers of the white race, needed assistance and education.

In 1898 another influential UDC member, Mary Ann Lamar Cobb Erwin of Athens, the daughter of Howell Cobb, envisioned a way to honor Confederate veterans. She combined her efforts with those of Atlanta's Sarah Gabbett to design the Cross of Honor medal, which was first bestowed by the Athens chapter of the UDC on Erwin's husband, Captain Alexander S. Erwin, in 1900. Nationally, the UDC bestowed thousands of crosses to veterans for honorable service. They continue to present medals to libraries for display today.

Athens native Mildred Lewis Rutherford was probably the most prominent member of the UDC. Rutherford led a crusade for what she believed to be the true history of the Confederacy in the late nineteenth and early twentieth centuries. Strongly opposed to woman suffrage, Rutherford argued that the ideal woman should be deferential to men and remain in the home. She believed that all women should hold the plantation mistress as a role model. In addition to defending secession, Rutherford glorified both the plantation system and slavery in antebellum Georgia. The textbooks she wrote, as well as her choice of which books to censor, serve as a testament to a Confederate history that attempted to legitimize the control of Southern elites. From 1899 to 1902 Rutherford served as the Georgia Division's president, and from 1911 to 1916 she served as historian general of the national organization.

Around 1915 Caroline Helen Jemison Plane, the president of the UDC Atlanta chapter, began the project that would culminate in the Confederate memorial carving on Stone Mountain. As leader of the Stone Mountain Memorial Association (incorporated in 1916 as the Stone Mountain Confederate Monumental Association), she solicited the support of the sculptor Gutzon Borglum and convinced the owners of the mountain to give the UDC access to the property. In addition to the carving of Confederate heroes, Plane wanted Ku Klux Klan members to appear in the design. Controversies, sculptor changes, funding problems, and the outbreaks of World War I (1917–18) and World War II (1941–45) forced the construction project to spread across decades.

From 1953 to 1955 Mabel Sessions Dennis served as president general of the national UDC. Born in De Soto, in Sumter County, she held many positions in the group before leading the national organization. During her administration she organized the national (General) Children of the Confederacy. Comprising thousands of members today, the organization inducts children under the age of eighteen who can provide proof that they are descendants of honorable Confederate soldiers. The membership creed states a "desire to perpetuate, in love and honor, the heroic deeds of those who enlisted in the Confederate Services" and "teach the truths of history (one of the most important of which is, that the War Between the States was not a rebellion, nor was its underlying cause to sustain slavery)."

By the 100th birthday of the UDC in 1995, the national organization had elected seven Georgia women to serve as president general. In 2009 more than sixty-five Georgia divisions of the UDC existed. Although membership and activism have slightly waned in the twenty-first century, the ideals, activities, and purposes of the UDC remain the same. The organization continues to erect monuments, to oversee the Children of the Confederacy organization, and to hold memorial events. Some critics, such as historian James M. McPherson, have accused the UDC of being an organization of white supremacists and neo-Confederates. Other people champion the organization for its memorial activities and college scholarship programs.

ANGELA ESCO ELDER

COMMEMORATIVE SITES AND ACTIVITIES

Tour buses at Stone Mountain, June 29, 1929. Courtesy of Georgia Archives, Vanishing Georgia Collection, cob162b.

} Cemeteries

Both during and after the Civil War, Georgians faced the task of burying the Confederate and Union soldiers who died within the state's bounds. Many of the fallen were later reburied either in existing cemeteries or in new ones specifically dedicated to Civil War soldiers. Nearly every sizable cemetery in Georgia contains individual graves of Confederate soldiers or veterans who died after the war was over, and several have entire sections devoted to Civil War dead. A few cemeteries hold only Confederate soldiers killed in the war; the Confederate Cemetery at Resaca was the first of these to be established in Georgia.

Approximately 120,000 Georgians served the Confederacy, and many thousands of them died over the course of the conflict, with estimates varying from around 11,000 to 25,000. Within the state itself, several major battles and numerous skirmishes left both Union and Confederate soldiers dead near farms, homes, hospitals, and towns. While many soldiers died on battlefields, many more died in hospitals from wounds and disease. Though most of the dead in Georgia were Confederates, a significant number of Union soldiers died as well. Such was the case at Andersonville Prison, where the Union dead were buried on site because of an inability either to preserve corpses or to move the dead.

Many fallen soldiers remained unidentified. The corpses were often very deteriorated after battle as the result of wounds and decomposition, and many were initially buried in mass graves near where they fell. For major engagements, such as those at Chickamauga, Resaca, and Atlanta, bodies were moved to nearby existing cemeteries or to new ones created just after the fighting.

Stone monuments or obelisks were often constructed in these cemeteries to honor both individuals and full companies and regiments that suffered significant losses. In addition, the United Daughters of the Confederacy (UDC), which formed a Georgia chapter in 1895, placed iron crosses of honor on many graves throughout the state. Later, soldiers' resting places were officially

Historic African American burial grounds in Georgia are being preserved in a variety of ways. Examples of **cemetery preservation** include the separate burial sections in the city cemeteries of Decatur and Atlanta (Oakland Cemetery); Porterdale, owned and maintained by the city of Columbus; Behavior, on Sapelo Island, overseen by the Hog Hammock community; and Laurel Grove-South, the major African American cemetery in Savannah.

—From online entry "Cemetery Preservation"

WWW.GEORGIAENCYCLOPEDIA.ORG

marked with regulation government headstones, noting their service to the Confederacy.

Kingston and Cassville Cemeteries

Each cemetery in Georgia has its own history relating to local events and politics during and after the Civil War. Kingston and Cassville, both in Bartow County, for example, established Confederate cemeteries after intense fighting in that area in May 1864, during the early part of the Atlanta campaign. There are 250 unknown Confederate and 2 Union soldiers buried in Kingston. The Cassville Cemetery holds approximately 300 unknown Confederate soldiers (including a general) who died in eight local hospitals. They were buried in the town cemetery after Union general William T. Sherman's troops set fire to Cassville. The UDC placed marble headstones on all the Cassville graves in 1899.

Marietta Cemeteries

Marietta boasts both a national cemetery and a Confederate cemetery. The national cemetery contains around 10,000 Union soldiers, only 7,045 of whom are known, who died during the Atlanta campaign. The Confederate cemetery, established in 1863, is the largest of its kind in the state. It holds 3,000 soldiers who died in local hospitals, in combat during the Battle of Chickamauga or the Atlanta campaign, or in an 1863 train wreck that occurred north of Marietta. In 1902 wooden markers at the Confederate cemetery were replaced by marble headstones.

The separate cemeteries in Marietta were created because local civilians objected to enemies lying together in death. A prominent Marietta businessman, Henry Green Cole, sought a combined Confederate and Union cemetery and donated land toward the project. When local officials objected, Cole gave the land to the federal government to be used for the burial of Union casualties only, and it was designated as such in 1866.

Oakland Cemetery

Oakland Cemetery in Atlanta, established in 1850, has 6,900 Confederates buried in its grounds, including 5 generals. It is Atlanta's oldest cemetery. The first soldiers were buried at Oakland as early as September 1863, following the Battle of Chickamauga. Soldiers who died in Atlanta while seeking treatment for wounds or disease were also buried there before the Battle of Atlanta in July 1864. During the Battle of Atlanta, Union soldiers vandalized the cemetery; they stole nameplates, broke into crypts, and exhumed Confederate dead in order to place Union corpses in their coffins. Wooden markers in the cemetery were replaced by marble ones in 1890.

A well-known monument to the Confederate dead, the "Lion of Atlanta," was erected at Oakland in 1894. Confederate vice president Alexander Stephens was briefly interred there after his death in 1883, but his body was later moved to his home at Crawfordville, in Taliaferro County.

Andersonville Cemetery

One of the best-known and most visited Civil War cemeteries is the burial ground at Andersonville, where more than 13,000 Union prisoners died and were laid to rest in 1864 and 1865. Due to the efforts of nurse Clara Barton, who worked to identify and mark the graves, the Andersonville cemetery was designated a national cemetery in 1866. It is one of fourteen cemeteries in the United States managed by the National Park Service, and one of only two in which American war veterans can still be buried.

LEAH RICHIER

Confederate Monuments

Confederate memorials honor Georgians who fought for the Confederacy during the Civil War, and are located across the state, in both large cities and small communities. One of the earliest Confederate memorial services was held in April 1866 at Columbus, marking the beginning of a national movement to honor the war's dead, both Confederate and Union.

Most memorials are monuments or markers, but others take different forms. Confederate memorials in Georgia include the beautiful depictions of Georgia's military leaders and battles in the stained-glass windows at Rhodes Hall in Atlanta, as well as the carving on Stone Mountain of Robert E. Lee, Stonewall Jackson, and Jefferson Davis, which is the largest Confederate memorial in the world. Memorials to individual soldiers include the large obelisk to Captain Henry Wirz (Andersonville) and statues to generals Patrick Cleburne (Ringgold), Nathan Bedford Forrest (Rome), John B. Gordon (Atlanta), Joseph E. Johnston (Dalton), Robert E. Lee (Richmond Hill), and James Longstreet (Gainesville). Countless other memorials to individual Confederate soldiers and sailors can be found in cemeteries across the state in the form of tombstones.

John B. Gordon emerged as one of the most successful military leaders produced by the Civil War. He began his Confederate service as an untrained captain of the "Raccoon Roughs," a company of mountain men from Georgia and Alabama, and ended it four years later as a major general in command of one half of General Robert E. Lee's army.—From online entry "John B. Gordon"

WWW.GEORGIAENCYCLOPEDIA.ORG

Markers consist primarily of signs or plaques that provide information about war-related individuals or events. Located throughout the state, they include government historical markers, markers installed under the Works Progress Administration (a New Deal program instituted by U.S. president Franklin D. Roosevelt), and markers placed by organizations or individuals. Examples of federal government markers are found in Georgia at Fort Pulaski, the battlefield at Chickamauga, and Kennesaw Mountain. Numerous state markers related to the Civil War discuss troop movements, engagements, or historical sites. Examples include the birthplace marker in Coweta County for William Thomas Overby, who is known as the "Confederate Nathan Hale," and the marker in Augusta's Magnolia Cemetery for the burial location of seven Confederate generals from Georgia.

Characteristics of Monuments

Georgia's Confederate monuments are made from a variety of materials, including fieldstone, marble, sandstone, granite, iron, and bronze, and are designed in a wide range of styles. The most common style is a shaft supported by a pedestal and topped by the figure of a Confederate soldier, but other styles include obelisks, columns, boulders, arches, tablets, cenotaphs, fountains, benches, and even one totem pole.

Inscriptions, ranging from the simple to the poetic to the highly political, grace Georgia's monuments. "Lest We Forget" or "Our Confederate Dead" are examples of simple sentiments found on numerous monuments. Typical expressions of extended sentiments include poet Theodore O'Hara's lines, "On fame's eternal camping ground / Their silent tents are spread, / And glory guards, with solemn round / The bivouac of the dead," which is found on the Colquitt County monument in Moultrie; and "They struggled for constitutional government as established by our Fathers and though defeated, they left to posterity and record [*sic*] of honor and glory more valuable than power or riches," found on the Randolph County monument in Cuthbert. Other monuments, especially some newer ones, list the names of men who were either native to or buried within the county in which the monument stands. Fine examples of this type are found in Blairsville (Union County), Carrollton, Dalton, Dawsonville (Dawson County), Elberton, LaFayette (Walker County), and Springfield (Effingham County).

Monument Construction

The construction of monuments began soon after the war, but most communities, financially wrecked by the conflict, had little money with which to honor the fallen. By 1900 three organizations, beginning with the Ladies Memorial Association and followed by the United Daughters of the Confederacy and the United Confederate Veterans, had undertaken a movement across the South to honor the veterans. These groups began to raise funds for monuments through bake sales, variety shows, lotteries, publication sales, donations, and socials.

Monuments were originally placed in a town's most prestigious location, such as along a major thoroughfare, on the grounds of the courthouse or city hall, or in a cemetery. Over the years, however, mostly due to changing traffic patterns, many monuments have been moved to safer locations; the monument in Albany has been moved at least four times.

The state's first dedicated monument, constructed to the memory of "Our Boys in Gray," was erected by the Linwood Sunday School in June 1866 and is located at Fort Gordon, outside Augusta. Although at least two other states claim the first Confederate monument, the monument at Fort Gordon predates both. One of the oldest monuments in Georgia is the chimney of Augusta's Confederate Powder Works, which was dedicated as a Confederate monument in 1872 to save it from demolition. The first large monument, the angel monument at Stonewall Cemetery in Griffin (Spalding County), was dedicated in 1869. About twenty-five monuments appeared during the nineteenth century, including those in Athens, Atlanta, Augusta, Columbus, Elberton, Macon, and Savannah. The monument in Elberton helped to begin a multimillion-dollar granite industry.

More than sixty monuments were built and dedicated during the first two decades of the twentieth century. These include many of the typical pedestal-shaft-soldier monuments found throughout Georgia. Examples exist in Brunswick, Cedartown (Polk County), Covington, Dublin, Eatonton, Gainesville, and Marietta. The first Confederate monument to women of the Confederacy was dedicated in Rome in 1910. The construction of new monuments waned in the first half of the twentieth century due to the hardships brought by World War I (1917–18), the Great Depression, and World War II (1941–45). From 1920 until 1980 approximately twenty-five monuments were dedicated in Georgia, including those in Canton, Commerce (Jackson County), Fairburn (Fulton County), and Toccoa (Stephens County), as well as the Confederate totem pole, which no longer exists, in Hall County at Blackshear Place.

A resurgence of interest in Confederate monuments, mainly among local chapters of the Sons of Confederate Veterans, resulted in the dedication of around thirty monuments between 1980 and 2005. Fine examples of the colorful monuments completed during this time period can be found in Colbert (Madison County), Chickamauga, Cumming, and Lawrenceville.

DAVID N. WIGGINS

 # Cyclorama

"Cyclorama" is the name given to the huge, late-nineteenth-century painting depicting the Civil War battle fought July 22, 1864, east of Atlanta. Housed in Atlanta's Grant Park and owned by the city, the Cyclorama is a national tourist attraction and cultural treasure. It is one of only two cycloramas in the United States, and at 42 feet tall and 358 feet in circumference, it is the largest painting in the country.

Cycloramic murals—building-sized paintings hung circularly for viewing from the inside—were a European innovation of the late nineteenth century. Frenchman Paul Philippoteaux supervised the painting of a cyclorama of the Battle of Gettysburg, which came to this country in 1884 and remains a prominent attraction at the Gettysburg National Military Park.

German artists also produced cycloramas, such as those depicting battles of the Franco-Prussian War. A number of them were recruited to America in 1883 by William Wehner of Milwaukee, who ran the American Panorama Company, dedicated to cycloramic art. Thirteen artists painted *The Battle of Missionary Ridge* in 1883–84 and then turned to the Battle of Atlanta as the subject for their next mural. The company's choice of subject was influenced by one patron, the Republican Illinois senator John A. Logan, who ran unsuccessfully for vice president in 1884 and was rumored to be a candidate for the presidential nomination in 1888. A former Union general, Logan commanded the Fifteenth Corps in the Battle of Atlanta and assumed command of the Army of the Tennessee after the death of General James B. McPherson.

Grant Park, Atlanta's first city-owned public park, is located on land that formed part of the field for the 1864 Battle of Atlanta. A Confederate battery, with a commanding position on the crown of a hill, was located on the battleground, along with Old Fort Walker and Confederate entrenchments.—From online entry "Grant Park"

WWW.GEORGIAENCYCLOPEDIA.ORG

In the summer of 1885 the Milwaukee artists came to Atlanta for field study. Twenty years after the war, histories of the battle were in print, but the artists received most of the technical advice from Union and Confederate veterans. Assisting was Theodore Davis, wartime illustrator for *Harper's Weekly*, who had followed General William T. Sherman's armies. With trench lines outside Atlanta still extant, the artists fixed as the point of reference a site just inside Union lines at the Georgia Railroad, running eastward from the city. From a forty-foot tower they studied the terrain and sketched layouts. After several months on site, they returned to their Milwaukee studio, where, supervised by F. W. Heine and August Lohr, the artists—all specialists in landscapes, figures, and animals—completed the painting.

At its debut in Detroit in February 1887, the work was billed as "Logan's Great Battle" (although the senator had died three months before). The heavy canvases were draped on wooden frames, which were moved and reassembled at Minneapolis and then Indianapolis, where the Cyclorama opened in May 1888. Wehner sold the painting to an Indianapolis art exhibit company, which in turn sold it in 1890 to Paul Atkinson of Madison, Georgia.

Atkinson, already the owner of the *Missionary Ridge* cyclorama, sent the Atlanta painting to Chattanooga, Tennessee, and brought the former to Atlanta, exhibiting it in a circular building on Edgewood Avenue until February 1892. *Missionary Ridge* then traveled to Nashville, Tennessee, where it was later destroyed in a hurricane; in its place, *The Battle of Atlanta* opened in Atlanta on February 22, 1892. Resale to various owners led to its purchase at the Edgewood Avenue exhibition hall by Atlanta businessman George V. Gress, who donated the painting to the city in March 1898 after providing it with housing in Grant Park. Grant Park is a public park established in 1883 and named for Atlantan Lemuel P. Grant, the donor of the park land, who as a Confederate engineer had surveyed for the fortifications around Atlanta.

The painting takes in a wide sweep of the area: the skyline of Atlanta, Kennesaw Mountain, Stone Mountain, and the smoke of a cavalry fight at Decatur. Details of the battle are as if the viewer stood just inside the Fifteenth Corps lines at about 4:30 p.m. on July 22. Near the Troup Hurt House, a two-story, red-brick building (destroyed during the war and placed erroneously by the artists too near the railroad), Confederates have broken through the Union lines and are resisting a Union counterattack. Farther off is Sherman's headquarters at the house owned by Hurt's brother Augustus, on the site of which is now the Carter Center. There Sherman is about to receive the ambulance carrying General McPherson's body. A prominent figure is the man who commissioned the painting, General John "Blackjack" Logan, galloping heroically to the battlefront ahead of reinforcements that will restore his lines. The painting also shows more distant fighting on other parts of the battlefield, especially Confederate attacks on the hill held by General Mortimer Leggett (an area now bisected by Interstate 20 at Moreland Avenue).

The Cyclorama has been housed at Grant Park since the 1890s. In 1921 a new building, designed by Atlanta architect John Francis Downing, took in the painting and, six years later, the locomotive *Texas*, famous in the Andrews Raid of 1862. In 1934–36, funded by the Works Progress Administration, artists Weis Snell, Joseph Llorens, and Wilbur Kurtz fashioned plaster figures for a diorama as foreground for the painting. Set on a flooring of red clay, the shrubbery, cannon, track, and 128 soldiers (twenty inches to fifty inches tall, to fit in perspective with the scale of the painting), give the painting more realism and extend it thirty feet toward the viewing platform. After Clark Gable visited the Cyclorama in December 1939 while in Atlanta for the premiere of *Gone With the Wind*, Mayor William B. Hartsfield had Snell make a figure of a Union corpse with a face painted to resemble Gable's Rhett Butler.

Deterioration of the painting and water damage led to an $11 million restoration of the Cyclorama in 1979–81. Under the supervision of Gustav Berger, the canvas was cleaned and treated, and the paint colors were restored. In the diorama the clay was replaced with a fiberglass and plastic flooring by Joseph Hurt (a descendant of Troup Hurt), and the plaster figures were reset. The building was remodeled and equipped with a 184-seat, tiered viewing platform, which rotates slowly as recorded narrative describes the painting. The upstairs museum was also updated, with artifacts given mostly by a former Cyclorama employee. The new Cyclorama reopened in June 1982 and continues to draw visitors from around the world.

STEPHEN DAVIS

 # Fitzgerald

Fitzgerald, the seat of Ben Hill County, is located in the heart of south central Georgia, twenty-five miles northeast of Tifton. Settled in 1896 by a land company under the direction of Philander H. Fitzgerald, the town is best known as a place of reconciliation among Civil War veterans. Fitzgerald, a former drummer boy in the Union army, had become a pension attorney with a thriving practice in Indianapolis, Indiana. His interest in the welfare of his fellow veterans was well documented in the publication of the widely read weekly newspaper *American Tribune*. Through his involvement Fitzgerald conceived the idea for a soldiers' colony in the more hospitable South. Georgia governor William J. Northen was eager to settle some of the sparsely populated areas in the wiregrass region of the Coastal Plain, and after some negotiation they settled on the area around the site of the former turpentine village of Swan on the Ocmulgee River.

When Georgia entered the war, **William J. Northen** joined the Confederate forces as a private, but an educator's exemption allowed him to opt out of combat duty in 1862. He then worked at Confederate hospitals in Atlanta and Milledgeville. After the war he established himself as a leading scientific planter and in 1890 was elected governor of Georgia.—From online entry "William J. Northen"

WWW.GEORGIAENCYCLOPEDIA.ORG

Early on, the prospect of so many Northerners inhabiting the Deep South was a strange concept, but as soon as settlement began, the locals offered their cooperation. An early nickname of Fitzgerald, the "Colony City," is still in use today. Through this harmony the idea that the town would be a spotlight of post-Reconstruction reconciliation was assured. There was little strife among the new colonists, who proved their dedication to unity by naming an equal number of streets in the city proper for Union and Confederate notables. In one of the first public-works constructions in the United States, a mammoth four-story hotel was built; it was named the Lee-Grant Hotel, to honor the leaders of the opposing sides of the Civil War.

In 1906 the town became the seat of the newly created Ben Hill County, named for prominent Confederate Georgia senator Benjamin Harvey Hill. The 2000 population of Fitzgerald was 8,758. Much attention has been brought to the town through the efforts of Beth Davis, founder and director of the Blue and Gray Museum. The museum hosts a Roll Call of the States, in which visitors from every state in the Union are photographed with their respective state flags. This idea was derived from an early custom in the colony in which representatives of the many Northern and Midwestern states paraded in unity through the center of town.

The city, while moving forward, is proud to maintain its links with the past and enjoys the distinction as the "City Where America Reunited."

BRIAN BROWN

 Stone Mountain

Stone Mountain, located in DeKalb County about ten miles northeast of downtown Atlanta, is the largest exposed mass of granite in the world. A town at the base of the mountain bears the same name. Before 1800, Native Americans used the mountain as a meeting and ceremonial place. Stone Mountain emerged as a major tourist resort in the 1850s, attracting residents of nearby Atlanta and other cities. The carving of a Confederate memorial on the side of the mountain attracted national and international attention during the twentieth century. Today, Stone Mountain is a tourist attraction that draws approximately 4 million visitors a year.

Two events brought Stone Mountain attention during the twentieth century: the founding of the second Ku Klux Klan (KKK) there in 1915 and the struggle from the 1910s to the 1960s to complete the Confederate memorial. Inspired by D. W. Griffith's silent film *Birth of a Nation* (which romanticized the earlier heyday of the Klan), William Simmons, a minister and organizer for fraternal associations, planned the induction ceremonies that awakened the KKK from its slumber of forty years to take place a week before the movie's opening in Atlanta. In 1914 the leader of the Atlanta chapter of the United Daughters of the Confederacy (UDC), Caroline Helen Jemison Plane, and the Stone Mountain Memorial Association (SMMA) had decided to carve a memorial on the side of Stone Mountain. Simmons may have selected Stone Mountain as the location of the ceremonies because of the planned memorial.

Even more than the birth of the second KKK, the Confederate memorial gave Stone Mountain notoriety throughout the twentieth century. A product of the Lost Cause era, the memorial was originally conceived as a symbol of the white South. In 1916 the recently incorporated Stone Mountain Confederate Monumental Association (SMCMA) hired the renowned sculptor Gutzon Borglum, a Northerner, to carve Robert E. Lee leading his Confederate troops across the mountain's summit. These whites hoped that the memorial would serve as a symbol of sectional reconciliation. World War I (1917–18) delayed the project until 1923. Then, in 1925, with only the head of Lee carved, a growing rift between the sculptor and the SMCMA over artistic control ended with the association firing Borglum, thereby halting construction. With the Great Depression of the 1930s, the Confederate memorial remained unfinished. In 1941 Governor Eugene Talmadge formed the Stone Mountain Memorial Association to continue work on the memorial, but the project was delayed once again by the U.S. entry into World War II.

It was not until the 1950s that interest in (and funding for) the completion of the Confederate memorial was revived. As the civil rights movement gained momentum, segregationists hoped that the memorial would serve as a reminder of white supremacy. In 1958 the state of Georgia purchased Stone Mountain, making it a state park, and Governor Marvin Griffin supported

In 1963 Stone Mountain Park employed **Butterfly McQueen**, the actress who played Prissy in the film *Gone With the Wind*, to live in a plantation house kitchen and greet visitors. She left the park in 1965, and by 1968 the park ceased using her photograph to promote the plantation attraction after she threatened a lawsuit.—From online entry "Butterfly McQueen"

WWW.GEORGIAENCYCLOPEDIA.ORG

plans to complete the memorial. The state and the Stone Mountain Memorial Association (SMMA; formed 1958) agreed to carve the images of Confederate icons Robert E. Lee, Thomas "Stonewall" Jackson, and Jefferson Davis on the mountain and to construct a plaza at its base. In 1970 planners dedicated the memorial, and an estimated 10,000 visitors came to witness its unveiling.

Since the 1980s Stone Mountain has remained a tourist attraction, although many groups denounce the memorial as racist. Millions of tourists from around the world marvel at the natural scenery. Other attractions include a reconstructed antebellum plantation built in the 1960s, a skylift, a waterside complex, and a thirty-six-hole golf course. The most popular attraction in the park is the laser show. This show now symbolizes the promise of a New South, imposing other Southern faces, including that of civil rights leader Martin Luther King Jr., over the Confederate icons.

BRUCE E. STEWART

 Civil War Heritage Trails

The nonprofit organization Georgia Civil War Heritage Trails (GCWHT) chronicles the Civil War era through historic driving routes and interpretive markers, patterned after Virginia's "heritage tourism" initiative. GCWHT, a tax-exempt corporation founded in 1999 and led by volunteers from throughout the state, works to raise public awareness of existing preservation opportunities while providing scenic and cultural benefits to those who follow its trails.

Another goal of GCWHT is to stimulate economic development in Georgia. With funds awarded by the federal government under the Transportation Equity Act for the Twenty-first Century, and with the support of scores of local communities, GCWHT has erected highway directional signs and a series of interpretive markers at many locations along or near some of the routes used by the Union and Confederate armies. Trails bypass interstate highways, instead leading visitors through rural counties. Communities along or near each trail benefit from this increased tourism.

The content of every marker is thoroughly checked by representatives of the National Park Service, the Georgia Park Service, academics, and local historians; documentation for all content is required. GCWHT markers include a map, photographs, and/or Civil War–era drawings. Most are installed adjacent to existing public parking; GCWHT coordinates with the Georgia Department of Transportation and with local jurisdictions and landowners to build adequate parking if none is nearby.

GCWHT divides the state into six distinct "trail regions," each representing a geographical area and/or a significant event from the Civil War period. Because the Atlanta campaign and the March to the Sea were two major Civil War events in Georgia, these trails were created first. Interpretive markers feature not only military campaigns but also such non-military topics as the roles of women and African Americans, hospitals, churches, railroads, and many other social and political subjects from the era. Each marker is linked along a trail route to national and state parks, museums, and other Civil War heritage attractions.

STEVE LONGCRIER

Tourism is one of Georgia's largest industries. The Civil War, African American heritage, Native American heritage, railways, and music are among the most popular areas of interest in the state for travelers who engage in **heritage tourism**. Communities enhance their appeal to such tourists by marketing historic downtowns and neighborhoods, house museums, landscapes, and archaeological sites, alongside nearby attractions.—From online entry "Heritage Tourism"

WWW.GEORGIAENCYCLOPEDIA.ORG

} National Civil War Naval Museum at Port Columbus

The National Civil War Naval Museum at Port Columbus, formerly the Confederate Naval Museum, is the only institution in the nation dedicated to telling the little-known maritime story of the Civil War. This 40,000-square-foot facility located on the Chattahoochee River in Columbus opened in 2001 and features the remains of two original Confederate Navy ships, along with full-scale reproductions of parts of three other famous Civil War ships and numerous artifacts. Port Columbus is operated as a public-private partnership project between the City of Columbus and the Port Columbus Civil War Naval Center, Inc., a private nonprofit organization. The first phase of the project was funded by nearly $8 million in private local donations.

A major feature of Port Columbus is the CSS *Jackson*, a 225-foot ironclad ship built in the Confederate Navy Shipyard, which is located less than a mile from the current museum. Though under construction for more than two years, the ship was not quite completed when a U.S. Cavalry column under General James Wilson captured Columbus in April 1865. All military and Confederate government property in Columbus was burned, including the shipyard and the CSS *Jackson*, which was set on fire and left adrift in the Chattahoochee River.

The Chattahoochee's waterpower made **Columbus** a manufacturing center. The river powered gristmills and sawmills as early as 1828 and a textile mill north of town by 1838. During the war Columbus expanded its industrial output and soon ranked among the top five Confederate producers. Factories tripled their output and shifted to war-related products.—From online entry "Columbus"

WWW.GEORGIAENCYCLOPEDIA.ORG

The fire persisted for nearly two weeks, until the ship finally burned to the waterline and sank about thirty miles south of Columbus, where it remained for ninety-six years. The *Jackson* was raised in 1961 and brought back to Columbus, where today it forms the nucleus of the museum. The CSS *Chattahoochee* also burned at the war's end; it too was recovered and returned in the early 1960s.

Port Columbus is designed to place its visitors inside the stories it tells. Reproduced ships, including the USS *Hartford*, the USS *Monitor*, and the ironclad CSS *Albemarle*, are open so that Civil War naval life can be experienced from the inside. A visitor can hear the ships creaking and the water lapping at their sides; in the *Albemarle*, visitors enter the ironclad combat "simulator" and witness the U.S. Navy fleet sailing up and sending 455-pound cannonballs bouncing off the casemate in which they stand.

Years of collecting have resulted in an extraordinary array of artifacts on display. The uniform coat worn by Catesby Jones, skipper of the CSS *Virginia* (popularly known as the "Merrimac"), on the day he fought the USS *Monitor* in one of naval history's most famous battles is featured, along with weapons, equipment, documents, paintings, and a stunning flag collection.

Special events are held year-round at Port Columbus and range from academic symposia to living-history activities in which an original Confederate Navy cannon is fired over the river. The museum's largest annual event is "RiverBlast," held in early March on the weekend nearest the anniversary of the facility's opening. Port Columbus also features educational opportunities; a teacher's guide is published, and special tours and programs are available to student groups visiting the museum.

BRUCE SMITH

Civil War Centennial

Between 1961 and 1965 the state of Georgia took part in the commemoration of the 100th anniversary of the Civil War. Following the lead of the federal government, which had established the Civil War Centennial Commission in 1957, Georgia created in 1959 a state commission, which subsequently encouraged local communities to carry out commemorative events in their areas. The commission's goals included using the anniversary as a means for education and reflection on the war and its legacy, as an opportunity for the collection and preservation of materials and documents related to the war, and as a vehicle for encouraging cultural tourism and economic development throughout the state.

A variety of events and programs occurred during the centennial, and several books, television documentaries, historical markers, and museums appeared as products of the commemoration. However, because the official centennial activities in Georgia took place entirely on the white side of the color line, the effort to encourage the public to reflect on the war's legacy of slavery and emancipation remained incomplete.

The anniversary coincided with the height of the civil rights movement in Georgia and the South. Some white Georgians used the commemoration to glorify the Confederacy, adopting its leaders, rhetoric, and symbols as a means for expressing resistance to civil rights ideals. While not all centennial efforts were driven by that agenda, the official commemorations upheld an idealized vision of antebellum plantation culture, celebrated Confederate military heroes, and omitted references to slavery as a cause for the war, all of which are characteristic of Lost Cause ideology.

Georgia Civil War Centennial Commission

Governor Ernest Vandiver Jr. issued an executive order creating the Georgia Civil War Centennial Commission on April 10, 1959. He named his executive secretary, Peter Zack Geer, as chairman and appointed seventeen commission members, all of whom were white. The commission members organized themselves into nine committees (arts participation, central research, education, finance, monuments/memorials/commemorations, official souvenirs, pageants and reenactments, publications, and publicity and promotions) and brought additional white men and women into their work.

With loaned staff assistance from the state chamber of commerce, and with $25,000 in funding, the commission set up an office in Atlanta and began to publicize its plans. An early goal of the commission was obtaining cooperation from educational and cultural groups across the state. State budget restrictions and a downsizing of state government staffing impeded the progress of the commission in its first months. Stanley Rowland Smith, a public relations professional, became the administrative director in October 1960, and he served for the remainder of the commemoration.

The Georgia Civil War Centennial Commission, from the beginning, encouraged counties to form groups that would carry out activities at the local level, and it published a pamphlet, *Civil War Centennial Manual for Georgians: A Guide to Local Committees,* to help them do so.

Centennial's First Year: 1961

Several patriotic organizations in Savannah organized the first commemorative activity of the centennial, which took place on January 3, 1961, to mark Georgia's seizure of Fort Pulaski from the United States 100 years earlier. A troop representing the Oglethorpe Light Infantry lowered the American flag and raised the Georgia flag. Governor Vandiver sent telegrams, using the words of Governor Joseph E. Brown, to the governors of other Southern states informing them of the transfer.

Rich's Department Store in Atlanta mounted a tableau of Civil War military leaders and an exhibition of weapons and artifacts in its downtown store. The *Atlanta Constitution* noted that the exhibition was "enough to turn Lee's head" because a statue of him was situated in the midst of the women's lingerie department.

From January 19 to 21 Milledgeville commemorated Georgia's secession with a parade, a tour of homes, and a reenactment of the secession convention at the old state capitol building. The inauguration of U.S. president John F. Kennedy in Washington, D.C., kept Governor Vandiver and commission chairman Geer from attending the Milledgeville events.

In March 1961 Atlanta sponsored a "re-premiere" of the movie *Gone With the Wind* (1939), as well as an antebellum-attire costume ball. Two of the film's stars, Vivien Leigh and Olivia de Havilland, along with producer David O. Selznick, attended the screening, which was held at Loew's Grand Theater, the site of the original premiere. The Atlanta events were envisioned as fund-raisers for the commission and its programming. However, despite the large crowd in attendance, the events did not produce the kind of profits that had been predicted.

The commission sponsored the production of a television and radio series entitled *Understanding the Civil War.* Ten thirty-minute presentations were recorded and aired on television stations across Georgia during 1961. Allen Phelps "Ned" Julian, the director of the Atlanta Historical Society and a former army colonel, served as the scholar and researcher for the programs.

In 1956 Georgia state legislators, angry over the recent *Brown v. Board of Education* rulings demanding the desegregation of public schools, passed legislation to substitute the square Confederate battle flag for the red and white bars on the most recent of the **state flags of Georgia**. Many saw the change as an appropriate way to mark the upcoming centennial of the Civil War.—From online entry "State Flags of Georgia"

WWW.GEORGIAENCYCLOPEDIA.ORG

Centennial's Second Year: 1962

In April 1962 local historians in northwest Georgia staged a reenactment of the Andrews Raid from Kennesaw to Chattanooga, Tennessee. The L&N Railroad allowed the reconditioned locomotive the *General* to be activated for the event. Two passenger-train cars full of spectators followed the locomotive, and other costumed spectators turned out to meet the trains as they passed through communities along the route. An estimated 200,000 people were present from one end of the line to the other. Walt Disney's film *The Great Locomotive Chase* (1956) was used as a background source for the reenactment.

Centennial's Third Year: 1963

In January 1963 Carl Sanders became governor, and Geer became lieutenant governor. Governor Sanders issued his own executive order,
which appointed insurance executive Beverly Dubose Jr. of Atlanta as
the new commission chairman. Dubose, one of the more active members of the original commission, came to the chairmanship full of ideas
for a heavy slate of commemorative programming. What he did not have
were the funds to implement them all.

During the summer and fall of 1963, Chickamauga National Battlefield Park held a series of "state days," which commemorated the participants from both Northern and Southern states who fought at the Battle
of Chickamauga in September 1863. Descendants of these soldiers were
invited, along with other cultural travelers, to visit the battlefield monuments erected at the park. The final state day was Georgia Day, which
featured a parade and a speech by the local congressman.

Centennial's Fourth Year: 1964

Given the level of military activity in Georgia in 1864, including Union
general William T. Sherman's Atlanta campaign and March to the Sea,
the commission designated 1964 as "Georgia's Year." The commission
developed a yearlong radio program series, *Georgia Civil War Centennial News*, which offered daily two-minute clips recounting events that
occurred on those dates. Battle reenactments took place along the route
of the Atlanta campaign, including events at Resaca, New Hope Church,
Kennesaw Mountain, Atlanta, and Jonesboro. The Resaca, New Hope
Church, and Jonesboro reenactments took place on portions of the original battlefield that were privately owned.

The Battle of Kennesaw Mountain reenactment took place on June 27,
the actual centennial date of the battle, but was held at a farm owned by
Cobb County, rather than on the actual battlefield. The National Park
Service, which owned the original battlefield, had a policy that prohibited reenactments on its sites. The Kennesaw reenactment came at the
end of a week of festivities, including a parade, memorial service, barbecue, costume ball, and tours. Despite intentions to make the reenactment as accurate as possible, it appeared to spectators, once the skirmish
started, that the ratio of Confederate to Union troops was not accurate

and that the Confederates were winning the battle (which history suggests should end in a draw). Approximately 7,000 people watched the mock battle, which featured 2,000 participants.

Development in the Atlanta area created difficulties in locating a site where the Battle of Atlanta could be reenacted. Ultimately, the event, which featured reenactments of maneuvers from multiple battles, took place at Stone Mountain, on the field in front of the carving of Confederate leaders Robert E. Lee, Thomas "Stonewall" Jackson, and Jefferson Davis. Four hundred people participated in the reenactment, and approximately three thousand spectators observed.

Another major event of 1964 was Atlanta's hosting of the Seventh Assembly of the National Civil War Centennial Commission and state commissions from across the United States. Historian James "Bud" Robertson, a graduate of Emory University in Atlanta, was the executive director of the national commission. After Dubose assured Robertson of the availability of integrated public accommodations in Atlanta, the event went forward and included a lecture by journalist Ralph McGill, tours of the Cyclorama and Stone Mountain, a band concert, a boat ride, and a wreath-laying.

Centennial's Final Year: 1965

Working with an Atlanta television station, the commission produced a thirty-minute film entitled *Death Knell*, which chronicles the fall of Atlanta and the effects of that battle's outcome on U.S. president Abraham Lincoln's reelection and on the final months of the war. The film was distributed to schools and was also used by Civil War Round Tables, a national historical society that organized programs in various cities. (The Atlanta Civil War Round Table, founded in 1949, is still active today.)

Working with the city of Atlanta, the commission mounted Georgia Historical Commission markers about the Battle of Peachtree Creek, the Battle of Ezra Church, and the Battle of Atlanta. Maps, wayside signage, and landscaped parking areas complemented the markers, creating small parks.

The commission also cooperated with the town of Fitzgerald to stage the drama *Our Friends, the Enemy* and to build the Blue and Gray Museum. Fitzgerald was established in the 1890s as a "colony" founded and settled by Union veterans from Indiana and other locations in the

North. Fitzgerald had lobbied the national commission to be the site of the closing event of the national commemoration, which did not come to pass; however, the Georgia commission scheduled its own disbanding to occur soon after Fitzgerald's "Blue and Gray Days" event, a gathering for descendants of Union and Confederate veterans, in 1965.

Other Legacy Projects

Around the period of the centennial, many other legacy projects not sponsored by the commission took place around the state. A visitors' center was built at Fort McAllister, a Confederate earthworks in Bryan County. In Columbus, underwater archaeologists worked to retrieve the remains of the ironclad CSS *Chattahoochee*, which later became the core of the collection at the Confederate Naval Museum (later the National Civil War Naval Museum at Port Columbus). Other historical markers were mounted, and collections of photographs, papers, and artifacts found their way into archives and museums to be preserved and shared with the broader public.

LAURA MCCARTY

 # Georgia Civil War Commission

The pastoral landscape of north Georgia served as the arena for contending Union and Confederate armies in one of the Civil War's most decisive and crucial campaigns during the summer of 1864. Many of the bloodstained fields and forests where those Americans fought and died have long since given way to the bulldozer's blade and are now marked by interstate exits, residential neighborhoods, fast-food restaurants, and other commercial facilities.

The Georgia Civil War Commission, formed by the General Assembly in 1993, coordinates the planning, preservation, and promotion of structures, battlefields, and other sites that are associated with the Civil War but not already managed by the state or federal government, as are Fort Pulaski and the battlefields at Chickamauga and Kennesaw Mountain. The commission consists of fifteen volunteers appointed by the governor, lieutenant governor, and Speaker of the Georgia House of Representatives.

Although the sites associated with the 1864 Atlanta campaign, nearly all located along the Interstate 75 corridor linking Atlanta with Chattanooga, Tennessee, are those most threatened by development, other Civil War–related properties across the state are equally valuable historic resources.

One of these, the battlefield at Griswoldville in middle Georgia (in Jones and Twiggs counties), was an early preservation victory for the commission. In June 1997 the group acquired seventeen acres at the site of the only infantry engagement prior to Union general William T. Sherman's arrival in Savannah during the March to the Sea. That land is now a state historic site.

From its formation, the commission focused on the preservation of the battlefield at Resaca, the first major engagement of the Atlanta campaign. In 2000 a major Civil War preservation victory was realized when the state purchased a 508-acre tract of that battlefield, located near Dalton in present-day Gordon and Whitfield counties. The commission was a key player in facilitating the sale.

In September 2002, commissioners brought together several parties to fund the purchase of a 190-acre tract in southwest Atlanta near the Utoy Creek battle site. The parcel, which was included on the national Civil War Preservation Trust's list of the nation's ten most endangered sites, is laced with a network of pristine earthworks dug by Union troops during the siege of Atlanta in August 1864.

In 1864 Union general William T. Sherman made his headquarters for a time in Calhoun, at what is now Oakleigh, the home of the Gordon County Historical Society. Each May the Battle of Resaca is reenacted on fields in the northern part of **Gordon County**, and the battle's fallen are commemorated in a ceremony at the Confederate cemetery there.—From online entry "Gordon County"

WWW.GEORGIAENCYCLOPEDIA.ORG

The commission publishes *Presence of the Past*, a color brochure available to visitors in Georgia's welcome centers and at other locations around the state. In 2010 it copublished a revised edition of *Crossroads of Conflict*, a detailed guidebook to the state's Civil War sites, with the University of Georgia Press, the Georgia Department of Economic Development, and the Georgia Humanities Council. It has sponsored and hosted national conferences and education and preservation forums and has networked extensively with local, state, and national preservation groups. Commissioners are regularly asked to endorse preservation efforts and serve as speakers at meetings and lectures.

Despite extremely limited funding, the Georgia Civil War Commission continues to raise awareness of preservation issues across the state and to promote contact between preservation groups.

DAN CHILDS

Reenacting

Reenactments of the Civil War are the most popular and widely known form of Civil War public commemoration in Georgia. Reenacting is a loosely organized hobby in which men and women dress as Union or Confederate soldiers or civilians to stage re-creations of Civil War battles, encampments, or marches. The hobby also offers fellowship, fun, and education to its participants and to its audiences. There are perhaps 2,000 active Civil War reenactors in Georgia. Additionally, many of the estimated 35,000 Civil War reenactors in the United States and 3,000 abroad visit Georgia to participate in reenactments.

Origins of Civil War Reenacting in Georgia

As an organized hobby, Civil War reenacting emerged in the early 1960s during the Civil War centennial. However, the tradition of reenacting battles is much older. Throughout the nineteenth century, town festivals often featured a historical play or pageant in which local residents dressed as Native Americans, early settlers, or soldiers in the Revolutionary War (1775–83) in order to portray the history of their community as they wished it to be remembered. This tradition of historical public performance, which later incorporated scenes from Civil War battles and the Reconstruction era, remained strong well into the twentieth century.

Before the Civil War, militia musters occasionally involved "sham battles," which were essentially practice maneuvers conducted with blank ammunition. During the Civil War, sham battles were conducted both as military training and as public spectacle. A series of three sham battles took place in the Confederate Army of Tennessee's winter camp near Dalton in March and April 1864, before a crowd of local residents and the commanders of the army. Volunteers training during the Spanish-American War (1898) camped, drilled, and held sham battles on the battlefield at Chickamauga, though none of these "battles" were intended as historical re-creations. The U.S. Army continued to use sham battles as part of its military training through the 1940s.

In the 1880s, reflecting renewed public curiosity about the war, many sham battles were conducted purely as entertainment. Although these sham battles were usually not attempts to re-create specific Civil War battles, they were conducted with strong undertones of both sectional pride and national unity. An estimated 20,000 people attended opening events of the Piedmont Exposition in Atlanta (held two years after the well-known Piedmont Exposition of 1887), where on October 16, 1889, a sham battle was staged by 10 Georgia militia companies, about 100 members of the Confederate Veterans' Association of Fulton County, and a mounted force of faux cowboys and Indians from Pawnee Bill's Wild West show, then camped on the exposition grounds. Newspaper editor and New South champion Henry W. Grady addressed the crowd, proclaiming the sham battle a symbol of "the imperishable union of American hearts, and of the indissoluble union of American states, now and forevermore." At the same time, the Confederate veterans were allowed to "win" the sham battle.

Henry W. Grady, the "Spokesman of the New South," served in the 1880s as managing editor for the *Atlanta Constitution*, often writing in support of care for Confederate veterans. His father, a major in the Confederate army, died in 1864 from wounds received at the siege of Petersburg.—From online entry "Henry W. Grady"

WWW.GEORGIAENCYCLOPEDIA.ORG

Civil War veteran reunions were often marked by military-style tented encampments and were occasionally accompanied by a sham battle or historical pageant. However, there is no evidence that Union and Confederate veterans ever actually reenacted a battle against each other; to have done so would have violated the spirit of national reconciliation inherent in these events.

In the 1930s Army National Guard units, U.S. Marines, and military school cadets began to stage what could be called the first true Civil War reenactments. These public performances used contemporary military formations, uniforms, and weapons to re-create actual battles on or near the anniversary dates of the battles. During the week of September 16–25, 1938, the seventy-fifth anniversary of the Battle of Chickamauga was marked by parades, races, fireworks, a horse show, and a historical pageant entitled "Drums of Dixie." On September 19, 700 soldiers from nearby Fort Oglethorpe reenacted the Battle of Chickamauga on Dyer Field, in the middle of the national park.

Reenacting during the Civil War Centennial

In the early 1960s middle-class affluence combined with commercialism, automobile travel, and the 100th anniversary of the Civil War to once again reinvigorate interest in the war and in re-creating its battles. On July 21–22, 1961, the National Park Service and the Civil War Centennial Commission helped sponsor a reenactment of the First Battle of Manassas (known in the North as the Battle of Bull Run) on the original ground at the Manassas National Battlefield Park in Virginia. The reenactment turned out to be a logistical, financial, and public relations nightmare for the organizers. The National Park Service faced unexpected costs, property damage, and legal liabilities as a result of 2,200 participants (including a contingent from Georgia) and around 50,000 spectators crowding into the park each day. The centennial commission faced public criticism for "celebrating" violence and a Confederate victory during a period of intense international tension and the domestic turmoil of the civil rights movement. Both organizations subsequently abandoned any further involvement in Civil War reenactments. As a direct result of this decision, reenactments are today not allowed on any property administered by the National Park Service.

Nevertheless, the momentum inspired by the 1961 Manassas reenactment influenced many amateur enthusiasts in the North-South Skirmish Association, a group of black-powder firearms buffs formed in 1950, who soon began forming their own groups devoted specifically to reenacting Civil War battles. In Georgia, small commemorations using amateur costumed participants were held at Milledgeville in 1961 and at Fort Pulaski in 1962 to mark the centennial of the state's secession from the Union. Similar commemorations marked the centennials of the Andrews Raid in April 1962 and the Battle of Chickamauga in September 1963.

In 1964 the Georgia Civil War Centennial Commission helped to sponsor a series of five reenactments to commemorate the 100th anniversary of the Atlanta campaign. The five battles reenacted were

- Battle of Resaca (May 16, 1964, on portions of original battlefield)
- Battle of New Hope Church (May 23, 1964, on portions of original battlefield)
- Battle of Kennesaw Mountain (June 27, 1964, on Cobb County farm)
- Battle of Atlanta (July 25, 1964, at Stone Mountain)
- Battle of Jonesboro (August 29, 1964, on farm outside Jonesboro)

The largest of the centennial reenactments in Georgia was the Battle of Kennesaw Mountain, which attracted more than 2,000 participants, including mounted cavalrymen, using cannons, mortars, and wagons. An estimated 7,000 spectators witnessed the event. Unlike the 1961 reenactment at Manassas, in which half the participants were National Guardsmen or military cadets, participants in the 1964 Georgia reenactments were volunteers who made their own uniforms and props; many used original Civil War arms and accoutrements. Thus was Civil War reenacting established as a true organized hobby.

The following year, on July 4, 1965, a small commemorative reenactment event occurred at "Unity Day" in the town of Fitzgerald, chosen for its symbolic value as a site of national reconciliation. Despite genuine efforts to promote North-South reconciliation, the centennial reenactments in Georgia bore a distinctively neo-Confederate flavor. Many participants saw the events as opportunities to advocate for states' rights, anti-integrationist, and white supremacist agendas. Thus was also established a reputation that still colors the reenacting hobby today.

Civil War Reenacting in the Twenty-first Century

Today the Civil War is not the only conflict simulated by hobbyists, but it is by far the most popular one in Georgia and in the United States. The Revolutionary War, World War I (1917–18), World War II (1941–45), and the Vietnam War (1964–73) are also reenacted; other hobbyists specialize in military and other aspects of the ancient, medieval, and Renaissance eras.

Civil War reenacting is a decentralized hobby based around small local organizations, or "units," that usually comprise ten to thirty regular participants. The units are named after actual Civil War regiments, batteries, or other formations. In 2010 there were roughly thirty-five reenacting units in the state portraying Georgia formations. Approximately fifteen of these were included in the Georgia Division Reenactors Association, a statewide umbrella organization founded in 1978. Many Georgia-based units portray either Union or Confederate soldiers. Additionally, units portraying Georgia formations exist in other states, including California and Illinois, as well as abroad.

Civil War reenacting units are often semifraternal organizations with members closely tied to one another by bonds of family, friendship, and a common outlook on their unit's role within the hobby. Within each unit, leaders are elected and afforded titles of military rank, such as sergeant or lieutenant; these ranks then correspond to leadership positions during a battle-reenactment performance. The average participant attends at least one significant weekend reenactment event per month, plus practice drills, unit meetings, or other informal gatherings.

The overwhelming majority of Civil War reenactors are white males in their late thirties or early forties, with middle-class incomes and suburban residences. Most Civil War reenactors express conservative political and social views. Some reenactors are also members of the Sons of Confederate Veterans or the Sons of Union Veterans of the Civil War. At the same time, there are increasing numbers of African Americans and women involved in the hobby, in both civilian and soldier roles.

The primary motivation for nearly all Civil War reenactors is a general fascination with history and a specific interest in how ordinary soldiers or civilians lived, dressed, and fought. Much of the pleasure of participation lies in trying to physically re-create the camp and battle experience of Civil War soldiers in all but the most dangerous aspects. Ultimately, one of the goals of participants is to achieve a "period rush," often defined as a burst of intense emotional connectedness when the Civil War seems "real" and tangible. To that end, reproduction clothing and gear are made to resemble as closely as possible the original items; camp activities, battle formations, and even meals are made to simulate those of the Civil War. Nevertheless, disputes over exactly what constitutes the proper level of authenticity in these respects (and many others) are common among units. The issue of women portraying male soldiers is an especially intense source of controversy within the hobby.

The Civil War reenacting hobby is also marked by friction between those who view participation in the hobby as a means of political expression or of honoring their ancestors and those who see it as a quest for personal experience and fun. Among Civil War reenactors there is no common consensus on the causes of the war or its relevance today. However, there is a consensus among reenactors that they re-create Civil War battles as a means of educating present-day audiences and honoring soldiers of both sides.

Although Georgia was the site of many Civil War battles, there are relatively few battle reenactments regularly held in the state. The Battle of Tunnel Hill is staged every year on the weekend after Labor Day in conjunction with a town festival in Whitfield County. The Battle of Resaca is held on the third weekend in May on a privately owned portion of the original battlefield in Paulding County. Begun in 1983, it is one of the longest-running annual reenactments in the United States. Other reenactments are held in conjunction with five- or ten-year anniversary dates, such as the 140th or 145th anniversary of the Battle of Chickamauga, which has been held in various locations near the actual battlefield in Walker County. Reenactments of the battles for Atlanta have been held at the Georgia International Horse Park near Conyers and on the Nash Farm Battlefield in Henry County. Occasionally, smaller reenactments, also known as "tacticals" or "immersion events," take place on private land solely for the benefit and experience of the participants and are not open to the public.

Nearly all national, state, and locally maintained battlefields, historic sites, and museums in Georgia periodically sponsor Civil War demonstrations or encampments using reenactors as living history interpreters. These events do not involve reenacting but can give visitors a sense of soldiers' lives and experiences during the war.

GORDON L. JONES

 # Archaeology

Archaeology offers a unique perspective on the Civil War, allowing archaeologists and historians to look at this defining event from a material perspective.

The Nature of Civil War Archaeology

In reconstructing the material context of the war, archaeologists study three main components: artifacts, features, and sites. *Artifacts* are man-made objects, such as bullets, pipe fragments, or uniform buttons. *Features* are similar to artifacts in that they are created by human hands, but unlike artifacts they cannot be physically separated from the landscape.

Examples of features include a military trench or the remains of a soldier's fire pit. *Sites* are defined as locations that contain a collection of artifacts and/or features, such as a battlefield or a fort. Civil War archaeologists look for the patterns of these three elements (often called the triad or trinity) as a means to interpret past behavior and activities.

Archaeologists place the triad of elements into a contextual framework through the study and application of letters, diaries, official military records, and other primary historical documents. An archaeological approach to the Civil War allows a wider array of wartime participants to enter the historical picture. Often the perspective of the common soldier, for example, can be presented only from an archaeological standpoint, given his more marginal representation in the written historical record.

Georgia is one of the birthplaces for the archaeological study of African American sites and artifacts. After the 1971 publication of an article detailing the excavation of a Georgia slave cabin, the choice of sites for the study of **African American archaeology** grew to include tenant farms, urban locations, rural communities, and cemeteries, resulting in a better understanding of African American landscapes, architecture, artifacts, and customs.—From online entry "African American Archaeology"

WWW.GEORGIAENCYCLOPEDIA.ORG

Archaeological investigations of Georgia's Civil War past may involve a number of different types of sites, including battlefields, training camps, bivouacs (encampments), earthen fortifications, masonry fortifications, and other strictly military features on the landscape. Other types of sites, such as mills, farms, and railroads, allow archaeological researchers to study aspects of the war that are not strictly military in origin and thus to glean a more complete picture of the war and how it affected all citizens, military and civilian.

Early Investigations in Georgia

One of the first archaeological investigations into the Civil War in Georgia was undertaken in the 1930s at Kennesaw Mountain in Cobb County. Archaeologist Charles Fairbanks undertook the documentation and limited excavation of Confederate earthworks at the battle site on top of the mountain. Fairbanks's early study was pioneering, as few archaeologists at the time recognized the value in investigating the Civil War from an archaeological perspective. Instead, most archaeologists focused their attention on much older sites. Not until the passage of the National Historic Preservation Act (NHPA) of 1966 did Civil War archaeology expand.

Section 106 of NHPA provides for the recording of archaeological and historic resources in an area to be disturbed by a federal undertaking (which would include local undertakings using federal funds, such as a road improvement project). The act's passage drew attention to Civil War sites as not only historic but also archaeological resources and led to numerous sites throughout the state being recorded and investigated for the first time by archaeologists. With the construction of MARTA during the 1970s, a number of Atlanta sites associated with the 1864 Battle of Atlanta and the Battle of Ezra Church, both of which took place during the Atlanta campaign, were studied and excavated. Previously, the sites had been known only to amateur collectors.

Archaeologists versus Relic Collectors

The practice of Civil War relic collecting began during the war itself and often took place immediately following a particular engagement, when local civilians would search the battlefield for souvenirs. The collection of such artifacts or "relics" has been and continues to be a popular pastime but differs from archaeology in both approach and intent. Now illegal on federal and most state property, the practice of relic collecting has led to an inherent bias in what remains of the archaeological record at Georgia's Civil War battlefields. Some relic collectors have aided archaeological studies greatly, however, by volunteering their knowledge and time to a common interest in the state's Civil War history.

Relic collectors introduced the metal detector, a tool that archaeologists were slow to embrace, in the late 1940s and 1950s. Collectors used surplus detectors, originally used to detect land mines during World War II, to look for artifacts on Civil War sites. Considered beneath the standards of the discipline, this practice was stigmatized for many years by the archaeological community. Some studies during the 1970s, such as the MARTA project, made attempts at using metal detectors but with limited application.

The pioneering National Park Service investigations of the 1980s at the Little Bighorn Battlefield in Montana demonstrated the capabilities of metal detectors in the hands of archaeologists. Recent investigations at Georgia's Civil War battlefields have incorporated the results of the Little Bighorn study, leading to a methodology that not only is an effective means of data acquisition but also has become the standard approach to Civil War battlefield research.

New Directions for Civil War Archaeology

Civil War archaeology in Georgia continues to utilize new technologies and approaches in order to better interpret site and artifact patterns. Many current studies use geographic information systems (GIS) technology, which allows researchers to project maps from the Civil War period into a modern mapping program. With GIS technology, researchers can pinpoint Civil War features on Georgia's modern landscape. This technology can also help with the monitoring of Civil War site preservation, which continues to be an ongoing struggle for the state. (In 1993 the state legislature established the Georgia Civil War Commission to coordinate the preservation and promotion activities of battle sites around the state.) Researchers today use such noninvasive technologies as ground-penetrating radar to help identify features long lost to urbanization.

Recent investigations into the Civil War archaeology of Georgia include examinations of the Chickamauga Battlefield in north Georgia and Tybee Island's coastal fortifications, as well as studies of the interaction between civilians and soldiers at Pickett's Mill Battlefield in Paulding County. In 2010, archaeology students at Georgia Southern University discovered the site of Camp Lawton, the prison camp built late in the war to relieve the overcrowding at Andersonville. Because it was previously unidentified and thus undisturbed, the site, located near Millen, in Jenkins County, is providing excavators with a far fuller and more varied collection of both artifacts and features than more well-established sites that have been subject to plunder over the years.

GARRETT W. SILLIMAN

LITERARY AND CINEMATIC PERSPECTIVES

Buster Keaton in *The General* (1927). Reproduced by permission from the Rohauer Collection/Douris UK Ltd. (In Administration). Image courtesy of the Academy of Motion Picture Arts and Sciences.

⟩ Journals, Diaries, and Memoirs

In *Patriotic Gore* (1962), his classic study of Civil War literature, the literary critic Edmund Wilson asked, "Has there ever been another historical crisis of the magnitude of 1861–1865 in which so many people were so articulate?" Historian Louis Masur later made the same point, stating that "the Civil War was a written war," one in which hundreds of participants and observers "struggled to capture the texture of the extraordinary and the everyday."

Georgians were certainly among those for whom the war became a "written war," and their accounts of what they experienced or observed took the form of letters; of diaries and journals, with entries made on a fairly regular basis during the war; and of memoirs and reminiscences, produced in hindsight, often many years after the war. Firsthand accounts in all these genres were written by soldiers as well as civilians, women as well as men, blacks as well as whites, collectively offering a remarkably multifaceted view of how the war was perceived and felt by both Georgians and those brought to the state's battlefronts and home fronts through a wide spectrum of circumstances.

A significant number of these accounts have made their way into print over the century and a half since the Civil War ended, and in numbers unmatched by any other war in American history. While some journals and diaries were published almost immediately after the war's end, it was in the mid-1870s that most memoirs began to be published, at rates that continued unabated until well after the turn of the twentieth century. Much of this trend was in response to a strong public interest in the military history of the war, which emerged in the late nineteenth century in both the North and the South, and also to the full flowering of the "Lost Cause" in the South, in which white Southerners sought to interpret the conflict in ways that justified both how and why the war was fought. The centennial of the war, from 1961 to 1965, inspired the publication of another round of wartime chronicles, many of which were reprinted, while others were published for the first time. That trend has been ongoing since, as newly found diaries, collections of letters, and other manuscripts continue to be edited and published in book form.

Atlanta Campaign

A number of diaries and memoirs by local residents capture the drama of the war in Atlanta, including the fall of the city and Union general William T. Sherman's subsequent occupation in 1864.

Perhaps the most widely read of all memoirs by a Confederate soldier is Sam Watkins's *Co. Aytch*, which offers a comprehensive and personal account of the Atlanta campaign from a Southern participant. An enlistee from Tennessee, Watkins spent the entire war in Confederate gray, and yet he claimed to "only give a few sketches and incidents that came under the observation of a 'high private' in the rear ranks of the rebel army." He first came into Georgia to fight at the Battle of Chickamauga and returned to fight in almost every other major engagement in the state, including those at Resaca, Kennesaw Mountain, Atlanta, and Jonesboro. (His descriptions of the destruction and death he witnessed at Chickamauga and at the "Dead Angle" on Kennesaw Mountain are among the most harrowing that have survived from any military eyewitness.) Watkins's narrative first appeared in his hometown newspaper in 1881 and 1882, and soon thereafter 2,000 copies were published, primarily for local consumption. In 1962, during the Civil War centennial, a new edition was published, and it has never been out of print since.

Sarah "Sallie" Conley Clayton's memoir, long held in the collection of the Virginia Historical Society, was published in 1999 under the title *Requiem for a Lost City*. The memoir provides a lively description of Clayton's life as an adolescent in Atlanta and the increasing tensions and hardships she and her wealthy family endured. She offers a detailed account of the Battle of Atlanta, which raged within sight of her home, and of her family's subsequent expulsion from the city.

Samuel Pearce Richards, a prominent merchant, kept a diary for sixty-seven years, and his thorough coverage of the war years is considered by many to be the best surviving portrait of the Atlanta home front. Surprisingly, the diary only made its way into print in 2009. Richards, the younger brother of artist Thomas Addison Richards, moved to Atlanta from Macon after the war was under way. His diary entries offer astute commentary on Confederate economic and military policy and the financial hardships he suffered as a result of both. He, like Clayton, wrote vividly about his forced exit from the city as well as his sojourn in New York, which lasted until he found it safe to return to Georgia in August 1865.

A very different perspective on Atlanta has also come to light in recent years. Cyrena Stone, a Vermont native who settled with her husband in Georgia in 1850, found herself part of a secret Unionist community in Atlanta when the war broke out, and she kept a diary about the experience. In 1976 that anonymous eighty-page document was sold to the University of Georgia library, where it was known simply as "Miss Abby's Diary" until the 1990s, when historian Thomas G. Dyer discovered not only Stone's identity but also that of many of her fellow Unionists, whom she referred to in code. From Stone's diary, Dyer produced a full history of the underground Unionist movement, entitled *Secret Yankees*, which details a much different response to the Battle of Atlanta and Sherman's occupation than do the chronicles of local Confederates.

Sherman's March

There are dozens of diaries and memoirs by Union troops who marched to the sea under Sherman. Historian Joseph Glatthaar wrote a book on the march based almost entirely on those firsthand accounts, including more than sixty diaries and reminiscences by enlisted men and junior officers. From their writings, Glatthaar was able to concentrate much of his analysis on their attitudes toward Sherman, toward his "total war" approach, and toward the many civilians and slaves they encountered en route.

Among the best-known civilian perspectives on Sherman's march are those of Joel Chandler Harris, Eliza Frances Andrews, and Dolly Sumner Lunt (Burge). Harris's thinly fictionalized *On the Plantation* (1892) includes a curiously benign account of the movement of Sherman's troops through Putnam County and the ransacking of Turnwold Plantation, where he lived and worked. Andrews's classic *War-Time Journal of a Georgia Girl, 1864–1865* (1908) recounts her harrowing retreat from her home in Washington; as Union forces approached, she moved across ravaged areas to find refuge at her sister's plantation in the southwestern part of the state. Lunt's *A Woman's Wartime Journal* (1918), reprinted under different titles since its original publication, recounts the hardships she faced in managing a

In addition to her *War-Time Journal of a Georgia Girl, 1864–1865*, **Eliza Frances Andrews** wrote three novels, more than a dozen scientific articles on botany, two internationally recognized botany textbooks, and dozens of articles, commentaries, and reports on topics ranging from politics to environmental issues.—From online entry "Eliza Frances Andrews"

WWW.GEORGIAENCYCLOPEDIA.ORG

plantation near Covington before, during, and after Sherman's men moved through the area.

The most widely read first-person chronicle of Sherman's activities in Georgia comes from Sherman himself. One of the first major military figures on either side to publish his account of the war, Sherman devoted more than a fourth of his memoir's 800-plus pages to the Atlanta campaign, the March to the Sea, the occupation of Savannah, and the policies toward freedmen that he initiated there. As much a historical treatise, full of facts and figures, as a personal memoir, Sherman's two-volume work (1875) was revised and updated twice before his death in 1891 and has appeared in numerous editions since, including several that include only the Georgia portion of the work, one of which is entitled "War Is Hell."

Women on the Home Front and Battlefront

Georgia women produced some of the most significant memoirs chronicling home-front activity in the state. Ella Gertrude Clanton Thomas, in Augusta, wrote a journal covering the years 1848 to 1889, a far broader time frame than most; selections from her journal were published under the title *The Secret Eye* in 1990. Her commentary over the war years demonstrates the typical arc that many Southern women experienced during the war, moving from initial enthusiasm for the Confederate cause to increasing resentment and war weariness as the conflict dragged into its third and fourth years.

Eleanor "Nellie" Kinzie Gordon, the Chicago-born wife of Savannahian William Washington Gordon II (and the mother of Juliette Gordon Low), found herself living with her in-laws when the war broke out. She spent most of the war in Georgia's port city, while her husband served as a Confederate captain, and for much of 1862 she kept a journal. Although she was publicly supportive of the Confederate cause at the beginning of the conflict, Gordon soon became disenchanted with the war, and inconsistencies in both her writings and her actions leave historians unsure of her true wartime loyalties. Edited portions of her journal were published by the *Georgia Historical Quarterly* in 1986. Another revealing Unionist perspective comes from a journal kept by Louisa Fletcher, who with her husband kept a hotel on the main square in Marietta. It was published as *Journal of a Landlady* in 1995.

More actively engaged women have also left behind narratives describing their wartime enterprises. Susie King Taylor's memoir is unique in that it is the only surviving wartime description by a black Georgia woman. A former slave, Taylor was born on a Liberty County plantation. She escaped in 1862 and joined the ranks of coastal contrabands in South Carolina, where she became a nurse to sick and wounded black Union troops as they moved down the coast from South Carolina, through Georgia, to Florida. She composed her account of that experience only at the turn of the twentieth century, and it appeared in print in 1902 under the title *Reminiscences of My Life in Camp*.

Two other nurses who served opposing armies in Georgia kept journals that were later published. Scotland native Kate Cumming traveled with the Army of Tennessee into Georgia and documented her work as a hospital matron in *A Journal of Hospital Life in the Confederate Army* (1866). It has appeared in multiple editions since then. Fannie Oslin Jackson, a Unionist in the north Georgia mountains, established a field hospital for Union troops on her farm during the fighting at nearby Resaca, and then followed the troops with a mobile hospital operation as they moved toward Atlanta. Her brief memoir of that experience, entitled *On Both Sides of the Line*, was composed soon after the war but not published until 1989.

Andersonville Prison

In addition to Sherman and his troops, other outsiders who experienced much of the war in Georgia were prisoners at Camp Sumter, known as Andersonville Prison, and other prisoner-of-war camps in the state. Dozens of different accounts of life at Andersonville, the most notorious of Confederate prison camps, appeared soon after the war, some as memoirs, many as published diaries and journals. These publications served as part of a propaganda campaign condemning the treatment of those held at Andersonville and demonizing Henry Wirz, the commandant whom many held responsible for the deplorable conditions there. The first of these publications, Connecticut native Robert Kellogg's *Life and Death in Rebel Prisons*, appeared late in 1865. In it, Kellogg states his intention of "kindl[ing] the fires of indignation" throughout the North for the treatment of Union troops, particularly at Andersonville, where he spent several months in 1864.

Perhaps the most widely reproduced prisoner's account of Andersonville Prison is Michigan sergeant John Ransom's *Andersonville Diary*, which has appeared in several editions (and under different titles) since its original publication in 1881. Ransom was among the first prisoners brought to Andersonville and spent six months there. Inaccuracies in facts and dates, as well as his harsh judgments of Wirz, the guards, and his fellow prisoners, have made his account suspect among historians, though the thoroughness of its coverage has made it one of the best-known narratives of life there. The graphic illustrations of the camp's deplorable conditions included in many of these accounts added to their use as effective propaganda by both former prisoners and vengeful Northern politicians seeking retribution from the South, almost to the end of the century.

Historical Value

In short, the written testimonials of those who witnessed or participated in the war in Georgia, whether on the home front, the battlefield, or in hospitals or prisons, have provided a vital part of the historical record on which scholars have drawn to recreate the struggle's human dimension from multiple perspectives. For soldiers, especially, their own accounts of battlefield action provide a sense of the confusion, the fear, the exhilaration, and the horror of warfare far better than do official records and other traditional military histories (which is why the best military histories now so often incorporate these firsthand accounts into their narratives). These personal accounts also reveal much about issues of shifting morale among both soldiers and civilians, as well as relationships between those two groups; of complex and sometime ambivalent loyalties; and of how individuals understood, remembered, and interpreted the most momentous period in their lives.

JOHN C. INSCOE

 Slave Narratives

One of the most valuable sources available for understanding the experiences of slaves in the American South is the testimony that they themselves produced in a variety of ways, both during and long after the existence of the "peculiar institution." These testimonials, generally referred to as slave narratives, include memoirs and autobiographies written by fugitive slaves who fled to the North and were assisted by abolitionists with the publication of their stories, as well as twentieth-century oral interviews with elderly former slaves that recorded their memories of life during slavery and the circumstances of their emancipation either during or after the Civil War.

Fugitive Slave Narratives

A number of autobiographies written by African Americans who escaped slavery were published in the first half of the nineteenth century, part of a large body of abolitionist literature intended to make clear to all readers the cruelty and immorality of slavery. Those published in the 1840s and 1850s helped fuel Northern opposition to slavery and intensified the sectional crisis that would lead to the breakdown of the Union in 1861. Two of the most significant of those late antebellum narratives come from Georgia. John Brown, though born in Virginia, spent much of his youth and early adulthood as the slave of Thomas Stevens, who moved Brown from Milledgeville to Decatur, before he escaped in the mid-1840s. Stevens's cruelties to Brown, along with those of Stevens's son, who inherited him, are laid out in full in Brown's *Slave Life in Georgia: A Narrative of the Life, Sufferings, and Escape of John Brown, a Fugitive Slave, Now in England*, written and published in England in 1855.

Even more sensational was the narrative of William and Ellen Craft, who escaped by train from Macon and then steamship from Savannah. The fact that they were husband and wife, that Ellen disguised herself as a white man, and that the journey northward was so harrowing made their book, *Running a Thousand Miles for Freedom: The Escape of William and Ellen Craft from Slavery* (1860), particularly popular. It has enjoyed a recent resurgence of interest and was reprinted in new editions in 1999 and 2000.

William and Ellen Craft were slaves who gained celebrity after a daring public escape from Macon in 1848. The daughter of an African American woman and her white master, Ellen looked white. She dressed as a Southern slaveholder in trousers, top hat, and short hair to avoid detection by slave catchers. Her darker-skinned husband, William, masqueraded as her slave valet.—From online entry "William and Ellen Craft"

WWW.GEORGIAENCYCLOPEDIA.ORG

Ex-Slave Interviews

After the Civil War, interest in the lives of African Americans faded, but in the late 1920s, anthropologists and sociologists at Fisk University in

Nashville, Tennessee; Southern University in Baton Rouge, Louisiana; and Prairie View State College in Prairie View, Texas, began to collect life histories of former slaves. Reasons for the scholarly attention included a renewed interest in African American culture; a desire to refute the "plantation myth" of historians like Georgia-born Ulrich Bonnell Phillips, whose book *American Negro Slavery* (1918) offered readers a rosy and comforting portrayal of benevolent masters and happy slaves; and researchers' realization that the last generation of people born in slavery was dying.

From 1937 to 1939 the Federal Writers' Project (FWP) collected interviews with African American men and women who had been born into slavery. More than 2,000 interviews were collected throughout the Southern states, approximately 2 percent of the total population of ex-slaves. Almost 200 narratives were collected in Georgia. Although the usefulness of the interviews is debated by historians, they remain an important and compelling resource for the study of slavery.

The FWP was created in 1935 by the Works Progress Administration (later Work Projects Administration), one of the New Deal agencies of U.S. president Franklin D. Roosevelt's administration, to provide jobs for white-collar workers during the Great Depression. In addition to writing the American Guide Series, guidebooks to every state and some major cities, the FWP was charged with collecting the life histories of ordinary citizens. John Lomax, a pioneer in the collection of folklore, led the project at its headquarters in Washington, D.C.

Some FWP units, including Georgia's, began interviewing small numbers of ex-slaves, and in 1936 the Georgia Writers' Project collected more than a hundred interviews. It was not until Lomax and other FWP administrators heard the interviews collected by members of an African American unit of the Florida Writers' Project that they were convinced of the value of preserving these stories. In 1937 instructions were sent to each of the Southern and border states directing FWP offices to begin interviewing former slaves.

Despite the prejudices of the interviewers, the vast majority of whom were white, and making allowances for the subjects' inability to be candid, these narratives contribute greatly to the understanding of the lives of African Americans before and during the Civil War. Unlike the antebellum slave narratives, the WPA interviews cover a wide spectrum of people who suffered under slavery. Most subjects were under the age of fifteen when the Civil War ended, but they lived in seventeen states;

hailed from cities and from the country, from small farms and large plantations; and worked in a number of tasks. Descriptions of clothing, food, living arrangements, family, and other aspects of daily life can all be found in the narratives.

The most vivid memories of many former slaves had to do with the war years and the circumstances that led to slavery's destruction and their own liberation. Georgians frequently recounted episodes involving Sherman's troops and the upheaval they brought to their master's plantations and the surrounding neighborhoods. Others recalled their experiences as refugees or fugitives, who left their homes and sometimes their families when presented with opportunities to do so. As freedmen and freedwomen during Reconstruction, many interviewees recalled their early efforts to establish themselves on farms of their own, to gain employment in towns and cities, or to learn to read and write. Confrontations with Ku Klux Klan members often stood out as particularly strong memories for many of those interviewed.

Publications

The effort to collect ex-slave narratives ended in 1939, and each state's office sent its manuscripts to Washington when the FWP was disbanded. The manuscripts became part of the collections of the Library of Congress in 1941. The Library of Congress made the ex-slave narratives available on microfilm, and a few small samplings, such as *Drums and Shadows* (1940), a collection of interviews with African Americans living on the Georgia coast, and Benjamin A. Botkin's *Lay My Burden Down: A Folk History of Slavery* (1945), made their way into print.

That remained the case until 1972, when George P. Rawick compiled and edited the multivolume *The American Slave: A Composite Biography*, a collection of the interviews held by the Library of Congress. The anthology is organized by state, and volumes 12 and 13 contain interviews from Georgia. The publication of *The American Slave* encouraged the discovery of additional slave narratives held in state collections, which were published in a supplement in 1977. Volumes 3 and 4 of the supplemental anthology contain Georgia materials. Two years later, Rawick published a second supplemental collection, which also included narratives from Georgia.

The Library of Congress has made the complete set of narratives available online as part of the American Memory Project, in the Born in

Slavery collection. A small set of audio recordings of interviews with ex-slaves, including two subjects from St. Simons Island, is also available online through the American Memory Project.

DIANE TRAP

 Macaria

Macaria; or Altars of Sacrifice, the third novel by Columbus native Augusta Jane Evans, was published in 1864, during the Civil War. The book served as propaganda for the Confederate cause and helped to redefine the role of Confederate women during the war. *Macaria* became a best seller in the Confederacy, with 20,000 copies in circulation by the war's end, and secured Evans's status as a leading female Southern writer. Northern generals banned the book for fear of its sympathetic Southern message taking hold among Union troops.

Themes

Evans believed that a primary purpose of literature was to provide moral instruction, and *Macaria* does this by focusing on the theme of sacrifice while also challenging the gender constructs of the day. The novel combines the genre of women's domestic fiction with the traditionally male war story to present two strong female heroines, Irene Huntingdon and Electra Grey, who expand their conventional gender roles through service to the Confederacy. The book's title is taken from the Greek mythological character Macaria, the daughter of Heracles, who saves Athens from invasion by sacrificing herself to the gods. In Greek, the word *macaria* means "blessed," and Evans depicts the lives of her unmarried heroines as blessed because they have greater opportunities for philanthropic work.

Columbus native **Augusta Jane Evans** wrote nine popular novels about Southern women. Her most successful novel, *St. Elmo* (1866), remained in print well into the twentieth century. During the war Evans sewed sandbags for community defense, wrote patriotic addresses, and set up a hospital dubbed "Camp Beulah" near her home.—From online entry "Augusta Jane Evans"

WWW.GEORGIAENCYCLOPEDIA.ORG

Evans relied on authentic accounts of the war and her own experiences to write *Macaria*, even lifting whole passages from her personal letters. The first part of the novel focuses on the lives of its motherless heroines, Irene and Electra, in the years prior to secession. Irene, who comes from a wealthy plantation family, befriends the poorer Electra, who lives with her aunt, Mrs. Aubrey, and Mrs. Aubrey's son, Russell. Mrs. Aubrey serves as a mother figure for the two girls. Troubled by his daughter's association with the Aubreys, Irene's father sends her to a Northern boarding school, where she studies not only domestic arts but also such classical subjects as astronomy.

The second part of *Macaria* centers on the heroines' lives during the war. Irene refuses to marry the cousin that her father chooses for her, but she also rejects her secret love, Russell Aubrey, sacrificing marriage in order to better serve the Confederacy. Electra also rejects marriage, choosing instead to pursue painting. Irene's choice to remain unwed and to nurse wounded soldiers echoes Evans's own decision in 1860 to break her engagement with James Spaulding, a Northern journalist, because of their differing political views. (It was nearly a decade later, in 1868, before Evans did marry; her husband was Confederate colonel Lorenzo Madison Wilson.)

In addition to its theme of sacrificing domestic comfort for a greater cause, *Macaria* also challenges long-held ideas about gender by advocating that unmarried women should have opportunities to support themselves. Despite her call for women's financial independence in the novel, however, Evans ultimately supported the South's traditional social hierarchies of race, class, and gender. According to the historian Drew Gilpin Faust, Evans backed away from some of her more unconventional ideas, particularly her somewhat radical stance on women, in the postwar years. She did not endorse women's political participation, for example, and after the war she spoke out against the feminist and woman suffrage movements of the North.

Editions

Although Evans's biographer William Perry Fidler claims that the novel first appeared in 1863, a copy of this edition has never been found, and most historians and bibliographers believe that the 1864 edition of *Macaria* is the first. The novel was published by West and Johnston in Richmond, Virginia, and printed by Evans and Cogswell in Columbia, South

Carolina. Evans was unaware during the war that the novel had also been printed in New York. A copy that she had given to a friend was smuggled past the Union's blockade of Georgia's coast and rivers to a Confederate-held port in Cuba. From there, the book traveled north, where it was published without the dedication to the "Army of the Southern Confederacy." The New York edition also includes changes to Evans's language, making it more accessible to Northern audiences.

By 1896 several new editions had been printed in the North. Some passages were shortened or clarified, and large passages of Confederate propaganda as well as passages critical of the federal government were cut out entirely. In 1992 Faust edited a new edition of *Macaria*, which reinstates the novel's original text.

HEATHER L. WHITTAKER

 # "Marching through Georgia"

"Marching through Georgia" is one of the best-known songs of the Civil War. Composed by Henry Clay Work and published soon after the war ended in 1865, it commemorates Union general William T. Sherman's march from Atlanta to Savannah in the fall of 1864. The song became very popular in the North and sold more than 500,000 copies in the first twelve years after its publication.

Work, a Connecticut native living in Chicago when the war broke out, was a printer by trade as well as a self-taught musician. In 1861 he signed a contract to produce sheet music for Root and Cady, a Chicago publishing firm. The firm's George F. Root was himself a well-known composer of popular music and Civil War songs.

"Marching through Georgia" is a five-stanza song with a recurring chorus and was published with a piano accompaniment. Like many Civil War songs, it served as a rallying cry for the North, even though the song did not appear until after the war had ended. Some historians have attributed the song's popularity to its morale-boosting effect as a celebration of the triumphant end of the war. As a testament to freedom and sacrifice, its inspirational lyrics also contain a comic undertone.

The first stanza calls for the rallying of the troops with the bugle call. The second stanza contains the line "How the darkies shouted when they heard the joyful sound" and claims that even sweet potatoes popped out of the ground as the "Yankees" approached. The third stanza is a nostalgic account of the Union soldiers as they see their flag raised. In the fourth stanza, the comedic tone returns with reference to "saucy rebels" who did not think the Northern troops could reach the coast. The final stanza describes the 300-mile-long March to the Sea, in which the Union army, in a 60-mile-wide column, "made a thoroughfare for freedom and her train." The chorus is written in four-part harmony for soprano, alto, tenor, and bass, to be performed by a group of people in response to a soloist singing the stanzas.

While this song remained quite popular in the North and became a standard at veterans' reunions and political rallies, Sherman did not like it and once stated that "if I had thought when I made that march that it would have inspired any one to compose the piece, I would have marched around the state."

"Marching through Georgia" became a popular tune for parade bands and inspired later composers, including Charles Ives. In Ives's early-twentieth-century composition for orchestra *Three Places in New England,* the first movement, "The 'St. Gaudens' in Boston Common," features a medley that interweaves Work's tune with Root's "Battle Cry of Freedom" and an old plantation song, "Old Black Joe." "Marching through Georgia" remains a recognizable song. It may be heard in the film *Gone With the Wind* (1939) and was used by Ken Burns in his documentary *The Civil War* (1990). Princeton University once adopted the tune as its football fight song.

Thomas "Blind Tom" Wiggins was an African American musician and composer. Blind from birth and born into slavery, he became well known for his piano virtuosity. In 1861, at the age of fifteen, Wiggins composed his most famous piece, "The Battle of Manassas," a song evoking the sounds of battle interspersed with train sounds and whistles, which Wiggins made himself.—From online entry "Thomas 'Blind Tom' Wiggins"

WWW.GEORGIAENCYCLOPEDIA.ORG

SONG LYRICS

Ring the good ol' bugle, boys, we'll sing another song,
Sing it with the spirit that will start the world along,
Sing it as we used to sing it 50,000 strong
While we were marching through Georgia.

[Chorus]: Hurrah, hurrah, we bring the jubilee!
Hurrah, hurrah, the flag that makes you free!
So we sang the chorus from Atlanta to the sea
While we were marching through Georgia!

How the darkies shouted when they heard the joyful sound!
How the turkeys gobbled which our commissary found!
How the sweet potatoes even started from the ground
While we were marching through Georgia! [Chorus]

Yes, and there were Union men who wept with joyful tears
When they saw the honored flag they had not seen for years.
Hardly could they be restrained from breaking forth in cheers
While we were marching through Georgia! [Chorus]

"Sherman's dashing Yankee boys will never reach the coast!"
So the saucy rebels said, and 'twas a handsome boast,
Had they not forgot, alas, to reckon with the host
While we were marching through Georgia! [Chorus]

So we made a thoroughfare for freedom and her train,
Sixty miles in latitude, 300 to the main.
Treason fled before us, for resistance was in vain
While we were marching through Georgia! [Chorus]

VANESSA P. TOME

 On the Plantation

On the Plantation: A Story of a Georgia Boy's Adventures during the
War (1892), written by famed New South journalist and folklorist Joel
Chandler Harris, is a fictionalized memoir of Harris's adolescence dur-
ing the Civil War. It is both an idealized portrait of plantation life on
Turnwold, the estate of Joseph Addison Turner in Eatonton (Putnam
County), and a sanitized treatment of the war. Purchased by publisher
S. S. McClure in New York for $2,500, the narrative was first serialized
in several national newspapers, beginning in 1891. A year later *On the
Plantation* appeared as a book published by D. Appleton and Company,
the same firm that had published Harris's first volume of Uncle Remus
stories. *On the Plantation* never achieved the popularity or critical ac-
claim of the Uncle Remus folktales, however, and most scholars subsequently ignored it.

Origins and Influences

Born in Eatonton in 1845, Harris was the illegitimate son of Mary Ann Harris and an Irish immigrant laborer. In March 1862 Harris found employment as a typesetter—or printer's devil—for Turner's *The Countryman*, a widely read Confederate newspaper. In return for his services, he received lodging on Turner's plantation. He remained there for the duration of the war, leaving in June 1866 to pursue a career in journalism. In his capacity as a journalist, Harris gained considerable recognition, especially in his efforts to foster reconciliation between the North and the South, but it was his stories—largely inspired by his experiences at Turnwold—that made him a cultural icon. While residing there, Harris spent hundreds of hours in the slave quarters. Much of his self-consciousness about his own origins receded during that time, and his humble background enabled him to form a bond with the slaves, which in turn gave him opportunity to learn their stories, language, and inflections. He later incorporated much of what he had absorbed during this time into his literary works, including *On the Plantation.*

Eatonton native **Joel Chandler Harris** gained national prominence for his Uncle Remus folktales. He published thirty-five books in his lifetime, including novels and short-story collections. Harris was also a prominent "progressive conservative" New South journalist, writing thousands of articles for the *Atlanta Constitution* over a twenty-four-year period.—From online entry "Joel Chandler Harris"

WWW.GEORGIAENCYCLOPEDIA.ORG

Portrayal of War

On the Plantation closely parallels Harris's adolescence on Turnwold Plantation between 1862 and 1866. In this semiautobiographical work of fiction, the Civil War years provide the narrative framework; the towns of Eatonton and Hillsborough, as well as the Turnwold Plantation, serve as the primary locales; and, in many instances, the names of Turner and of Harris's slave acquaintances remain unchanged. Harris did, however, replace his own name with that of Joe Maxwell. The first chapters detail Maxwell's childhood in Eatonton, including the circumstances that led him to Turnwold; descriptions of the adjustments to his new job and setting; and colorful sketches of plantation acquaintances, both black and white. The reader is made especially aware of a romanticized portrayal of slavery. On Harris's fictionalized plantation, the slaves are happy, loyal, and well behaved, and they purportedly enjoy comfortable lives, never considering desertion or rebellion. The remaining chapters detail how Turnwold and its residents internalize and adapt to the realities and aftermath of the Civil War.

The ways in which Harris chose to remember his Civil War experience and, in turn, to fictionalize it often do not conform to reality. Many salient aspects of Harris's life on the home front are omitted and/or significantly downplayed, creating an account that does not accord with the memories of most middle Georgians who lived through similar experiences. Although *On the Plantation* chronicles life on Turnwold during the Civil War years, Harris does not introduce details of the conflict until well into his work, and when he does, they receive cursory treatment.

Particularly surprising, considering the magnitude of the event for both whites and blacks, is Harris's scant attention to Union general William T. Sherman's March to the Sea. The left wing of Sherman's army—led by General Henry Slocum—did, in fact, raid areas of Putnam County in November 1864. Turnwold was invaded on November 20–21, 1864, and Union soldiers stole horses and other valuables from the plantation. Neighboring properties suffered more extensive damage; however, Harris, through Joe Maxwell, characterizes these invaders as good-natured and sometimes even benevolent. Few, if any, Georgians would have concurred with Harris's depiction of Sherman's troops, and the reader has little sense of the hardships and deprivations that Georgians suffered during the war.

In the final chapters of *On the Plantation*, after Sherman vacates middle Georgia, Turner frees his slaves. However, in Harris's version of events, most of the Turnwold slaves choose to remain with their master, where "peace and quiet reigned on the plantation." In point of fact, "peace and quiet" most probably never typified Turnwold prior to hostilities and certainly did not typify it afterward; financially ruined by the Civil War, Turner lost his plantation and died in 1868 at the age of forty-one.

While writing *On the Plantation* and numerous other stories, Harris doubled as an associate editor for the *Atlanta Constitution*. Along with Henry W. Grady, his close colleague and friend, Harris was a significant voice for the New South. Together, as highly placed journalists, Harris and Grady promoted racial and especially regional reconciliation, hoping to soften Northern animosities toward the South. Harris's arguably sanitized portrayal of the Civil War in *On the Plantation* may have helped to foster some harmony between the North and South at a time when it was most needed.

KATHERINE E. ROHRER

} *The General*

The General, released in 1927, is a classic silent film directed by and starring Buster Keaton, one of the major comic filmmakers of the silent era. It was one of several films loosely based on the Andrews Raid of 1862, a key event of the Civil War in Georgia.

On April 12, 1862, Union raiders staged a daring seizure of a Confederate train pulled by the *General*, a locomotive traveling north from Big Shanty (present-day Kennesaw, in Cobb County) toward Chattanooga, Tennessee. The raiders' dramatic trek toward Union lines was marred by setbacks; they ultimately abandoned the train and were captured by Confederate forces. Eight of their number, including leader James J. Andrews, were executed.

Earlier Cinematic Precedents

There were several antecedents to *The General*. In 1903 Edison Studios, established by inventor and entrepreneur Thomas Edison, produced *The Great Train Robbery*, a short film that set a new standard for cinematography. Approximately twelve minutes in length, the film depicts a train robbery and a gunfight in which several of the robbers are killed. *The Great Train Robbery* is widely remembered for its closing scene, in which one of the robbers fires his pistol directly at the camera.

In 1911 the Kalem Company produced *Railroad Raiders of '62*. This film, also about twelve minutes in length, does not make an overt reference to the Andrews Raid but is clearly based on that event. As the plot unfolds, the audience sees a woman waving frantically to stop a Confederate train, before she faints alongside the tracks. When the train crew stops to help her, they are overpowered by a group of raiders—including the "woman," who turns out to be a man in disguise. The Confederates pursue the raiders, first on a handcar and then by locomotive, dealing with torn-up rails along the way. The chase ends with gunfire, and the raiders are either shot dead or burned alive when

The Southern Museum of Civil War and Locomotive History, located in Kennesaw, houses the *General*, the train engine stolen from Big Shanty during Andrews Raid. In addition to commemorating the raid, the museum highlights other aspects of the war's history in **Cobb County**, as well as railroad and locomotive history.—From online entry "Cobb County"

WWW.GEORGIAENCYCLOPEDIA.ORG

the Confederates set fire to a barn in which they are hiding. Edison's film clearly influenced the *Railroad Raiders of '62*, but the Kalem Company nonetheless took some pains to incorporate elements of the actual Andrews Raid into the script.

Between November 1914 and February 1917, Kalem produced another antecedent to *The General,* a serial entitled *The Hazards of Helen.* One of the longest serialized films in the history of cinema, with 119 episodes totaling more than twenty-three hours, *The Hazards of Helen* includes a reformatted version of *Railroad Raiders of '62,* which was released in 1915 as episode number 19. The episodes depict the ongoing story of Helen (played by four different actresses), who is always involved in some kind of escapade, such as chasing train robbers or preventing a train wreck. Helen is sometimes rescued by a man, but most of the time she manages to extricate herself, unaided, from dangerous situations.

The General

Along with Charlie Chaplin and Harold Lloyd, Buster Keaton is remembered as one of the great comedic geniuses in the history of early American film. *The General* is perhaps Keaton's best work and continues to garner the most recognition from present-day audiences. It was one of the most expensive films produced during the silent era, and despite its popularity with audiences, Keaton made very little money from the picture, owing in part to his meticulous production standards, as well as to his naivete in matters of studio finances.

In the film, Keaton portrays Georgia native Johnnie Gray, a train engineer with similarities to the real-life train conductor William Fuller. Keaton selected Marion Mack to portray his erstwhile fiancée, Annabelle Lee, and cast his own father, Joe Keaton, as a Union general. Keaton filmed most of the movie in Oregon during the summer and fall of 1926. Unlike the later Walt Disney film *The Great Locomotive Chase* (1956), Keaton adopted a distinctly Southern perspective for *The General.*

While the film is clearly based on the Andrews Raid, it is wildly inaccurate and full of improbable scenes, included primarily for comic effect. Keaton's character, Johnnie Gray, attempts repeatedly to join the Confederate military but is turned down because he is more valuable as a locomotive engineer. His fiancée and her father misinterpret the situation and attribute his continued civilian status to cowardice. Neither will be seen in public with such a man. When Union spies steal the *General* in

Marietta (one of several actual place names incorporated into the narrative), Annabelle Lee is on board the train. Johnnie Gray, apparently motivated by devotion to his fiancée and not to the Confederacy, pursues the *General* in a second locomotive, the *Texas*. As the chase proceeds, the pursuer ultimately becomes the pursued, as Johnnie Gray abandons his train, falls down an embankment, and reboards the locomotive at a lower elevation.

The carefully choreographed movements of the train chase sequence occupy only a small portion of the film. Johnnie Gray later rescues Annabelle Lee from the headquarters of a Union general, fends off an attack by a bear, and takes back his locomotive from the middle of a Union encampment (a reversal of the Andrews theft at Big Shanty). He is then chased back to Confederate lines (setting a bridge on fire in the process), where he warns the Confederate commander of an impending Union attack, inadvertently takes part in a battle, saves the day, captures a Union general, and is given a commission in the Confederate army, thus winning the undying love of Annabelle Lee.

In assessing *The General*, it is important to note that the film's most obvious factual inaccuracies involve reversals of the actual course of events. In much the same way that the Redeemers (former Confederates) were able to reverse public perceptions of what had happened in the South during Reconstruction and the decades of the late 1800s, the film establishes the Southerner as the focus of all the action and turns him into the hero.

One of twelve films made by Buster Keaton Productions between 1921 and 1928, *The General* is an odd mix of Keaton's trademark physical—often slapstick—comedy and action adventure, but it is grounded far more fully in historic circumstances than any other of his films. Critics have long recognized the work as Keaton's crowning cinematic achievement. *The General* was added in 2007 to the American Film Institute's list of the 100 greatest films of all time, ranked at number 18. Only one other silent film—Charlie Chaplin's *City Lights* (1931)—is ranked higher.

ALBERT CHURELLA

} *Gone With the Wind* (Novel)

Atlanta native Margaret Mitchell's 1936 novel of the Civil War and Reconstruction in Georgia, *Gone With the Wind*, occupies an important place in any history of twentieth-century American literature. Dismissed by most academic literary critics for being uneven, flawed, and conventionally written in an age marked by literary experimentation, and attacked by some cultural commentators as promulgating racist myths and undermining the very foundations of its basically feminist paradigm, the best-selling novel of the twentieth century continues to withstand its detractors.

Influences and Historical Background

Upon its publication, reviewers drew comparisons with William Makepeace Thackeray's *Vanity Fair* and Leo Tolstoy's *War and Peace*. Margaret Mitchell claimed not to have read Thackeray's novel until after she had completed her Civil War saga and confessed her inability ever to get very far in Tolstoy's monumental work. She did admit her saturation in Charles Dickens and her sense that her work was a "'Victorian' type novel." Mitchell chose an epic moment in American history and never flinched in bringing it to life on a grand scale; a creative energy reminiscent of the nineteenth century drives the work. From the memorable first sentence through the Twelve Oaks barbecue on the eve of the war, the fall of Atlanta, Scarlett O'Hara's unforgettable journey back home to Tara, and her beginning struggles during Reconstruction, Mitchell's narrative power (at the very top of its form) propels the reader through the limning of a culture (its grace and color and folly and weakness), a vivid evocation of the cauldron of war, and a bitter picture of the devastation following.

The author spoke often of her research in accounts and memoirs of the period, but probably more important was her knowing people who had lived through the era. A child naturally drawn to old people and to the great drama of her region,

Margaret Mitchell was a fourth-generation Atlantan. Her grandfather Russell Mitchell fought in the Civil War and suffered two bullet wounds to the head during the fighting at Antietam. In 1926, to relieve the boredom of being cooped up with a broken ankle, she began to write *Gone With the Wind.*—From online entry "Margaret Mitchell"

WWW.GEORGIAENCYCLOPEDIA.ORG

Mitchell had gone horseback riding with Confederate veterans, sat listening in the parlors of faded belles, and taken every literary advantage of her exposure to the past. The result is a Balzacian sense of the texture of the period—Scarlett O'Hara's green morocco slippers, the bright rag rugs in her bedroom at Tara, Melanie Hamilton's black lace mittens—that leads to the capturing of color and movement in great scenes like the Twelve Oaks barbecue and the ball in Atlanta. Alternating with such scenes are remarkably evocative descriptions of the languorous beauty of the landscape.

Characters and Setting

Though her four major characters have now become stereotypes, when she drew them, with the exception of the Byronic Rhett Butler, they were not. Scarlett is a full-blooded woman, selfish, deluded, conflicted, but driven by her own strength of will. Melanie is far from the foolishly duped Amelia of Thackeray's novel; underlying her sweetness and Christian charity is enormous strength and purpose. And the Hamlet-like Ashley Wilkes is not the beau ideal of the Southern planter or Confederate stalwart.

Mitchell's upland Georgia is also not the dreamy land of a Thomas Nelson Page plantation novel. She is insightful on the social structure, its closeness to pioneer days, and its mixture of old bloodlines and new men. She is astute about the violence lying not far submerged beneath the surface of all classes. She is unsentimental about the Lost Cause, tracing its origins to unreconstructed women, not to the men who fought the war. And she is remarkably good as a novelist of manners, understanding the mores and shibboleths of the culture she is examining and bringing them skillfully into play.

Thematic Motifs

Like many of the omnibus novels of the nineteenth century that influenced it, *Gone With the Wind* is a powerful, flawed, uneven, and sometimes disturbing novel that explores diverse facets of the human experience.

Sexuality. The novel also contains the stuff of great romance. Two great loves—one a misplaced, deluded infatuation, and the other a thwarted union of two passionate spirits—share equal focus with the story of people swept along by the forces of history. Additionally, the novel is sexually charged. Scarlett's Bovaristic attraction to Ashley could not be sustained were she not given proof at two significant points in the novel that he responds to her sexually, that he wants, in his own phrase, to "take" her. The powerful sexual chemistry dramatized between Scarlett and Rhett provides a running tension of the novel, countered as it is by Scarlett's incredibly dogged and willful attachment to her first romantic ideal. It is testimony to Mitchell's skill that these basic sexual and emotional tensions could be sustained for 1,037 pages in the original Macmillan edition.

Survival. Mitchell's *Gone With the Wind* is one of the great novels of survival, and therein lies much of its appeal. In chapter 43 Mitchell gives to Rhett Butler a version of the speech that we know now her own mother had given her when she was a child. He is speaking, in the war's aftermath, about Ashley Wilkes:

> Whenever the world up-ends, his kind is the first to perish. And why not? They don't deserve to survive because they won't fight—don't know how to fight. This isn't the first time the world's been upside down and it won't be the last. . . . But there are always a hardy few who come through and, given time, they are right back where they were before the world turned over.

The Darwinian message is made flesh in Scarlett O'Hara. But Mitchell is clear-sighted enough to see that a moral and emotional price is often paid for survival against great odds. That fact is borne out in a number of ways in the novel's conclusion.

Feminism. Mitchell also wrote a distinctly feminist novel. She sounds the note early with the narrator's comment that "at no time, before or since, had so low a premium been placed on feminine naturalness," and she mercilessly exposes a Southern patriarchy that requires that women be flatteringly subservient to males, no matter how much less intelligent and capable. But even more telling than its overtly repeated feminist message, it is a novel dominated by strong women—Scarlett, Melanie, Ellen O'Hara, Mrs. Tarleton, Grandma Fontaine, Mrs. Meade, and Mammy. Mitchell takes pains to show the spine of a Southern matriarchy secretly underlying a patriarchy.

Some critics have argued that Scarlett's feminist success story is undercut by a sexual desire to be engulfed and dominated. Mitchell does problematize human sexuality. Ashley Wilkes's own fear of being passionately released but then engulfed and dominated by Scarlett is a case in point. "You would want all of a man," he laments. In Mitchell's failure to bend sexual desire to some clinically theorized, balanced, emotionally healthy paradigm, she is a modern.

Representations of African Americans

The inherent racism of the novel is more difficult to defend. Characteristic of her generation of Southerners is Mitchell's unquestioning acceptance of the essential inferiority of African Americans, whom she presents, in a few distasteful instances, in nonhuman terms. Melded with that prejudice, contradictorily, is evidence of her great respect for some members of the race. Such a bifurcated vision is the very dilemma that Mississippi author William Faulkner wrestled with his entire writing career. In the novel Mitchell merely accepts the institution of slavery and fails to recognize the strength and courage of those who rebelled against their status as slaves.

What she presents well is an array of portraits of an unlettered African American peasantry, ranging from the nobility, shrewdness, loyalty, and affection of Mammy to the foolishness of Prissy. Like William Shakespeare, Mitchell has her fools among all classes. No one has yet criticized her portrayal of Honey Wilkes. Margaret Mitchell was proud of the fact that she had tried to convey accurately the speech of the old African Americans of her acquaintance without resorting to the entangled dialect of Joel Chandler Harris, and she reacted against all the stock figures, white and black, of the sentimental plantation novels that preceded *Gone With the Wind*.

Mitchell is most open to criticism in the last third of the novel. The narrative drive diminishes, returning only in fits and starts. Historical background is too often telegraphed, rather than blended, into the fabric of the novel. And Mitchell appears to succumb to a nightmare vision of white female purity under attack by black bestiality only to be saved by the Ku Klux Klan. The model here, which Mitchell halfway acknowledges in a letter, is Thomas Dixon's racist novel *The Clansman* (1905), made into what is often regarded as the first masterpiece of American cinema, *The Birth of a Nation*, in 1915—both works lying solidly behind the reemergence of the Klan in the twentieth century.

Mitchell's conflicted sensibility is apparent when she has Scarlett comment about one such incident, "Probably the girl hadn't been raped after all. Probably she'd just been frightened silly." And she has Scarlett deliberately and foolishly expose herself to danger, against all advice, by her stubborn drive through Shantytown, where the homeless and desperate have collected. And even though the black man's assault upon her seems closer to a robbery than a rape attempt, still by introducing the situation of the imperiled white female threatened by the powerful black man and the resulting Klan vengeance, Mitchell's novel invites the same criticism heaped on Dixon's work.

Conclusion

With its richly detailed evocation of a former age, its narrative engagement, its compelling portrait of the archetypal human instinct for survival, and its reflection of the contrariness of romantic dreams, *Gone With the Wind* continues to capture, entertain, excite, and sometimes exasperate readers. As well as being a gripping novel of epic proportions, it is valuable as a historical document—though one that must be carefully read. A vivid record of a segment of life in the nineteenth-century South, the novel is also the record of a twentieth-century sensibility's engagement with the region's past.

HUBERT H. MCALEXANDER

 Gone With the Wind (Film)

Few films are so closely identified with a geographical region as *Gone With the Wind* is identified with Georgia and the Civil War South. The 1939 adaptation of Margaret Mitchell's 1936 novel, produced by David O. Selznick, featured such well-known actors as Clark Gable (Rhett Butler), Olivia de Havilland (Melanie Wilkes), and Leslie Howard (Ashley Wilkes), and made a star of actress Vivien Leigh (Scarlett O'Hara). It remains one of the most popular and commercially successful films ever made. Its main theme, from the Max Steiner score, is recognized throughout the world. In its use of color, scene design, and cinematography, it set new standards. The film won eight Academy Awards, more than any film up to that time.

Adapting the Novel

The film is a relatively faithful adaptation of the novel, despite a hand-ful of significant changes. The novel offers detailed information about the early lives of Gerald and Ellen O'Hara that is largely missing from the film. The film significantly simplifies Scarlett's life (removing, for ex-ample, two of her children) and discards much of the novel's social con-text. The novel's racial attitudes were softened—offensive language and references to the Ku Klux Klan were removed, and the sexual overtones of the attack on Scarlett in the freedmen's settlement were deleted. The novel was sexually explicit for its day, but this too was toned down, in ac-cord with the Hays Code; Rhett Butler's rape of Scarlett and Melanie's childbirth were treated in indirect or euphemistic terms.

Seldom has a successful film been the product of such chaos and dis-organization. The time between Selznick's purchase of the rights to the novel and the actual premiere was three and a half years; in the 1930s most movies were produced and premiered within a matter of months. The search for actors to play the leading characters became the stuff of American legend: 1,400 interviews and ninety screen tests were nec-essary before Selznick cast Vivien Leigh, a twenty-six-year-old British actress, as Scarlett. Clark Gable was a popular choice as Rhett Butler, though Selznick had to sell MGM an interest in the film to gain permis-sion to use him. Gable did not want to play the part. Leslie Howard was embarrassed by the Ashley Wilkes role. Olivia de Havilland, on the other hand, actively sought to play the part of Melanie Wilkes.

Perhaps as a way of generating publicity, and to create the proper atmosphere, Selznick did look for Southern actors. A casting call in Atlanta, held at the Biltmore Hotel, brought a mob of hun-dreds of young women hoping to play Scarlett. In the end, only a few minor roles went to South-erners. Gable was from Ohio and refused to use a Southern accent; Leigh and Howard were from England.

Two Georgians, Susan Myrick and Wilbur G. Kurtz, served as advisors to Selznick on matters of cultural and historical accuracy. Selznick wanted to produce an epic drama that was historically ac-curate. The film was largely shot in California,

Despite a journalism career with the *Macon Telegraph* that spanned half a century, **Susan Myrick** is best known as the technical ad-visor for the film *Gone With the Wind* (1939). She also held many other titles in her long and colorful life—educator, soil conservation advocate, civic leader, amateur theater doyenne, and painter.—From online entry "Susan Myrick"

WWW.GEORGIAENCYCLOPEDIA.ORG

with artists, painters, scene designers, and architects working together to create a convincing simulation of the Southern landscape. The work of production designer William Cameron Menzies and costume designer Walter Plunkett and the attention to detail in costumes, buildings, and set design are major reasons for the film's success.

George Cukor was Selznick's original choice as director. Cukor spent two years on the project and was actively involved in casting the film and developing major characters. Nineteen days after shooting began, however, Selznick fired Cukor, because they disagreed on how filming should proceed. Selznick then turned to Victor Fleming, who was just completing work on *The Wizard of Oz* (1939). Fleming reshot many scenes already filmed by Cukor and demanded that filming proceed in a more conventional fashion. Although Fleming was credited as director, a number of others also had a role in directing, especially Cukor, who had a lasting influence on the film.

Fitting the events of this 1,000-plus-page novel into a film that could be viewed in one sitting would have been a formidable task for any screenwriter. (At just under four hours, it was one of the longest Hollywood films ever made.) Any screenwriter would have found it a challenge to satisfy Selznick. Pulitzer Prize–winning dramatist Sidney Howard wrote several drafts of the screenplay before withdrawing from the project, frustrated by Selznick's interference. Selznick attempted to write and rewrite sections of the screenplay himself, often composing scenes the night before they were shot. Others worked on the script as well. The playwright Ben Hecht was hired to work on the script, and finally Howard was brought back to get it in shape, even as filming was under way.

The Film

Often touted as the epic story of the Old South, *Gone With the Wind* focuses almost entirely on the Civil War and the years immediately following, ending around 1872. Such events as the start of the war, Gettysburg, the siege of Atlanta, Sherman's march through Georgia, and Reconstruction provide a historical background for the main focus—Scarlett O'Hara, her unrequited love for Ashley Wilkes, and her marriages, especially her turbulent relationship with her third husband, Rhett Butler.

Geographically, the film moves between the O'Hara plantation, Tara, which Scarlett struggles to save, and Atlanta, which both film and novel treat as a symbol of hope and promise for Georgia's future. Scarlett is identified with Tara, but more strongly with Atlanta, especially because

of her fierce independence, her disdain for convention, and her growing concern with money (a concern more evident in the novel than the
film). Ultimately, both Scarlett and Atlanta symbolize the post–Civil War
South, struggling to survive and rebuild.

Politically, the film offers a conservative view of Georgia and the
South. In her novel, despite her Southern prejudices, Mitchell showed
clear awareness of the shortcomings of her characters and their region.
The film is less analytical. It portrays the story from a clearly Old South
point of view: the South is presented as a great civilization, the practice of slavery is never questioned, and the plight of the freedmen after
the Civil War is implicitly blamed on their emancipation. A series of
scenes whose racism rivals that of D. W. Griffith's film *The Birth of a Nation* (1915) show Reconstruction mainly as a time when Southern whites
were victimized by freed slaves, who themselves were exploited by Northern carpetbaggers.

Although the film provides a compelling if romanticized portrait of
the Southern planter class, it vilifies the white lower class (mainly represented by the overseer Jonas Wilkerson), and slaves and ex-slaves are
viewed both as clowns and as faithful servants. *Gone With the Wind* was
hardly alone in the 1930s in its caricature of African American characters, and it did offer previously unavailable opportunities to such black
actors as Hattie McDaniel (Mammy), Butterfly McQueen (Prissy), and
Eddie Anderson (Uncle Peter).

A major theme in the film is the contrast between the land, which
the O'Haras value, and the commercial environment of the city. Some
of the most compelling scenes center on the land: Gerald O'Hara's insistence to his daughter Scarlett that "land's the only thing in the world
worth working for. Worth fighting for, worth dying for. Because it's the
only thing that lasts"; Scarlett's discovery after her retreat from Atlanta
that Tara still stands, unburned by the Union army; and the scene in
which she raises her fist to the sky and vows, "As God is my witness, I'll
never be hungry again." Other notable scenes focus on the Battle of Atlanta, wounded soldiers laid in the city's immense railyard, and a grue-
some battlefield traversed by Scarlett during her retreat.

Premiere and Posterity

Gone With the Wind premiered at the Loew's Grand Theater in Atlanta
on December 15, 1939. The theater's façade had been renovated to resemble a Southern mansion. A three-day celebration preceded the pre-

miere. Mayor William B. Hartsfield declared a holiday and gave the city's workers a half day off. A crowd of 18,000 gathered in front of the theater on opening night, eager for a glimpse of the stars. Most of the major actors in the film attended the premiere, with the exception of Howard and McDaniel (the black actors were not invited). Margaret Mitchell attended as well, and after being escorted to the stage by Gable and Leigh, she gave the film and Selznick her blessing.

Gone With the Wind was widely praised as a landmark achievement, and critics continue to regard it as important for its cinematography, art direction, and special effects, and for its ambitious portrayal of history. In a year that produced some of the best American films ever made, *Gone With the Wind* received thirteen Academy Award nominations in twelve categories (plus two nominations in special categories) and won eight awards, including Best Picture, Best Screenplay, Best Director, Best Actress (Vivien Leigh), Best Supporting Actress (Hattie McDaniel, a first for a black actress), Best Art Direction, Best Film Editing, and Best Cinematography, as well as a special award to William Cameron Menzies for use of color.

In its first run the film played for slightly more than two years and was seen by more than 25 million viewers. Many more have seen it in subsequent releases and on home video. Frank S. Nugent asked in his *New York Times* review of the film, "Is it the greatest motion picture ever made? Probably not, although it is the greatest motion mural we have seen and the most ambitious filmmaking venture in Hollywood's spectacular history." A *McCall's* reviewer wrote that the film, "fantastic in scope, extraordinary in detail, played better than any movie I've ever seen, and more colossal, stupendous, gigantic and terrific than any picture ever has been." *Gone With the Wind* is fourth on the American Film Institute's list of the "100 Greatest American Movies of All Time." It is probable that more people have seen *Gone With the Wind* than any other film ever made.

HUGH RUPPERSBURG

} The Great Locomotive Chase

The Great Locomotive Chase is an action-adventure film produced by Walt Disney in 1956. To date it is the last of several films depicting the Andrews Raid of 1862, which took place in north Georgia during the Civil War.

On April 12, 1862, Union raiders staged a daring seizure of a Confederate train pulled by the *General*, a locomotive headed north from Big Shanty (present-day Kennesaw, in Cobb County) toward Chattanooga, Tennessee, and the Union lines. The Disney film was produced nearly thirty years after *The General* (1927), a silent-film version of the story by comedian Buster Keaton, and offers a far more serious and straightforward telling of these events. While Keaton casts the Confederates as the heroes of his narrative, *The Great Locomotive Chase* focuses on the raiders and portrays their leader, James J. Andrews, as the film's protagonist.

The Source Material

William Pittenger, a participant in the Andrews Raid, wrote several narrative accounts of the event. Born in Ohio in 1840, Pittenger joined the Union army in 1861 and the following year rode north in a Western and Atlantic boxcar during the raid, until he was captured by Confederate forces. In 1864 he became a Methodist minister and subsequently spent much of his life attending veterans' reunions and writing a series of books chronicling the raid.

Pittenger's first book about the raid, *Daring and Suffering*, appeared in 1863, and he revised the work several times. He later admitted that "*Daring and Suffering*, like a number of similar sketches published in newspapers, magazines, and pamphlets, was a hasty narrative of personal adventure, and made no pretense of completeness." His next work about the raid, *Capturing a Locomotive: A History of Secret Service in the Late War* (1881), greatly exaggerates Pittenger's own importance in the raid. His last major work, *The Great Locomotive Chase: A History of the Andrews Railroad Raid into Georgia in 1862* (1889), is dedicated to "The Grand Army of the West, which, under command of General Sherman, in one hundred days of continuous battle, followed us and conquered where we only dared."

The Film

The Great Locomotive Chase, directed by Francis D. Lyon, is a fairly accurate depiction of William Pittenger's various accounts of the raid; in fact, the film includes a shot of Pittenger's book cover, but not of the raid itself. The action sequences were filmed in Habersham and Rabun counties in northeast Georgia, and the tracks of the old Tallulah Falls Railroad were brought back into service for the locomotive chase scenes. Walt Disney himself spent several weeks on location in the north Georgia mountains.

The film begins with Edwin M. Stanton, the secretary of war, presenting the Congressional Medal of Honor to the surviving members of the raid team, including Pittenger (played by John Lupton), who serves as the film's narrator. This scene moves quickly into a flashback, with Pittenger introducing civilian James J. Andrews (played by longtime Disney stalwart Fess Parker) as the "man of mystery" who conceives of the daring scheme; Andrews is quickly established as the film's hero. The narrative details Andrews's recruitment of his volunteer raiders and dramatizes their secret advance into Georgia, the taking of the locomotive, the suspense-filled chase that ensues, and the ultimate failure of the mission, culminating in the execution of Andrews and other captives.

While Pittenger's early books vilified the Confederacy, in his later life he gave high praise to William Fuller, the Western and Atlantic conductor who doggedly pursued the stolen train. The film reflects this later, more conciliatory attitude, and Fuller (portrayed by Jeffrey Hunter) emerges as a minor hero in his own right. (His character is a more realistic version of the Southern protagonist played by Buster Keaton in *The General*.)

Despite its Northern bias, the film ultimately emphasizes reconciliation between North and South. When Pittenger sees a Confederate soldier, he muses, "That soldier—he's supposed to be my enemy—I'm supposed to hate him," but he can't bring himself to do so. At the end of the film, as Andrews is about to be executed, he shakes hands with

Nearly 1,000 men from **Habersham County** joined the Confederate army, and the Habersham Iron Works and Manufacturing Company produced arms during the war. In 1864 Confederate troops defeated Union troops at the Battle of Narrows (also called the Battle of Currahee), which was fought at a mountain pass in the county.—From online entry "Habersham County"

WWW.GEORGIAENCYCLOPEDIA.ORG

Fuller—something that never occurred in real life but is symbolic of the reconciliation between North and South. The film is most critical not of the South but of the dangers of unrestrained emotion. As the Pittenger character notes, "My companion was the giant Bill Campbell—he had a violent temper—one such powder keg could blow the expedition sky-high."

As the narrator, Pittenger also recognizes the waste and futility of war itself and sees the raid as an attempt to prevent further bloodshed, saying, "I believe in the federal Union, and I hope we can preserve it without any more Shilohs—we could stop it." Thus, the film is ultimately not about a conflict between North and South but is rather an homage to the little man (or men) who fight the good fight against mass society. The film ultimately emphasizes the individual value of personal honor and bravery in wartime.

ALBERT CHURELLA

 The Andersonville Trial (Play) and *Andersonville* (Film)

A play, *The Andersonville Trial,* and two television films, *The Andersonville Trial* and *Andersonville,* have focused on the most notorious prison camp of the Civil War.

In 1959 dramatist Saul Levitt wrote his award-winning play *The Andersonville Trial,* which was produced that same year by William Darrid, Daniel Hollywood, and Eleanore Saidenberg. The play recounts the trial of Captain Henry Wirz, the Swiss doctor who commanded the Confederate garrison at Andersonville. Eleven years later, in 1970, George C. Scott, a cast member in the original Broadway production of Levitt's play, directed a critically acclaimed film adaptation also entitled *The Andersonville Trial.* In 1996 *Andersonville,* a film produced by David W. Rintels and directed by John Frankenheimer, appeared on Turner Network Television (TNT). This miniseries followed the experiences of Union soldiers imprisoned at the camp.

The Andersonville Trial

Levitt's two-act play *The Andersonville Trial* was first performed in New York City at Henry Miller's Theater on December 29, 1959. The original Broadway production was directed by José Ferrer, and the cast included Herbert Berghof, Albert Dekker, Lou Frizzell, Russell Hardie, and George C. Scott. Levitt used the official record of Wirz's 1865 trial as his primary source. In the play, Captain Wirz's defense maintains that he was simply following orders as he watched thousands of Union soldiers die at the prison. The prosecution argues that orders should not shield Wirz from being held responsible for the deaths. The play ends with the court sentencing Wirz to death. (Wirz was the only man tried and executed for war crimes committed during the Civil War.) Although much of the play's dialogue consists of direct testimony from the trial transcript, the play deviates from history in having Wirz testify on his own behalf and in making the ethical dilemma a central element of the case.

In 1970 Scott brought Levitt's play to television. The cast of Scott's film includes Richard Basehart as Henry Wirz, William Shatner as the government prosecutor, with Jack Cassidy as Otis Baker, Buddy Ebsen as Dr. John Bates, Cameron Mitchell as General Lew Wallace, and Martin Sheen as Captain Williams. The only member of the original Broadway cast to star in Scott's adaptation was Lou Frizzell. Like the play, the television production recounts through courtroom testimony such conditions as overcrowding, disease, malnutrition, and rat-infested living quarters. The movie presents the same ethical dilemma of Levitt's play, that of military officials who must decide when to disobey orders to save lives. The production won both an Emmy Award and a Peabody Award in 1971.

Andersonville

The two-part miniseries *Andersonville*, which aired on TNT in March 1996, was loosely based on MacKinlay Kantor's Pulitzer Prize–winning novel of the same name, published in 1955. The story follows a Massachusetts regiment from its capture through its stay at Andersonville. Frankenheimer constructed the set of *Andersonville* by building a stockade and barracks modeled after the original prison, and the cast and crew filmed on location in Turin (Coweta County), Georgia; North

Carolina; and California. Carmen Argenziano, Jarrod Emick, Frederic Forrest, and Ted Marcoux star in the miniseries.

Unlike *The Andersonville Trial*, the miniseries emphasizes tensions that emerge among the prisoners themselves. The plot focuses on the Union soldiers as they dig tunnels in an attempt to escape, resist dysentery by soaking up rainwater in their clothes to drink, and fight Union raiders, other captives who murder and steal from fellow prisoners. The climactic scene of the miniseries focuses on the trial of the raiders, in which they are found guilty.

Frankenheimer, whose long Hollywood career includes the films *The Birdman of Alcatraz* (1962), *The Manchurian Candidate* (1962), and *Seven Days in May* (1964), claimed that *Andersonville* was the most difficult film he ever directed. Andersonville garnered generally positive reviews from critics, and Frankenheimer received an Emmy Award for his direction.

BARTON MYERS

⧘ *Jubilee*

Margaret Walker's novel *Jubilee*, published in 1966, is one of the first novels to present the nineteenth-century African American historical experience in the South from a black and female point of view. The winner of Houghton Mifflin's Literary Fellowship Award, the novel is a fictionalized account of the life of Walker's great-grandmother, Margaret Duggans Ware Brown, who was born a slave in Dawson in Terrell County and lived through Reconstruction in southwest Georgia. It is based on stories told to Walker by her maternal grandmother. Walker herself was not a Georgian by birth. Born in Alabama, she spent most of her teaching career in Mississippi and earned her doctorate at the University of Iowa, where she wrote most of *Jubilee*, which served as her dissertation.

Walker also learned much about the life of her great-grandfather, a free man from birth. While on a speaking engagement in nearby Albany in 1947, Walker visited Dawson, where she found a man who had known her great-grandfather Randall Ware, who worked as a blacksmith and operated a gristmill, which she was able to visit. Walker based the description of the Dutton plantation, where most of her story is set, on an antebellum house that she discovered while visiting Bainbridge.

Walker's narrative is divided equally into sections on the antebellum era, the Civil War, and Reconstruction. Each section contains eighteen to twenty-two chapters. Despite the lengthy narrative passages and the demands on the reader imposed by the various dialects, *Jubilee* moves its heroine, Vyry, from the slave cabin to the "Big House," and from slavery to freedom.

Jubilee draws on both history and folk traditions. The treatment of the slaves is based on numerous slave narratives Walker researched in archives and libraries in Georgia, North Carolina, and the National Archives. The Civil War section of *Jubilee* traces the battles, historically, from Tennessee to Sherman's march through Georgia. The African American male characters Randall Ware and Brother Zeke, who are both literate, function in dual roles as spies for the Union army and foot soldiers in the Confederate army. As the Union soldiers storm and destroy the plantations, including the Dutton place, Vyry's role changes from that of chattel slave to primary protector of the property and caretaker of her master's daughter and two grandchildren.

Violence instigated by the **Ku Klux Klan in the Reconstruction era** was used to control freedpeople's social behavior. Black churches and schools were burned, teachers were attacked, and freedpeople who refused to show proper deference were beaten and killed. While these attacks surely terrorized some freedpeople, they failed to destroy the cultural and social independence blacks had gained with emancipation.—From online entry "Ku Klux Klan in the Reconstruction Era"

WWW.GEORGIAENCYCLOPEDIA.ORG

The book's final section begins with the war's end. It does not bring immediate freedom for Vyry. In addition to her caretaking duties, she, along with a "contraband" freedman named Innis Brown, must work the crops, as she anxiously awaits word from Randall Ware, her husband. When she receives news that Ware is dead, her heart will not allow her to believe it. Innis Brown, however, expresses interest in Vyry, befriends her children, and asks her to marry him. His hard work and his dream of owning his home and farm persuade her to do so. They leave the Dutton plantation and move to Alabama. After several temporary homes, including one burned by the Ku Klux Klan, Vyry and her family settle in Greenville, Alabama. The building of the new house is a community effort. Vyry's midwifery and the marketing of her vegetables establish a bond between blacks and whites in the community. The house-building celebration concludes with quilting bees, plenty of food, and the solidarity of the "neighborhood watch."

With a home and a farm in place, Randall Ware, who survived the Civil War after all, fulfills Vyry's dream of schooling for her children. After seven years of military duty, work in his smithy and gristmill in Dawson, and service as a charter member of the Georgia Equal Rights Association, Ware traces Vyry and her family to Greenville. He knows of her marriage to Innis Brown, but his mission is to take his son, Jim, to a training school in Selma, Alabama. The final section of *Jubilee* thus shifts its focus to the education of blacks during and after Reconstruction.

The ending of *Jubilee* suggests a connection between the events the novel has described during Reconstruction and the civil rights movement of the 1960s. The narrative ends on a train bound for Selma. As Jim and his father board the train, the conductor announces the segregated seating order—colored up front and whites in the rear.

JACQUELINE MILLER CARMICHAEL

 # *The Wind Done Gone*

Few novels have captured the popular American imagination more strongly than Margaret Mitchell's 1936 book, *Gone With the Wind.* Its sweeping, romantic story of the South and the Civil War has entranced readers since the day of its publication. Many readers, however, especially African Americans, have complained that the novel demeans the role of blacks and that its portrayals of such characters as Mammy and Prissy are racist stereotypes. For them, *Gone With the Wind* has little to tell us about the real experiences of African Americans in the South during and after the Civil War.

In 2001 Alice Randall, a Harvard literature graduate and Nashville, Tennessee, writer of songs and scripts, set out to put the record straight. Her novel *The Wind Done Gone* tells the story of *Gone With the Wind* from the perspective of the daughter of Mammy and Gerald O'Hara and thus the half sister of Scarlett O'Hara. Her name is Cynara (taken from the same Ernest Dowson poem that gave Mitchell her title), and she narrates the novel through diary entries about her life.

Randall loosely based her characters on Mitchell's, though she gave them different names and to some extent redefined them. Gerald O'Hara is Planter, his wife is Lady, Scarlett is Other, and Rhett Butler is

R. The plantation Tara becomes Tata. Some of the slaves have altered names as well: Pork becomes Garlic, for instance. Planter is a drunk easily manipulated by Garlic, who in fact runs the plantation. Because his wife is sexually cold, Planter takes Mammy as his mistress. Rhett Butler, in Mitchell's novel a swaggering, virile figure, in Randall's is aging and gray-haired. Scarlett, the strongest character in Mitchell's novel, is weak and given to hysteria in Randall's.

Parody or Appropriation?

Alice Randall has described her book as a parody, a novel that stands in a long tradition of writing that makes fun of other literary works. But the estate of Margaret Mitchell and its lawyers interpreted *The Wind Done Gone* differently. They saw it as appropriating without permission the characters and situations of *Gone With the Wind*. Tom Selz, an attorney for the Mitchell estate, argued that Randall's novel commits "wholesale theft" by borrowing characters, scenes, and situations from the Mitchell novel. Mitchell's lawyers sought to suppress publication of the novel on these grounds, and the first court ruling granted their request. According to Judge Charles Pannell: "When the reader of *Gone With the Wind* turns over the last page, he may well wonder what becomes of Ms. Mitchell's beloved characters and their romantic, but tragic, world. Ms. Randall has offered her vision of how to answer those unanswered questions. . . . The right to answer those questions and to write a sequel or other derivative work, however, legally belong to Ms. Mitchell's heirs, not Ms. Randall."

Randall appealed, and with the support of such well-known writers as Arthur Schlesinger, Harper Lee, Pat Conroy, Charles Johnson, James Alan McPherson, Larry McMurtry, Shelby Foote, and Toni Morrison, she argued that as a parody her book offered a time-honored literary response to another novel. Randall compared her book to the eighteenth-century English novel *Shamela* by Henry Fielding, which makes light of Samuel Richardson's novel *Pamela*.

On May 25, 2001, the Eleventh Circuit Court of Appeals in Atlanta agreed with Randall's argument and ruled in her favor. *The Wind Done Gone* was published shortly thereafter and quickly became a best seller, remaining on the *New York Times* list for many weeks. Randall and the Mitchell Trusts reached an out-of-court settlement in May 2002 that ended the dispute.

A Different Point of View

The Wind Done Gone recounts many of the events in *Gone With the Wind*, but from a different point of view and with numerous satiric twists. Behind the fumbling white inhabitants of the plantation are the slaves and former slaves who keep things going and manage to get what they need to survive and prosper by manipulating their owners. Randall shows a deep understanding of Mitchell's novel, and her book is not without compassion for the white characters, whom she sees as victims of their own foibles and weaknesses. At the same time, she demonstrates that *Gone With the Wind* did not accurately portray the historical world of the nineteenth-century South and that Mitchell misunderstood the African American slaves on whom the white plantation owners depended to run their plantations, pick their cotton, work in their homes, and make their lives comfortable.

An important theme in *The Wind Done Gone* is African American self-determination. Many of the black characters actively work to protect themselves and their loved ones, to improve their positions, and to provide for the future. While Mitchell presents Mammy as a selfless and devoted servant, Randall presents her as capable of any act that protects the welfare of herself and her loved ones. To maintain control over the household, for example, she has stealthily murdered at birth each of Planter's sons: she wants to remove any male heir who in the future might challenge her authority. Moreover, while Mitchell's novel

Early adolescence for **slave women** was often difficult because of the threat of exploitation and abuse from masters and mistresses, overseers, male slaves, and members of the planter family. House servants were on call twenty-four hours a day tending to the needs of their plantation mistresses.—From online entry "Slave Women"

WWW.GEORGIAENCYCLOPEDIA.ORG

does not acknowledge the possibility of love in the lives of the slaves at the O'Hara plantation, Randall gives Cynara a full romantic existence, especially in the novel's second half.

In many ways *The Wind Done Gone* moves well beyond the novel it parodies. Rather than surviving to live another day, like Scarlett in Mitchell's story, the Scarlett figure dies. Cynara then follows R to Washington, D.C., where she meets important figures of the Reconstruction era, including Frederick Douglass, author of the famous slave narratives, as well as an African American congressman with whom she falls in love. As the novel concludes, with the end of Reconstruction and the days of Jim Crow laws looming, she takes steps to provide for the future welfare of her own descendants. She thus manages, in the pages of this novel written in the form of her diary, to chart the course of her own history.

The Wind Done Gone as Literature

As an African American response to *Gone With the Wind*, *The Wind Done Gone* is interesting and sometimes entertaining; however, it is not great literature. Randall leaves too many plot lines undeveloped or incomplete, and most of the characters, including Planter, Other, and Cynara, are hazily indistinct. Randall's own intentions seem unclear—is she writing a parody, as she seems to be doing in the book's first half, or is she writing about a young woman's discovery of her life's purpose?

The novel shows the mark of numerous influences, including Alice Walker, Margaret Walker, Frederick Douglass, Toni Morrison, and even William Faulkner, and it never develops its own style and identity. In some ways it substitutes for the myths of Mitchell's Old South another mythology all its own. But as a statement embodying African American reaction to the myths underlying *Gone With the Wind*, it is an important literary and historical document.

HUGH RUPPERSBURG

} Fictional Treatments of Sherman in Georgia

The presence of Union general William T. Sherman in Georgia during the Civil War has inspired numerous novels. These fictional accounts, some obscure and some quite prominent, have centered on characters caught up in either the Atlanta campaign, during the spring and summer of 1864, or the subsequent March to the Sea, in the late fall of that year.

Perhaps one reason that these events have attracted so many novelists is that both the campaign and the march involved interactions among many different types of people, including soldiers and civilians, Northerners and Southerners, blacks and whites, and the rich and the poor. Such interactions provide ample fodder for dramatic situations and compelling characters, as the works discussed here demonstrate. Both individually and collectively, these novels reflect the tensions, traumas, and social complexities of an invading force whose presence caused tremendous upheaval in the lives of Southerners, both urban and rural, in its path.

Probably the first fictional account of Sherman's march appears in the Joel Chandler Harris work *On the Plantation: A Story of a Georgia Boy's Adventures during the War* (1892). Harris's semiautobiographical account, drawn from his experiences as a boy on Turnwold Plantation in Putnam County, includes a dramatic description of Union forces raiding the county and the plantation early in the March to the Sea. Perhaps the most curious novel dealing with the war in Georgia during 1864 is *Goldie's Inheritance: A Story of the Siege of Atlanta* (1903), by Vermont writer Louisa Bailey Whitney. For the novel Whitney drew heavily on her sister Cyrena Bailey Stone's diary of the war years in Atlanta. The diary came to light after historian Thomas G. Dyer at the University of Georgia discovered it to be a key piece of source material for the history of the Atlanta community of "secret Yankees," or Unionists, of which Stone was a part.

Certainly the most popular account of the Atlanta siege and its aftermath occurs in Margaret Mitchell's *Gone With the Wind* (1936). The burning of Atlanta and the efforts of protagonist Scarlett O'Hara to flee the city make for some of the most dramatic sequences in both the novel and its 1939 film adaptation. (Kentucky writer Caroline Gordon made the Battle of Chickamauga, fought in Walker County in 1863, the centerpiece of her novel *None Shall Look Back*. Published in 1937 and thus overshadowed by *Gone With the Wind*'s appearance a year earlier, it remains a critically acclaimed work that focuses on the plight of two families in Kentucky and Georgia.)

In more recent years several writers have constructed novels based on the events of 1864 in Georgia. Cynthia Bass's short novel *Sherman's March* (1994) recounts the Union army's trek across the state through the voices of three protagonists: a Union captain from Illinois, a young Confederate widow on a plantation near Milledgeville, and Sherman himself. Each character narrates a third of the book.

Two novels, Daniel R. Burow's well-regarded *Sound of the Bugle: The Adventures of Hans Schmidt* (1973) and John Jakes's *Savannah; or A Gift for Mr. Lincoln* (2004), are set in Savannah. Both novels recreate the turmoil in and around the city as the Union army approached and ultimately occupied it, and both focus on the experiences of local residents, black and white, who are forced to interact with the Northern invaders in a variety of circumstances, some more hostile than others.

Two novels published early in the twenty-first century have been particularly well received and are recognized as among the most accomplished and historically accurate treatments of the subject. Athens-based novelist Philip Lee Williams's *A Distant Flame* (2004) is told from the viewpoint of Georgia natives, many of whom experience the conflict on their home turf. E. L. Doctorow's *The March* (2005), told primarily from a Northern viewpoint, focuses on the campaign in the southern half of Georgia and beyond. Very different in terms of character and plot, these novels complement each other. While both offer graphic, powerful battle scenes, Williams effectively portrays battle from the individual soldiers' points of view, while Doctorow gives a deeper, broader sense of war as a phenomenon.

A Distant Flame

Philip Lee Williams's *A Distant Flame* is about the struggle of an old man, Charlie Merrill, to make sense of his memories and his life. The novel received the 2004 Michael Shaara Prize for Civil War Fiction, and in 2005 was listed among the Georgia Center for the Book's top twenty-five notable books by Georgia authors.

In 1864 **Madison** resident and politician Joshua Hill reportedly convinced Sherman not to burn the town during the March to the Sea. The Union army did spare Madison's center, although a number of public buildings and some surrounding plantations were burned. While accounts vary, Madison has become known in local folklore as "the town too pretty to burn."—From online entry "Madison"

WWW.GEORGIAENCYCLOPEDIA.ORG

A Confederate veteran and small-town newspaper editor, Charlie is known nationally for his columns and books. Through alternating chapters set in 1861–63, 1864, and 1914, Williams's novel recounts a love story, a war story, and Charlie's later reflections on these events. The novel's final chapter is set in 1918.

The chapters covering 1861–63 follow the relationship between Charlie, who lives in fictional Branton, Georgia, and Sarah, a girl from Boston, Massachusetts, who has come to live with her uncle in Branton while her parents are divorcing. (Branton is loosely based on Madison, where Williams grew up.) Their romance ends in 1864, when Sarah leaves for England to live with her father. The chapters set in 1864 recount Charlie's experiences as a soldier and sharpshooter with the Confederate army as it retreats before Sherman's forces during the Atlanta campaign. The remaining chapters, set in 1914, are told from the vantage point of Charlie, now an old man, as he prepares to deliver a speech commemorating the fiftieth anniversary of the Battle of Atlanta. While doing so he recalls his wartime experiences and his affair with Sarah.

Although the novel focuses mainly on the white inhabitants of a small Georgia town, it also documents the social realities of the times in which they lived, including the institution of slavery. Williams shows a close relationship between the Merrill family and some of their slaves, but he also makes clear that the lives of the slaves were severely constrained. As an old man, Charlie is convinced that slavery was an evil.

Williams's research into the Civil War never overwhelms the novel but provides a rich historical context. In an afterword Williams describes how he studied the way men and women from that era talked and thought by reading letters, journals, diaries, and other accounts from those years.

A Distant Flame, with its credible, intense, and realistic portrayals of battle, conveys an understanding of the unpleasant and unworldly horrors of war, not only the violence and carnage but also the disease-ridden conditions in which solders lived and often died.

The March

One of America's most acclaimed historical novelists, E. L. Doctorow offers *The March* as his first work set during the Civil War era. Focusing on Sherman's March to the Sea and subsequent foray into the Carolinas, *The March* won the National Book Critics Circle Award for 2005 and the Pen/Faulkner Award for 2006. (Only the first third of the novel is set in Georgia.)

The narrative method in *The March* is reminiscent of Doctorow's best-known novel, *Ragtime* (1975), in that he combines historical details gleaned from meticulous research with an array of fictional and nonfictional characters, both soldiers and civilians. The stories of the various participants in the march are interwoven, demonstrating the varied impact of Sherman's forces as they passed through Georgia, South Carolina, and North Carolina.

Although no single protagonist guides the novel, several important characters emerge: the slave girl Pearl, who follows the Northern troops as they leave Macon; Emily Thompson, the daughter of a Southern patriarch who dies while Northern soldiers occupy their house; Dr. Sartorius, a brilliant Northern field surgeon devoid of feeling; a British reporter; a photographer; and Arly and Will, two no-account Confederate soldiers who change allegiance from North to South and back depending on the needs of the moment. And, of course, there is Sherman himself.

Some of the characters are present in *The March* from beginning to end; others enter for a time and are killed or simply fall out of view. All engage in a continual process of personal redefinition as their circumstances change, especially as a result of the war. For the Southern characters, change often requires adjustment to the destruction of their familiar world; they often become entirely different people, engaging in behaviors that they would never have considered prior to Sherman's arrival. To the Northern characters, change often means confronting personal successes and failures as the war progresses.

Doctorow portrays the march as loosely organized anarchy. Sherman has some control over the direction in which his troops move but little control over their individual actions. (This is especially evident when the troops ignore his orders and burn Columbia, South Carolina.) Sherman is the book's most fascinating character. He desires greatness, wants recognition for his achievements, and feels overlooked, especially when commanding officers blame him for a disastrous battle over which he had little control. Although Doctorow might have paid Sherman more attention in this novel, to have done so would have violated its essential premise and narrative structure, which allows none of its characters prominence over the others.

Doctorow's basic theme in *The March* is that war is evil. It alters or destroys lives. It is a naturalistic force that destroys landscapes and nations. It roils on in chaos and disrepute, and people, voluntarily or not, become caught up in it. Although the novel occasionally acknowledges such political and historical causes of the Civil War as slavery, more often than not it depicts war as an event with little connection to historical causes and political movements.

HUGH RUPPERSBURG
JOHN C. INSCOE

Selected Bibliography

General

Boney, F. N. *Rebel Georgia.* Macon, Ga.: Mercer University Press, 1997.

Brown, Barry L., and Gordon R. Elwell. *Crossroads of Conflict: A Guide to Civil War Sites in Georgia.* Athens: University of Georgia Press, 2010.

Bryan, T. Conn. *Confederate Georgia.* Athens: University of Georgia Press, 1953.

DeCredico, Mary A. *Patriotism for Profit: Georgia's Urban Entrepreneurs and the Confederate War Effort.* Chapel Hill: University of North Carolina Press, 1990.

Fowler, John D., and David B. Parker, eds. *Breaking the Heartland: The Civil War in Georgia.* Macon, Ga.: Mercer University Press, 2011.

"Georgians at War, 1861–1865." Special issue, *Georgia Historical Quarterly* 79 (Spring 1995).

Inscoe, John C., and Robert C. Kenzer, eds. *Enemies of the Country: New Perspectives on Unionists in the Civil War South.* Athens: University of Georgia Press, 2001.

Lenz, Richard J. *The Civil War in Georgia: An Illustrated Traveler's Guide.* Watkinsville, Ga.: Infinity Press, 1995.

Miles, Jim. *Civil War Sites in Georgia.* Nashville: Rutledge Hill Press, 1996.

Mohr, Clarence L. *On the Threshold of Freedom: Masters and Slaves in Civil War Georgia.* Athens: University of Georgia Press, 1986.

Morgan, Chad. *Planters' Progress: Modernizing Confederate Georgia.* Gainesville: University Press of Florida, 2005.

Weitz, Mark A. *A Higher Duty: Desertion among Georgia Troops during the Civil War.* Lincoln: University of Nebraska Press, 2000.

Williams, David, Teresa Crisp Williams, and David Carlson. *Plain Folk in a Rich Man's War: Class and Dissent in Confederate Georgia.* Gainesville: University Press of Florida, 2002.

Sectional Crisis

Carey, Anthony Gene. *Parties, Slavery, and the Union in Antebellum Georgia.* Athens: University of Georgia Press, 1997.

Crutcher, Luke F. "Disunity and Dissolution: The Georgia Parties and the Crisis of the Union, 1859–1861." PhD diss., University of California, 1974.

Davis, William C. *The Union That Shaped the Confederacy: Robert Toombs and Alexander H. Stephens.* Lawrence: University Press of Kansas, 2001.

Freehling, William W., and Craig M. Simpson, eds. *Secession Debated: Georgia's Showdown in 1860.* New York: Oxford University Press, 1992.

Johnson, Michael P. *Toward a Patriarchal Republic: The Secession of Georgia.* Baton Rouge: Louisiana State University Press, 1977.

Phillips, Ulrich Bonnell. *Georgia and State Rights: A Study of the Political History of Georgia from the Revolution to the Civil War, with Particular Regard to Federal Relations.* Washington, D.C.: U.S. Government Printing Office, 1902.

Phillips, Ulrich Bonnell, ed. *The Correspondence of Robert Toombs, Alexander H. Stephens, and Howell Cobb.* Washington, D.C.: n.p., 1913.

Shryock, Richard Harrison. *Georgia and the Union in 1850.* 1926. Reprint, New York: AMS Press, 1968.

Atlanta Campaign and Sherman's March

Bailey, Anne J. *The Chessboard of War: Sherman and Hood in the Autumn Campaigns of 1864.* Lincoln: University of Nebraska Press, 2000.

―――. *War and Ruin: William T. Sherman and the Savannah Campaign.* Wilmington, Del.: SR Books, 2003.

Barnard, George N. *Photographic Views of Sherman's Campaign.* New York: Dover Publications, 1977.

Bonds, Russell S. *War like a Thunderbolt: The Battle and Burning of Atlanta.* Yardley, Pa.: Westholme, 2009.

Castel, Albert E. *Decision in the West: The Atlanta Campaign of 1864.* Lawrence: University Press of Kansas, 1992.

Davis, Stephen. *Atlanta Will Fall: Sherman, Joe Johnston, and the Yankee Heavy Battalions.* Wilmington, Del.: Scholarly Resources, 2001.

Ecelbarger, Gary L. *The Day Dixie Died: The Battle of Atlanta.* New York: Thomas Dunne Books, 2010.

Evans, David. *Sherman's Horsemen: Union Cavalry Operation in the Atlanta Campaign.* Bloomington: Indiana University Press, 1996.

Glatthaar, Joseph T. *The March to the Sea and Beyond: Sherman's Troops in the Savannah and Carolinas Campaigns.* New York: New York University Press, 1985.

Hitt, Michael D. *Charged with Treason: Ordeal of 400 Mill Workers during Military Operations in Roswell, Georgia, 1864–1865.* Monroe, N.Y.: Library Research Associates, 1992.

Kennett, Lee B. *Marching through Georgia: The Story of Soldiers and Civilians during Sherman's Campaign.* New York: HarperCollins, 1995.

Luvaas, Jay, and Harold W. Nelson, eds. *Guide to the Atlanta Campaign: Rocky Face Ridge to Kennesaw Mountain.* Lawrence: University Press of Kansas, 2008.

McCarley, J. Britt. *The Atlanta Campaign: A Civil War Driving Tour of Atlanta-Area Battlefields.* Atlanta: Cherokee Publishing Co., 1989.

McDonough, James Lee, and James Pickett Jones. *War So Terrible: Sherman and Atlanta.* New York: Norton, 1987.

McMurry, Richard M. *Atlanta 1864: Last Chance for the Confederacy.* Lincoln: University of Nebraska Press, 2000.

Miles, Jim. *To the Sea: A History and Tour Guide of Sherman's March.* Nashville, Tenn.: Rutledge Hill Press, 1989.

Petite, Mary Deborah. *The Women Will Howl: The Union Army Capture of Roswell and New Manchester, Georgia, and the Forced Relocation of Mill Workers.* Jefferson, N.C.: MacFarland Press, 2008.

Scaife, William. *The Campaign for Atlanta.* Saline, Mich.: McNaughton and Gunn, 1993.

Secrist, Philip L. *The Battle of Resaca: Atlanta Campaign, 1864.* Macon, Ga.: Mercer University Press, 1998.

Wortman, Marc. *The Bonfire: The Siege and Burning of Atlanta.* New York: Public Affairs, 2009.

Local and Regional Studies

Bohannon, Keith S. "The Northeast Georgia Mountains during the Secession Crisis and Civil War." PhD diss., Pennsylvania State University, 2001.

Bragg, C. L., Charles D. Ross, Gordon A. Baker, Stephanie A. T. Jacobe, and Theodore P. Savas. *Never for Want of Powder: The Confederate Powder Works in Augusta, Georgia.* Columbia: University of South Carolina Press, 2007.

Bragg, William Harris. *Griswoldville.* Macon, Ga.: Mercer University Press, 2000.

Bryant, Jonathan M. *How Curious a Land: Conflict and Change in Greene County, Georgia, 1850–1885.* Chapel Hill: University of North Carolina Press, 1996.

Coleman, Kenneth. *Confederate Athens.* Athens: University of Georgia Press, 1968.

Corley, Florence Fleming. *Confederate City: Augusta, Georgia, 1860–1865.* Spartanburg, S.C.: Reprint Co., 1995.

Davis, Robert S., Jr. *Cotton, Fire, and Dreams: The Robert Findlay Iron Works and Heavy Industry in Macon, Georgia, 1839–1912.* Macon, Ga.: Mercer University Press, 1998.

Durham, Roger S. *Guardian of Savannah: Fort McAllister, Georgia, in the Civil War and Beyond.* Columbia: University of South Carolina Press, 2008.

Dyer, Thomas G. *Secret Yankees: The Union Circle in Confederate Atlanta.* Baltimore: Johns Hopkins University Press, 1999.

Jones, Jacqueline. *Saving Savannah: The City and the Civil War.* New York: Alfred A. Knopf, 2008.

Jones, James Pickett. *Yankee Blitzkrieg: Wilson's Raid through Alabama and Georgia.* Athens: University of Georgia Press, 1976.

Lane, Mills. *Savannah and the Civil War at Sea.* Savannah: Ships of the Sea Maritime Museum, 2001.

Marvel, William. *Andersonville: The Last Depot.* Chapel Hill: University of North Carolina Press, 1994.

Misulia, Charles A. *Columbus 1865: The Last True Battle of the Civil War.* Tuscaloosa: University of Alabama Press, 2010.

O'Donovan, Susan E. *Becoming Free in the Cotton South.* Cambridge: Harvard University Press, 2008.

O'Neill, Charles. *Wild Train: The Story of the Andrews Raiders.* New York: Random House, 1956.

Sarris, Jonathan Dean. *A Separate Civil War: Communities in Conflict in the Mountain South.* Charlottesville: University Press of Virginia, 2006.

Tuck, Glenn. *Chickamauga: Bloody Battle in the West.* Indianapolis: Bobbs-Merrill, 1961.

Turner, Maxine. *Navy Gray: A Story of the Confederate Navy on the Chattahoochee and Apalachicola Rivers.* Tuscaloosa: University of Alabama Press, 1988.

Wetherington, Mark V. *Plain Folk's Fight: The Civil War and Reconstruction in Piney Woods Georgia.* Chapel Hill: University of North Carolina Press, 2005.

Whites, LeeAnn. *The Civil War as a Crisis in Gender: Augusta, Georgia, 1860–1890.* Athens: University of Georgia Press, 1995.

Williams, David. *Rich Man's War: Class, Caste, and Confederate Defeat in the Lower Chattahoochee Valley.* Athens: University of Georgia Press, 1998.

Woodworth, Steven E., ed. *The Chickamauga Campaign.* Carbondale: Southern Illinois University Press, 2010.

———. *Six Armies in Tennessee: The Chickamauga and Chattanooga Campaigns.* Lincoln: University of Nebraska Press, 1998.

Postwar Era and War's Legacy

Blight, David W. *Race and Reunion: The Civil War in American Memory.* Cambridge: Harvard University Press, 2001.

Cimbala, Paul A. *Under the Guardianship of the Nation: The Freedmen's Bureau and the Reconstruction of Georgia, 1863–1870.* Athens: University of Georgia Press, 1997.

Clinton, Catherine. *Tara Revisited: Women, War, and the Plantation Legend.* New York: Abbeville Press, 1995.

Conway, Alan. *The Reconstruction of Georgia.* Minneapolis: University of Minnesota Press, [1966].

Drago, Edmund L. *Black Politicians and Reconstruction in Georgia: A Splendid Failure.* 1982. Reprint, Athens: University of Georgia Press, 1992.

Foster, Gaines M. *Ghosts of the Confederacy: Defeat, the Lost Cause, and the Emergence of the New South.* New York: Oxford University Press, 1987.

Haskell, Molly. *Frankly, My Dear: "Gone with the Wind" Revisited.* New Haven, Conn.: Yale University Press, 2009.

Horwitz, Tony. *Confederates in the Attic: Dispatches from the Unfinished Civil War.* New York: Pantheon, 1998.

LaCavera, Tommie Phillips. *The History of the Georgia Division of the United Daughters of the Confederacy, 1895–1995.* Atlanta: Georgia Division United Daughters of the Confederacy, 1995.

Nathans, Elizabeth S. *Losing the Peace: Georgia Republicans and Reconstruction, 1865–1871.* Baton Rouge: Louisiana State University Press, [1968].

Wiggins, David N. *Georgia's Confederate Monuments and Cemeteries.* Charleston, S.C.: Arcadia, 2006.

Wilson, Charles Reagan. *Baptized in Blood: The Religion of the Lost Cause, 1865–1920.* Athens: University of Georgia Press, 1980.

Memoirs, Journals, and Diaries

Andrews, Eliza Frances. *The War-Time Journal of a Georgia Girl, 1864–1865.* Edited by Spencer Bidwell King Jr. 1908. Reprint, Macon, Ga.: Ardivan Press, 1960.

Benson, Berry. *Berry Benson's Civil War Book: Memoirs of a Confederate Scout and Sharpshooter.* Edited by Susan Benson Williams. Athens: University of Georgia Press, 2007.

Broadwater, Robert P., ed. *Chickamauga, Andersonville, Fort Sumter and Guard Duty at Home: Four Civil War Diaries by Pennsylvania Soldiers.* Jefferson, N.C.: McFarland and Co., 2006.

Clayton, Sarah Conley. *Requiem for a Lost City: A Memoir of Civil War Atlanta and the Old South.* Edited by Robert Scott Davis Jr. Macon, Ga.: Mercer University Press, 1999.

Cumming, Kate. *The Journal of a Confederate Nurse.* Baton Rouge: Louisiana State University Press, 1998.

Fletcher, Louisa Warren. *Journal of a Landlady: The Fletcher/Kennesaw House Diary.* Edited by Henry Higgins, Connie Cox, and Jean Cole Anderson. Chapel Hill, N.C.: Professional Press, 1995.

Gay, Mary A. H. *Life in Dixie during the War.* Edited by J. H. Segars. 1892. Reprint, Macon, Ga.: Mercer University Press, 2001.

Jackson, Fannie Oslin. *On Both Sides of the Line.* Baltimore, Md.: Gateway Press, 1989.

Kellogg, Robert H. *Life and Death in Rebel Prisons.* 1865. Reprint, Freeport, N.Y.: Books for Libraries Press, 1971.

Lunt, Dolly Sumner. *The Diary of Dolly Lunt Burge, 1848–1879.* Edited by Christine Jacobson Carter. Athens: University of Georgia Press, 1997.

Ransom, John L. *John Ransom's Andersonville Diary.* Edited by Bruce Catton. Middlebury, Vt.: P. S. Erikson, 1986.

Richards, Samuel Pearce. *Sam Richards's Civil War Diary: A Chronicle of the Atlanta Home Front.* Edited by Wendy Hamand Venet. Athens: University of Georgia Press, 2009.

Robertson, Mary D., ed. "Northern Rebel: The Journal of Nellie Kinzie Gordon." *Georgia Historical Quarterly* 70 (Fall 1986): 477–517.

Sherman, William T. *Memoirs of General W. T. Sherman.* Edited by Michael Fellman. New York: Penguin Books, 2000.

Smith, Charles Henry [Bill Arp]. *Bill Arp's Peace Papers: Columns on the Civil War and Reconstruction, 1860–1873.* Edited by David B. Parker. Columbia: University of South Carolina Press, 2009.

Taylor, Susie King. *Reminiscences of My Life in Camp: An African American Woman's Civil War Memoir.* Athens: University of Georgia Press, 2006.

Thomas, Ella Gertrude Clanton. *The Secret Eye: The Journal of Ella Gertrude Clanton Thomas, 1848–1889.* Edited by Virginia Ingraham Burr. Chapel Hill: University of North Carolina Press, 1990.

Watkins, Samuel R. *Co. Aytch: A Side Show of the Big Show.* New York: Collier Books, 1962.

Fiction and Drama

Doctorow, E. L. *The March.* New York: Random House, 2005.

Evans, Augusta Jane. *Macaria; or Altars of Sacrifice.* Edited by Drew Gilpin Faust. Baton Rouge: Louisiana State University Press, 1992.

Gordon, Caroline. *None Shall Look Back.* New York: Charles Scribners' Sons, 1937.

Harris, Joel Chandler. *On the Plantation: A Story of a Georgia Boy's Adventures during the War.* New York: D. Appleton and Co., 1892. Reprint, Athens: University of Georgia Press, 1980.

Jakes, John. *Savannah; or A Gift for Mr. Lincoln.* New York: Dutton, 2004.

Kantor, Mackinlay. *Andersonville.* Cleveland: World Press, 1955.

Levitt, Saul. *The Andersonville Trial.* New York: Dramatist Play Service, 1960.

Mitchell, Margaret. *Gone With the Wind.* New York: Macmillan, 1936.

Walker, Margaret. *Jubilee.* Boston: Houghton Mifflin, 1966.

Williams, Phillip Lee. *The Campfire Boys.* Macon, Ga.: Mercer University Press, 2009.

———. *A Distant Flame.* Macon, Ga.: Mercer University Press, 2004.

Wright, Charles. *Chickamauga.* New York: Farrar, Strauss, and Giroux, 1995.

} Contributors

Jarrod Atchison, Wake Forest University
   The Countryman

Anne J. Bailey, Georgia College and State University
   Sherman's March to the Sea

Keith S. Bohannon, University of West Georgia
   Battle of Chickamauga
   Guerrilla Warfare

Katherine Brackett, West Virginia University
   Nancy Harts Militia

William Harris Bragg, Georgia College and State University
   Griswoldville
   Reconstruction

Brian Brown, Fitzgerald, Ga.
   Capture of Jefferson Davis
   Fitzgerald

Anthony Gene Carey, Auburn University
   Secession

Jacqueline Miller Carmichael, Georgia State University
   Jubilee

Dan Childs, Cumming, Ga.
   Georgia Civil War Commission

Albert Churella, Southern Polytechnic State University
   The General
   The Great Locomotive Chase

Levi Collins, University of Georgia
   Naval War on the Chattahoochee River

Robert Scott Davis Jr., Wallace State College
  Andersonville Prison
  Confederate Gold

Stephen Davis, Marietta, Ga.
  Andrews Raid
  Atlanta as Confederate Hub
  Atlanta Campaign
  Cyclorama

Caroline Matheny Dillman
  Roswell Mill Women

Dan Du, University of Georgia
  Industry and Manufacturing

Angela Esco Elder, University of Georgia
  United Daughters of the Confederacy

John D. Fowler, Dalton State College
  Battle of Kennesaw Mountain
  Overview: The Civil War in Georgia

Lisa Tendrich Frank, Florida State University
  Women

Laverne W. Hill, Athens, Ga.
  State Constitution of 1861

Melvin B. Hill Jr., Athens, Ga.
  State Constitution of 1861

Richard Houston, University of Georgia
  Union Blockade and Coastal Occupation

Stephen Huggins, University of Georgia
  CSS *Savannah*

Jun Suk Hyun, University of Georgia
  Battle of Pickett's Mill

John C. Inscoe, University of Georgia
   Fictional Treatments of Sherman in Georgia
   Georgia in 1860
   Journals, Diaries, and Memoirs
   Unionists

Edwin L. Jackson, University of Georgia
   Milledgeville

Gordon L. Jones, Atlanta History Center
   Reenacting

George W. Justice, Valdosta State University
   Georgia Platform
   Secession
   State Constitution of 1861

Steve Longcrier, Civil War Heritage Trails
   Civil War Heritage Trails

Jason Manthorne, University of Georgia
   Wilson's Raid

Hubert H. McAlexander, University of Georgia
   Gone With the Wind (Novel)

Laura McCarty, Georgia Humanities Council
   Civil War Centennial

David H. McGee, Central Virginia Community College
   Fort Pulaski

Samuel B. McGuire, University of Georgia
   Desertion

Clarence L. Mohr, University of South Alabama
   Black Troops

Barton Myers, Texas Tech University
   The Andersonville Trial (Play) and *Andersonville* (Film)
   Georgia Military Institute
   Sherman's Field Order No. 15

Susan E. O'Donovan, University of Memphis
    Emancipation

Kyle Osborn, University of Georgia
    Sectional Crisis

Leah Richier, University of Georgia
    Cemeteries

Katherine E. Rohrer, University of Georgia
    On the Plantation
    Wanderer

Hugh Ruppersburg, University of Georgia
    Fictional Treatments of Sherman in Georgia
    Gone With the Wind (Film)
    The Wind Done Gone

Franklin C. Sammons Jr., University of Georgia
    Confederate Veteran Organizations

Cindy Schmid, University of Georgia
    Civil War Photojournalist: George N. Barnard

Glenna R. Schroeder-Lein, Lincoln Legal Papers Project
    Confederate Hospitals

Garrett W. Silliman, Atlanta, Ga.
    Archaeology

Bruce Smith, National Civil War Naval Museum
    National Civil War Naval Museum at Port Columbus

Bruce E. Stewart, Appalachian State University
    Stone Mountain

Vanessa P. Tome, University of Georgia
    "Marching through Georgia"

Diane Trap, University of Georgia Libraries
    Slave Narratives

James C. Turner, Georgia College and State University
    Old Governor's Mansion

Sean H. Vanatta, University of Georgia
    Industry and Manufacturing

Debra Reddin van Tuyll, Augusta State University
    Newspapers

James H. Welborn III, University of Georgia
    Union Blockade and Coastal Occupation

Heather L. Whittaker, University of Georgia
    Macaria

David N. Wiggins, Carrollton, Ga.
    Confederate Monuments

Chris Wilkinson, National Park Service
    Prisons

David Williams, Valdosta State University
    Dissent

David S. Williams, University of Georgia
    Lost Cause Religion

Robert J. Wilson III, Georgia College and State University
    Milledgeville

Brad Wood, University of Georgia
    USS *Water Witch*

Denise Wright, Elberton, Ga.
    Welfare and Poverty

Jeffrey Robert Young, Georgia State University
    Slavery

Kevin W. Young, University of Georgia
    Battle of Resaca

} Index

Page numbers in italics represent full-chapter entries in the book.

Enlistment, of Georgia troops, 6, 161
Erwin, Mary Ann Lamar Cobb, 203
Etowah River, 76, 87
Evans, Augusta Jane, 167, 248–50
Evans, Clement, 194, 196, 198–99
Ezra Church, Battle of, 80–81

Fairbanks, Charles, 234
Fannin County, 154
Farmers, 18, 26
Farragut, David G., 93
Faulkner, William, 261, 276
Faust, Drew G., 249, 250
Fayetteville, 156
Federal Writers' Project, 246
Felton, Rebecca Latimer, 202–3
Fernandina Beach, Fla., 68
Field Order No. 15 (Sherman), 9, 69, 174, *177–78*, 187
Fifteenth Amendment, 192
Fifty-fourth Massachusetts Regiment, 54, 69
Findlay Iron Works, 130
Fingal (ship), 52
First Georgia State Volunteers (Union), 155
First Georgia Volunteers, 141
First Reconstruction Act, 188–89
Fitzgerald, 200, *215–16*, 225–26, 226, 231
Fitzgerald, Philander H., 215
Fleming, Victor, 264
Fletcher, Louisa, 156, 242
Fontaine, Francis, 125
Food shortages, 8, 159, 161–62, 165, 170–71, 187
Foote, Shelby, 2
Foreign-born, in Georgia, 25
Forrest, Nathan Bedford, 7, 99, 210
Fort Gordon, 211
Fort McAllister, 54–55, 94, 226; photographed by Barnard, 105–6, 119

Fort Oglethorpe, 230
Fort Pulaski, 6, *49–51*, 56–57, 68, 157, 168, 210
Fort Sumter, attack on, 6, 38, 161
Fort Wagner, S.C., attack on, 54
Fourteenth Amendment, 188–89, 191
Frankenheimer, John, 269, 270–71
Freedmen's Bureau, 175, 178, 187–88
Freedpeople, 174–76, 177–78, 186–87, 191, 194, 246–47; fictional depictions of, 272–73, 275
Fremont, John C., 32, 33
Fugitive Slave Act, 31, 38
Fuller, William, 66–67
Fulton County Confederate Veterans Association, 198
Fulton County Jail, 139

Gabbett, Sarah, 203
Garrard, Kenner, 138
Gatewood, John P., 63, 155
Gay, Mary Harris, 167
Geer, Peter Zack, 222–24
General (locomotive), 66–67, 223, 267
General, The (film), 67, *255–57*, 267
Georgia Civil War Centennial Commission, 222, 230–31
Georgia Civil War Commission, 86, *226–28*, 236
Georgia Department of Natural Resources, 86
Georgia Division Reenactors Association, 232
Georgia Historical Commission, 169–70
Georgia in 1860, *24–29*; population of, *24–25*
Georgia Military Institute, *125–26*, 138
Georgia Platform, 29, 31, *34–35*

National Park Service, 51, 209, 219, 224, 230, 234
National Prisoner of War Museum, 146
Naval blockade (Union): along Atlantic coast, 45, *51–55*; of Chattahoochee River, *59–62*
Naval Iron Works (Columbus), 60–62, 132
Naval stores, 28
Navy (Confederate), 52, 60–61, 219–20
New Hope Church, Battle of, 76–77, 87–88; reenactment of, 231
Newspapers, 46, *149–52*; antebellum, 149–50; in Atlanta, 149, 151; and dissent, 150–51, 163; in Savannah, 149
Nisbet, Eugenius A., 5, 36–37
None Shall Look Back (Caroline Gordon novel), 277
Northen, William J., 215
Nurses, 127; memoirs by, 243

Oakland Cemetery, 135, 208–9
Ocmulgee River, 140, 215
Ogeechee River, 54, 94
Oglethorpe Light Infantry Association, 197–98, 222
Okefenokee Swamp, 64
Old Governor's Mansion, *41–42*, 94, 222
Olmstead, Charles H., 50, 53
On the Plantation (Harris), 241, *252–54*, 277
Oostanaula River, 67, 76, 83, 86
Ossabaw Island, 58, 68
Overby, William Thomas, 210

Page, Thomas Nelson, 259
Paulding County, 87, 233
Peace movement, 150–51

Peachtree Creek, Battle of, 77, 80, 125
Penitentiary (Milledgeville), 133
Phillips, Ulrich Bonnell, 246
Pickens County, 161
Pickett's Mill, Battle of, 45, 76–77, *87–89*; archaeological site, 89, 236
Pierce, Franklin, 31–32
Pierce County, 64
Pittenger, William, 267–69
Plane, Caroline Helen, 203, 217
Poe, Orlando, 82–83
Polk, Leonidas, 72, 84
Pollard, Edward A., 194
Ponder, Ephraim, 117, 135
Poor whites, 26, 171–72
Pope, John, 189
Population, Georgia, 17–18, 24–25, 185
Port Columbus, 219–21
Port Royal, S.C., 50, 52, 56
Poverty, 26, *170–72*
Powder works, 129–32
Preservation. *See* Battlefield preservation
Presidential election: of 1856, 32; of 1860, 33–35; of 1864, 5, 10, 73–74, 83; of 1868, 191–92
Prisoner exchange, 140
Prisoners of war, 140–42; black, 69; women, 138
Prisons, *139–42. See also* Andersonville prison
Pulaski, Casimir, 49
Putnam County, 152–53, 241

Rabun County, 268
Radical Republicans, 177
Railroad Raiders of '62 (film), 255–56
Railroads, 6–7, 28–29, 52, 84, 129–30, 133

Sherman, William T., 1, 9, 10, 98, 250; and Atlanta campaign, 74–83; attitude of, toward black troops, 68–69, 173; and Field Order No. 15, *177–78*; on guerrilla warfare, 64; memoirs of, 242; photographed by Barnard, 105, 109, 118; at Resaca, 84–85; in Savannah, 177–78; and siege of Fort Pulaski, 50

Sherman's Field Order No. 15, 9, 69, 174, *177–78*, 187

Sherman's March (Bass novel), 277

Simmons, William, 217

Slave Life in Georgia (John Brown slave narrative), 245

Slave narratives, *244–48*, 272; ex-slave interviews, 245–47; by fugitive slaves, 245

Slave patrols, 163

Slave property, 25–26

Slave reparations, 178

Slavery, *16–22*; depicted by Joel Chandler Harris, 253–54; fictional depictions of, 253–54, 261–62, 271–72, 273–75, 277–79; legalities of, 18–19, 23; national debate over, 29–30; political defense of, 19; and secession, 21–22, 35–37; wartime destruction of, 8–9

Slaves: in Atlanta, 134; debates over arming, 151; in Georgia Lowcountry, 20–21; importation of, 17, 22–23; as industrial workforce, 28, 133; plantation life of, 20; population of, in Georgia, 17, 25, 185; as prison-camp workers, 142; as sailors and pilots, 70; and Sherman's march, 94, 96, 173–74; as troops, 68–70

Slave trade: African, 17, 22–23, 39–40; in District of Columbia, 31

Slocum, Henry W., 93, 254

Smith, James M., 193

Social structure, antebellum, 17–18, 25–26

Sons of Confederate Veterans, 139, 199–200, 212, 232

Sons of Union Veterans, 232

Sound of the Bugle (Burow novel), 277

Southern Confederacy (newspaper), 134, 151

Southern Historical Society, 201

Southern Loyalists Convention (1866), 188–89

Southern Museum of Civil War and Locomotive History, 255

Southern Rights Convention (1850), 30–31

Spanish-American War, 229

Sparta, 28

Special Field Order No. 15 (Sherman), 9, 69, 174, *177–78*, 187

Stanton, Edwin M., 177–78, 268

Steedman, James, 155

Steedman, Joseph B., 64

Stephens, Alexander, 5–7, 19, 29–31, 34, 36–37, 39, 188; capture of, 100; and defense of slavery, 29–30; election of, as Confederate vice president, 6, 38; as postwar candidate, 186

Stephens, Linton, 39

Stevens, Thaddeus, 177

Stone, Cyrena, 156, 168, 241, 277

Stone Mountain, *216–18*; carvings on, 181, 203, 210, 217–18; Ku Klux Klan at, 217; reenactment at, 225

Stone Mountain Memorial Association, 203, 217–18

Stout, Samuel H., 127–28

Streight, Abel D., 7

St. Simons Island, 52–54, 68, 167, 248

Sumner, Charles, 177

Wilson, James H., 11, 98–101, 169

Wilson's Raid, 11, 61–62, *98–101*, 169, 220

Wind Done Gone, The (Randall novel), *273–76*

Wiregrass (Ga.), 24, 215; deserters in, 158–59, 162

Wirz, Henry, 144–46, 210, 243–44; capture of, 100; execution of, 11, 145

Wofford, W. T., 65–66

Women, 8, *164–68*; and bread riots, 161–62, 166, 170; as hospital workers, 127, 243, 248; as industrial workforce, 133, 165; journals and memoirs by, 241–43; and Lost Cause, 194–96, 201–4, 207, 211, 217; as militia unit, 168–70; as mill workers, 138–39, 165; monument to (Rome), 212; as plantation mistresses, 46, 164–65; poor white, 46, 165–66; as reenactors, 232; and Sherman's march, 166; slave, 46, 96, 166, 275; as Unionists, 156–57, 167–68

Wood, Thomas J., 72, 87–88

Work, Henry Clay, 250

Works Progress Administration, 210, 214, 246

Worth County, 64